D1547359

Jackie Robinson

Recent Titles in Black History Lives

W.E.B. Du Bois: A Life in American History
Charisse Burden-Stelly and Gerald Horne

Thurgood Marshall: A Life in American History
Spencer R. Crew

Barack Obama: A Life in American History
F. Erik Brooks and MaCherie M. Placide

Harriet Tubman: A Life in American History
Kerry Walters

Zora Neale Hurston: A Life in American History
Stephanie Li

Rosa Parks: A Life in American History
Darryl Mace

Jackie Robinson

A LIFE IN AMERICAN HISTORY

Courtney Michelle Smith

Black History Lives

ABC-CLIO®

An Imprint of ABC-CLIO, LLC
Santa Barbara, California • Denver, Colorado

Copyright © 2021 by Courtney Michelle Smith

All rights reserved. No part of this publication may be reproduced, stored in a retrieval system, or transmitted, in any form or by any means, electronic, mechanical, photocopying, recording, or otherwise, except for the inclusion of brief quotations in a review, without prior permission in writing from the publisher.

Library of Congress Cataloging-in-Publication Data

Names: Smith, Courtney Michelle, 1978- author.
Title: Jackie Robinson : a life in American history / Courtney Michelle
  Smith.
Description: Santa Barbara : ABC-CLIO, [2021] | Series: Black history lives
  | Includes bibliographical references and index.
Identifiers: LCCN 2020036226 (print) | LCCN 2020036227 (ebook) | ISBN
  9781440872686 (hardcover) | ISBN 9781440872693 (ebook)
Subjects: LCSH: Robinson, Jackie, 1919-1972. | African American baseball
  players—Biography. | Negro leagues—History. | Discrimination in
  sports—United States—History—20th century.
Classification: LCC GV865.R6 S635 2021 (print) | LCC GV865.R6 (ebook) |
  DDC 796.357092 [B]—dc23
LC record available at https://lccn.loc.gov/2020036226
LC ebook record available at https://lccn.loc.gov/2020036227

ISBN: 978-1-4408-7268-6 (print)
        978-1-4408-7269-3 (ebook)

25 24 23 22 21   1 2 3 4 5

This book is also available as an eBook.

ABC-CLIO
An Imprint of ABC-CLIO, LLC

ABC-CLIO, LLC
147 Castilian Drive
Santa Barbara, California 93117
www.abc-clio.com

This book is printed on acid-free paper ∞

Manufactured in the United States of America

Contents

Series Foreword

The Black History Lives biography series explores and examines the lives of the most iconic figures in African American history, with supplementary material that highlights the subject's significance in our contemporary world. Volumes in this series offer far more than a simple retelling of a subject's life by providing readers with a greater understanding of the outside events and influences that shaped each subject's world, from familial relationships to political and cultural developments.

Each volume includes chronological chapters that detail events of the subject's life. The final chapter explores the cultural and historical significance of the individual and places their actions and beliefs within an overall historical context. Books in the series highlight important information about the individual through sidebars that connect readers to the larger context of social, political, intellectual, and pop culture in American history; a timeline listing significant events; key primary source excerpts; and a comprehensive bibliography for further research.

Preface

On April 15, 1947, a major historical event happened at Ebbets Field in Brooklyn. Twenty-eight-year-old Jack Roosevelt Robinson donned the blue-and-white jersey of the Brooklyn Dodgers, a team in the National League of Major League Baseball, and ran onto the field alongside his teammates. The newest Dodger, in his number 42 jersey, stood out from his teammates and from the players on the opposing team because of the color of his skin. Aside from Robinson, all the other players at Ebbets Field and the other ballparks across the Major Leagues were white. Robinson made history on April 15, 1947, because he became the first African American to play for a Major League team since the late nineteenth century. Robinson's presence at Ebbets Field added an extra layer of anticipation to Opening Day in Brooklyn since the fans in attendance witnessed something that had not happened in most of their lifetimes. No one, Robinson included, knew what would happen once the home plate umpire yelled "play ball" to officially start the season. Many people, Robinson included, knew that he represented a test case. If Robinson succeeded, then other African American ballplayers would follow him into the Major Leagues. If Robinson failed, then African American ballplayers would continue to receive a cold shoulder from Major League franchises and would continue to toil in the segregated Negro Leagues.

When Robinson took the field on April 15, 1947, he reintegrated Major League Baseball and symbolized the end to the unwritten "gentlemen's agreement" that had been in place since the 1890s. Prior to the 1890s, a few African Americans had played on teams that belonged to the leagues that constituted the "major" and "minor" leagues in the late nineteenth century. Major League Baseball, therefore, had a brief period of integration before the long period of segregation that ended with Robinson's arrival. The black players who integrated the majors in the late nineteenth century endured the racism and discrimination that flowed throughout American society and that facilitated a system of legalized racial segregation known as "Jim Crow." A written rule that never existed kept black ballplayers out of the Major Leagues. Instead, the owners of Major League franchises adhered to an unwritten "gentlemen's agreement" that they would not sign any African Americans. That agreement held until October 1945, when Branch Rickey, the general manager of the Brooklyn Dodgers, signed Robinson to a contract and assigned him to the Dodgers' top minor league team, the Montreal Royals. Rickey took that step in an atmosphere of intense pressure from politicians and others who wanted to end the racial segregation of professional baseball. In Robinson, Rickey saw the ideal person who could reintegrate the Major Leagues and who could usher in the arrival of other black players. Robinson proved Rickey correct and disproved all the assumptions and myths that had kept the "gentlemen's agreement" in place for approximately fifty years.

Nearly a half century after his death, Robinson's story remains a critical story for understanding the history, society, and culture of the United States in the twentieth century. Robinson's life represents a valuable lens for studying phenomena such as the Great Migration, segregation in American sports, the societal changes related to World War II, and the evolution of the civil rights movement. Robinson's success indelibly changed the game of baseball, but his significance goes beyond the world of sports. He showed that athletes should not simply stick to sports; he showed that athletes could use their fame to advocate for political causes and press political leaders to fulfill the promises of America's founding documents. Diabetes and heart disease cut Robinson's life short; he died at the age of fifty-three in October 1972, ten days after making his final public appearance at that year's World Series. At that appearance, he delivered a brief speech in which he challenged Major League Baseball to continue the reintegration he had started and to expand that process to the coaching ranks.

This work on Robinson strives to situate his life and career within the broader context of American history, society, and culture. It seeks to contribute to the rich scholarship surrounding Jackie Robinson, the Negro Leagues, and Major League Baseball. Robinson himself contributed to the scholarship with an autobiography, *I Never Had It Made: An Autobiography of Jackie Robinson*, that was published a few days after his death. Robinson had a ghostwriter for his autobiography, as he had for many of the items that appeared under his byline. His autobiography revealed the deep pain that Robinson endured as he reintegrated the Major Leagues and a reassessment of the views he held earlier in his life. Along with that autobiography, Jules Tygiel's *Baseball's Great Experiment: Jackie Robinson and His Legacy*, which was first published in 1983, continues to serve as a necessary starting point for anyone interested in scholarship about Robinson.

Tygiel provides a thoughtful and groundbreaking analysis of the "experiment" that brought Robinson and other African American players to the Major Leagues. In more recent years, works by Jonathan Eig, James W. Johnson, and Arnold Rampersand enriched the scholarship on Robinson. Eig's *Opening Day: The Story of Jackie Robinson's First Season* was published nearly sixty years to the date after Robinson's debut with the Dodgers and offers a book-long examination of Robinson's rookie season. Johnson's *The Black Bruins* examines Robinson's career at UCLA and provides an important context for understanding the experiences that made him an ideal candidate to break Major League Baseball's color barrier. Rampersand's *Jackie Robinson: A Biography* reads like an autobiography since he worked closely with Rachel, widow of Robinson, and received invaluable insight into their shared life away from sports. Rampersand also delves into the triumphs and frustrations Robinson faced in his retirement as he tried to press politicians on civil rights and enact his dream of having both political parties actively campaign for African American voters.

In addition to those books, the scholarship on Robinson includes a rich collection of articles that analyze the role of the black press in reintegrating Major League Baseball. David K. Wiggins's "Wendell Smith, *The Pittsburgh Courier*, and the Campaign to Include Blacks in Organized Baseball, 1933–1945" led the way in highlighting the central role of Smith and his newspaper in bringing Robinson to the Major Leagues. Brian Carroll wrote several of those articles—including "A Tribute to Wendell Smith," "A Crusading Journalist's Last Campaign: Wendell Smith and the Desegregation of Baseball's Spring Training," and "'It Couldn't Be Any Other Way': The Great Dilemma for the Black Press and Negro League Baseball." In addition to honoring the work of Smith, Carroll's articles cover a paradox at the heart of the campaign to reintegrate the Major Leagues. With Robinson and other black players entering the Major Leagues, the Negro Leagues quickly became irrelevant, and African Americans lost important sources of black entrepreneurship and capital.

This book has been organized to cover Robinson's life and legacy in both a chronological and thematic fashion. The early chapters situate Robinson's life and career within the legacy of slavery and the deferred dreams of African Americans in the immediate post–Civil War era. Those chapters also provide readers with an overview of the Negro Leagues and Smith's successful campaign to reintegrate Major League Baseball. Smith worked for the *Pittsburgh Courier*, one of the largest black newspapers in the country, and served as the conduit who linked Robinson to Rickey. Three chapters cover Robinson's historic season with the Montreal Royals and then his historic rookie season with the Brooklyn Dodgers. The later chapters move away from baseball as Robinson himself moved away from the sport during his retirement. Those chapters cover Robinson's often-frustrating quests to exert political influence, find the ideal Republican politician who would welcome African American voters, and push for civil rights. The final chapter covers Robinson's dream of building a suburban oasis and his heartache at losing his eldest son and namesake in a car accident in 1971.

With its focus on Robinson's life from his birth in 1919 to his death in 1972, this book aspires to tell a story about the United States in the twentieth century by telling a story about Robinson. His life follows the trajectory of the lives of many African Americans in the twentieth century—a life that included moving away from the segregated South, entering fields that were once the exclusive domain of white Americans, and enduring both the promises and frustrations of the civil rights movement. Like other African Americans, Robinson understood the frustrations of living in a country that treated some citizens as second class due to the color of their skin. Like other African Americans, Robinson understood the opposition that came with entering a world dominated by white Americans and challenging long-held beliefs about racial superiority. Robinson, therefore, serves as an ideal gateway to learning about American history in the twentieth century and the wide scope of segregation as well as integration in American society. Robinson stands as the most important and consequential African American athlete of the twentieth century. This book seeks to tell his story and build upon the legacy of other authors who made their contributions to the rich scholarship on Robinson, Smith, Rickey, and others who transformed American society through baseball.

1

The World That Made Jackie Robinson

On January 31, 1919, thirty-year-old Mallie Robinson of Cairo, Georgia, gave birth to her fifth child—Jack "Jackie" Roosevelt Robinson. Mallie and her husband, Jerry, had four other children—sons Edgar, Frank, and Matthew "Mack" and a daughter, Willa Rae. Ironically, Jackie's middle name of "Roosevelt" foreshadowed many of the forces that he would confront as the first African American player in Major League Baseball in the twentieth century. Mallie gave her youngest son that middle name in honor of President Theodore Roosevelt. The first President Roosevelt served two terms from 1901 to 1909 and died shortly before Jackie's birth. While serving as president, Roosevelt invited Booker T. Washington, one of the most prominent black Americans, to the White House. President Roosevelt's decision sparked an outcry that demanded he apologize for the decision and back away from any insinuation that he supported equal rights for African Americans. In the early twentieth century, many Americans could not and would not abide their president treating even a respected black man such as Washington as an equal. Many Americans regarded racial inequality as the norm and expected the president as well as other politicians to uphold that standard.

Both Mallie and Jerry Robinson had familial roots in the Deep South. Mallie's family, the McGriffs, came from a class of black farmers in Georgia who owned their land and sent their children to school. Both of Mallie's parents were born into slavery and impressed the importance of education as well as religion upon her and her siblings. Jerry's family came from less fortunate circumstances. His father, Tony, had moved to Georgia from Florida and labored on land belonging to a white family named Sasser. Jerry never received any formal education and followed in his father's footsteps by laboring on the same land, then owned by James Madison Sasser. Mallie first met Jerry in 1906 when she was only fourteen years old, and her father tried to steer her toward someone else. Her father's efforts failed, and Mallie and Jerry married in 1909. The young couple then moved into a rented cabin on the Sasser land and embarked upon a union marked by poverty and frequent separations.

Similarly to many other white landowners, Sasser kept his black laborers and tenants in a state of dependency. He required that all his laborers ask him for products produced on the farm and shop in a store he maintained on the plantation. The situation did not suit Mallie, who successfully persuaded Jerry to ask Sasser for a sharecropping contract. According to the terms of the contract, Sasser provided housing, land, and other materials to Jerry, and Jerry kept half of what he grew on that land. While the arrangement improved the couple's financial situation, it could not save their marriage. Jerry wanted a life away from the plantation, and he started a relationship with a married black woman whose family owned land near the Sasser plantation. A pattern emerged where Jerry would leave Mallie for brief periods and then return once Mallie forgave him for his actions. In the middle of that pattern, Mallie gave birth to the couple's five children. The pattern ended six months after their youngest child's birth, when Jerry ostensibly left his family to visit a brother in Texas. Jerry never headed to Texas, and Mallie refused to welcome him back into her home and her marriage when he returned for a final time.

With Jerry's departure, Mallie faced the wrath of Sasser and eventually made a life-altering decision for herself and her five children. After forcing her into a smaller house on his plantation and unsuccessfully pressuring her to work as his cook, Sasser evicted Mallie and her children. Sasser also tried to use local law enforcement to force Mallie to accept Jerry back into her home and tried to block Mallie's attempts to find work away from his plantation. With the help of her family, Mallie decided to move to Pasadena, California, at the behest of one of her half brothers. Other family members joined Mallie and her children, including the then sixteen-month-old Jackie, on the cross-country voyage that began in May 1920. They arrived in southern California one month later. While the voyage meant that Jackie Robinson escaped a childhood and adulthood in the Deep South, he could not escape a life shaped by a culture and other events with roots deep in American and world history.

ROBINSON AND SLAVERY'S LEGACY

With his birth in 1919 in the American South, Jackie Robinson entered a world scarred by the long arm of slavery. Slavery first arrived in the future

United States three hundred years before Robinson's birth. In 1619, John Rolfe recorded in his diary the arrival in Jamestown of a Dutch ship that carried approximately twenty slaves. For the rest of the seventeenth century, the practice of slavery became a key feature of the economies, societies, and cultures of Virginia and other southern colonies. While slavery also existed in northern colonies, the practice of slavery established its deepest roots in the southern colonies. Planters in those colonies used slaves to tend to their crops that consisted of products, such as tobacco, that enriched them at the expense of their slaves. Planters also used the laws of their colonies to define the scope of slavery, deny autonomy and rights to slaves, and use violence to maintain their power.

When delegates gathered in Philadelphia to debate independence from Great Britain and later to write a constitution for the United States, they also engaged in debates concerning slavery. Ideas such as natural rights, liberty, and freedom led some to equate the situation facing the American colonies with slavery and led others to question the practice of slavery. Thomas Jefferson, the lead author of the Declaration of Independence, embodied the paradox surrounding slavery's place within a country devoted to life, liberty, and the pursuit of happiness. Jefferson wrote those words, along with the famous phrase asserting the equality of all men, while owning slaves in his native Virginia. At the Second Continental Congress in Philadelphia, delegates voted to remove a passage that Jefferson wrote, condemning the King for imposing slavery on the colonies. Eleven years later, another group of delegates made compromises on the issue of slavery in order to garner support for the new Constitution. Their compromises counted slaves as three-fifths of free people for the purpose of determining a state's representation in the House of Representatives. The delegates also included a fugitive slave provision in the Constitution and prohibited the new government from removing the United States from the Trans-Atlantic Slave Trade for twenty years.

Those debates reflected the growing geographic division of slavery in the United States. Beginning in 1780, northern states such as Pennsylvania enacted gradual emancipation laws, and the Northwest Ordinance of 1787 forbade the practice of slavery in future states in the northern Midwest. In the southern states, however, the practice of slavery continued unabated and flourished well into the nineteenth century thanks to the invention of the cotton gin. While the United States ceased participation in the Trans-Atlantic Slave Trade in 1808, an internal slave trade thrived until the eve of the Civil War (1861–65). Slave owners in the upper South turned profits by selling "excess" slaves to slave owners in the Deep South who needed the labor for their cotton plantations. Despite any personal misgivings he may have held about slavery, Jefferson maintained the practice throughout his life and likely had children with his slave Sally Hemmings. He publicly

PENNSYLVANIA

Though Pennsylvania allowed slavery during the colonial era, it also was the place that displayed some of the earliest sentiment and movement against slavery. In 1688, Francis Daniel Pastorious and three other German Quakers wrote an antislavery petition that likely represents the first antislavery petition written in the English North American colonies. Pastorious had worked closely with the colony's founder, William Penn, on advertising Pennsylvania to potential settlers and on attracting German Quakers and Mennonites to a settlement called Germantown. The settlement lay close to the city of Philadelphia, the colony's main city and point of settlement.

Even though the antislavery petition did not spark a movement among other Quakers in Pennsylvania in the seventeenth century, it did foreshadow that Quakers would emerge as some of the earliest abolitionists. Quakers in Pennsylvania did move away from slavery in the eighteenth century, and in 1775, they did help support the founding of the first abolitionist society, the Pennsylvania Abolitionist Society (PAS), in the future United States. Benjamin Franklin served as the PAS's first president, and he brought his antislavery views to the Constitutional Convention in 1787. In that same year, Philadelphia witnessed the birth of the Free African Society (FAS), a self-help organization that helped to make Philadelphia an important center of free black society in the antebellum era.

Antislavery sentiment manifested itself in Pennsylvania in another way. On March 1, 1780, the Pennsylvania legislature passed An Act for the Gradual Abolition of Slavery. The act marked the first time that one of the states in the new United States of America passed such a law. While the law prohibited the importation of new slaves into the state, it did not prohibit slave owners from other states from bringing their slaves with them into Pennsylvania. Slave owners from other states could do so provided they did not stay past a certain amount of time in the state.

advocated for colonization for freed slaves because he believed that they could never attain equality with white Americans.

In addition to embodying the hypocrisy and paradox associated with slavery, Jefferson also embodied the power and influence associated with slave owners in the United States. Jefferson served as the first secretary of state and the third president of the United States. George Washington, also a slave owner from Virginia, served as the head of the Continental Army and the first president of the United States. Until the Civil War, the majority of the men who served as president of the United States owned slaves at some point in their lives. A few of them, including Washington and Jefferson, owned slaves while serving as president. Due to a balance between the number of free and slave states, the United States Senate contained an equal number of Senators from free and slave states. Those slave-owning presidents, along with slave-owning Senators and members of the House of Representatives, successfully blocked any federal action against slavery until the 1860s. In southern state governments, slave owners held sway in the legislatures and governor mansions and pushed their states to adopt uncompromising positions on slavery. Those positions hardened as the country acquired more territory and eventually led those states to decide upon secession as the only course of option to preserve the practice of slavery.

As the geographic division of the country into free and slave states hardened, enslaved and free black Americans sought ways to push back against the peculiar institution. The American South witnessed only a handful of slave revolts. Most slaves sought to resist the dehumanizing effects of slavery by working slowly, developing their own culture in slave quarters, and earning money to purchase their freedom. Some slaves made the risky decision to flee to northern states and live within free black communities. While northern states had committed themselves to abolishing slavery, they had not committed themselves to abolishing racial discrimination. Free black Americans faced discrimination in nearly every aspect of public life and relied upon organizations, such as the Free African Society, for support and mutual aid. In the mid-nineteenth century, as the abolitionist movement arose, some black Americans such as Frederick Douglass (ca. 1818–95) and Sojourner Truth (1797–1883) spoke publicly about the evils of slavery. Douglass noted how the institution undermined America's founding ideals, while Truth spoke about the additional dangers that enslaved women faced from their masters.

The culture and society of antebellum era and the Civil War defined the world of Jackie Robinson's enslaved ancestors. Both of Mallie's parents were born into slavery, meaning that only one generation separated Robinson from the practice of legalized slavery. Slaves such as Robinson's grandparents provided the labor for the cotton plantations that powered the economy of Georgia, his home state, and other states in the Deep South. Slavery remained a profitable enterprise for white planters until the Civil War, though the slaves themselves reaped few, if any, benefits from those profits. The profitability of slavery meant that the rise of an antislavery political party, the Republican Party, threatened the livelihoods of white planters in Georgia and other slave states. Abraham Lincoln's victory in the 1860 presidential election triggered a secession crisis across the South. South Carolina made the first move to secede from the United States in December 1860; Georgia followed in January 1861. Those states, along with nine other slave states, formed the Confederate States of America and engaged in a war with the United States in order to gain independence and preserve the practice of slavery. Georgia and the other Confederate states lost that war and, in the war's aftermath, faced an uncertain future as the

United States sought to heal wounds and establish a country dedicated to the abolishment of slavery.

Robinson's parents, Mallie and Jerry, came of age in an era defined by the failed promises of the post–Civil War era. In the immediate aftermath of the Civil War, Republican Congressional leaders such as Thaddeus Stevens sought to use the power of the federal government to enforce not only the end of slavery but also some measure of racial equality. The three Reconstruction Amendments (Thirteenth, Fourteenth, and Fifteenth) to the Constitution sought to permanently enshrine not only the end of slavery but also the extension of citizenship rights to black Americans and voting rights to black men. States such as Georgia, however, evaded the federal government and succeeded in reestablishing a post–Civil War society akin to the society present under legalized slavery. Georgia and other states passed laws that effectively denied voting rights to black men, and that kept black Americans dependent upon white Americans for their livelihoods. By the end of the 1870s, northern states and the federal government had effectively turned their backs on the goals of the Civil War and left southern states free to establish racially segregated societies.

Sharecropping represented one key way that white southerners instituted a society based upon racial inequality. With sharecropping, tenants such as Jerry Robinson agreed to work for a white landowner and to provide that landowner with labor and a share of the crops grown through that labor. In return, the white landowner provided the black tenants with some supplies and a place to live. The legal arrangement kept the black tenants impoverished and dependent upon white landowners. Many sharecroppers such as Jerry Robinson lacked the ability to read and write, meaning that they lacked access to other means to support themselves and their families. Jerry's youngest son, therefore, entered a world not far removed from legalized slavery. Sharecropping mimicked the power dynamics present in slavery, and the promises associated with the Reconstruction Amendments had long disappeared. Though Robinson spent only sixteen months in the Deep South, the legacy of slavery followed him across the country and for the remainder of his life.

ROBINSON AND WORLD WAR I'S LEGACY

In addition to entering a world scarred by the long arm of slavery, Robinson also entered a world still reeling from a devastating global conflict, World War I (1914–18), known as the Great War. World War I began in the summer of 1914 when European leaders decided that war represented the best means to resolve long-simmering tensions. Leaders of various

European countries—including Austria-Hungary, Germany, Russia, France, and the United Kingdom—foolishly plunged their countries into a war that they believed would end in a few months. The resulting conflict exceeded their imaginations. Within a few months of the war's beginning, the conflict ground into a stalemate that lasted until the fall of 1918. In the meantime, the warring powers launched often-futile offensives that resulted in high causalities but little change in the war's progress. The war destroyed centuries-old monarchies in countries such as Austria-Hungary, Germany, Russia, and the Ottoman Empire. By the time the war ended, the Austro-Hungarian and Ottoman Empires had dissolved, while Russia witnessed a revolution that brought the world its first communist dictatorship. The war touched all parts of the world, but Europe took the brunt of the conflict and entered the postwar era with a generation haunted by the prolonged conflict.

Robinson's birth in January 1919 came in the uncertain interim between the armistice that concluded the war in November 1918 and the final resolution of that war at a peace conference in Paris, France. The conference convened on January 18, 1919, and marked the first time that a sitting president of the United States, Woodrow Wilson, left the country and visited Europe. Wilson attended the conference because he wanted his ideals for a postwar world to shape the Great War's resolution and prevent a similar war from occurring. He first announced his ideals, known as the Fourteen Points, as part of his State of the Union message in 1918. Though the United States had not entered the war until 1917, Wilson had some leverage to implement his ideals since the United States' intervention helped bring the war to its conclusion. The United States also provided aid to the victorious powers, and Germany agreed to an armistice with the understanding that the Fourteen Points would serve as the basis of the war's final resolution. While the peace conference remained in session from January to June 1919, people around the world waited with a mix of hopefulness and hesitation to see how Wilson and his fellow leaders decided to build a new world order.

The treaty that Wilson and other leaders produced established the foundation for a second global conflict that ensnared the men and women of Robinson's generation. The treaty, known as the Treaty of Versailles, blamed Germany for the conflict, saddled the country with a reparations bill that stretched into the billions of dollars, and stripped the country of its means to wage war. Faced with the threat of fighting a war it lacked the resources to fight, the new German government signed the treaty and never escaped the stain of that decision. The treaty's provisions harmed the German economy and psyche and provided fertile ground for the rise of a demagogue who promised to punish Germany's enemies and reestablish the nation's greatness.

Within the United States, many Senators balked at the treaty's provisions, particularly the provisions related to the creation of a new organization called the League of Nations. Those Senators believed that the organization undermined Congress's authority to declare war and would unnecessarily involve the country in future conflicts. Wilson refused to compromise because the League of Nations represented one of his Fourteen Points and one of the lynchpins of his vision for a new world order. Even though he went on a speaking tour in support of the treaty, he failed to rally public support to his side. Wilson also suffered a debilitating stroke, something he tried to hide from the public, and remained hapless as the Senate rejected the treaty. The treaty's harsh provisions, combined with the failure of the United States to join the League of Nations and partake in world leadership, helped to create an unsettled world in the 1920s and 1930s. That world produced totalitarian regimes, such as the ones in Nazi Germany and imperial Japan, that again sought to use war to settle scores and bring glory to their nations.

In addition to framing the world of Robinson's childhood and young adulthood, Wilson also played an important role in shaping the domestic world of Jackie's early life. Prior to serving as president of the United States, Wilson served as president of Princeton University and as governor of New Jersey. Wilson, however, was not a native of New Jersey; he was born in Staunton, Virginia, in 1856, five years before the outbreak of the Civil War. Consequently, Wilson spent his formative years in a culture that regarded slavery in a positive light, disagreed with the lofty goals of the immediate post–Civil War era, and valued reconciliation at the expense of equal rights for black Americans. Wilson maintained that worldview while he served as president of the United States. He segregated parts of the federal government and welcomed a showing of the film *The Birth of a Nation* (1915), a film that glamorized the Ku Klux Klan, in the White House. Wilson's elevation to the presidency embodied the harsh reality that faced families such as the Robinsons. The federal government had long abandoned any commitment to enforcing the goals of the Civil War, and many in the United States considered legalized racial segregation as a perfectly normal feature of American society.

Ironically, Wilson's administration also sparked the Great Migration, the term given to the mass migration of African American families from southern states. Since the late nineteenth century, industry leaders in northern cities relied upon immigrants as a source of cheap labor. The outbreak of the Great War reduced the number of immigrants from Europe, but the demands upon the American economy grew since the country supplied belligerent nations before the country formally entered the war. Those factors led industry leaders to turn to a new source of cheap labor—black Americans from southern states. The inducement of better jobs and

"Lost Cause" Mythology

The mythology about the Civil War that framed Woodrow Wilson's formative years was known as the "Lost Cause" mythology. That mythology appeared soon after the Civil War ended, as a way for white Southerners to cope with losing the war and to reframe the war as an unnecessary mistake. According to the tenets of the "Lost Cause" mythology, slavery did not represent the cause of the Civil War. Instead, northern aggression against the sovereign rights of southern states caused the Civil War, and the southern states mounted an honorable defense against that aggression. Believers in the "Lost Cause" mythology asserted that slavery was in decline in 1860, and it would have ended naturally without a bloody and destructive war. Believers, furthermore, contended that antebellum southern society represented a glorious and genteel time during which the black and white races lived in harmony. In the antebellum South of the "Lost Cause" mythology, paternalistic slaveowners cared for all their slaves, and the slaves happily served their masters.

The "Lost Cause" mythology defied all facts about the antebellum South, the viability of slavery, and the actual cause of the Civil War. Despite its lack of factual foundation, the "Lost Cause" mythology remained strong at the time of Woodrow Wilson's presidency and Jackie Robinson's birth. The mythology manifested itself in popular culture through a popular novel *The Clansman* and its movie adaptation *Birth of a Nation*. Both the novel and the film glorified the emergence of the Ku Klux Klan and the reconciliation that helped to usher in the Jim Crow era in the United States. Wilson loved the film and screened it in the White House. He also presided over the formal racial segregation of jobs available within the federal government, a symbol of the mythology's enduring impact upon the world of Robinson's birth.

escape from the endless drudgery of sharecropping enticed many black Americans to join the Great Migration and move to northern cities. Black Americans in northern cities still felt the sting of racial inequality, and a race riot erupted in Chicago in 1919. Black Americans in northern cities, however, did serve as customers for black-owned businesses and as spectators for sports events, including black professional baseball.

When the Robinsons trekked across the United States in 1920, they too participated in the Great Migration and experienced both the promises and limitations that came with the movement. Like many other black families, however, the Robinsons discovered that their new environs still carried the legacy of the country's racial history. Though Mallie Robinson had received an education and could read and write, the only jobs available to her in Pasadena came in service to the city's white residents. She worked long hours to provide for her five children, and within a few years, she succeeded in saving enough money to purchase a property with two separate houses in a white neighborhood. The Robinsons' presence angered their white neighbors. Those neighbors signed a petition designed to force the Robinsons out of the neighborhood; that petition failed, and the Robinsons remained in the neighborhood. Other times, the white neighbors called the police to complain about Jackie and his older brothers. Instead of striking back in anger, Mallie responded with kindness and tried to turn her white neighbors away from their racism. While Mallie could not shield her children from their neighbors' racism, she did provide an example of resolve in the face of racism that her youngest son emulated later in his life.

Though Pasadena stood a continent away from the states that had formed the Confederacy, the city contained some of the same vestiges of inequality that the Robinsons had faced in Georgia. Pasadena ranked as one of the country's wealthiest cities per capita, yet black families saw little of that wealth. White Pasadenans sought to keep black families out of their neighborhoods, and many occupations remained off-limits to Pasadena's black residents. As a result, many black Pasadenans endured long stretches of unemployment, hunger, and poor living conditions. Though Mallie maintained a steady job and bought property, Robinson recalled periods of hunger in his childhood and remained acutely aware of the racism in his midst. Mallie sought to instill good qualities in her youngest son, but he went through a rough period in his childhood that could have taken him on a very different path in his life.

As a child, Robinson displayed few of the qualities that made him suited to reintegrate Major League Baseball. He joined a gang, known as the Pepper Street Gang, and often found himself in trouble with the local police. Robinson and his fellow gang members engaged in some minor crimes, such as theft from local stores, and some mischief, such as stealing golf balls and selling them back to their owners. As Robinson later recalled, the Pepper Street Gang attracted nonwhite kids like himself who came from poor families. They joined the gang because it provided them with a sense of community and a means to release the resentment they experienced while living near wealthier white neighbors. Robinson and the other Pepper Street Gang members saw the privileges that their white neighbors enjoyed, privileges denied to them because of the color of their skins. Robinson's time with the Pepper Street Gang did not lead him toward a life of crime, but it did demonstrate the frustrations he felt and his recognition of the racial disparities in American society.

Robinson credited two men with helping him leave the gang and putting his life on a firmer path—Carl Anderson and Rev. Karl Downs. Both of those men served as father figures for Robinson and helped him form a closer bond with his mother. According to Robinson, Anderson challenged him to consider how his mother would react if he continued his membership in the Pepper Street Gang. Reverend Downs, who worked at the church Mallie attended with her children, helped Robinson appreciate the role religious faith could play in building a community. Through his efforts, Reverend Downs brought Robinson closer to his religious faith and helped provide him with advice as he made the transition from childhood to adulthood. Both men filled a void left in Robinson's life due to his father's absence and succeeded in steering him away from the gang and toward more healthy pursuits, such as sports.

PASADENA AND THE BEGINNING OF ROBINSON'S CAREER

During Robinson's childhood, the city of Pasadena had a thriving sports culture as symbolized by the completion of the Rose Bowl in 1922. Located near the campus of the University of California at Los Angeles (UCLA), the Rose Bowl served as the site of one of the country's premiere college football bowl games and, in later years, as the home field for the UCLA Bruins football team. The Rose Bowl's size reflected the spectacle surrounding top-level college football in American society and the sport's role in defining athletic cultures at institutions such as UCLA. Talented players on teams such as the Bruins received special privileges and benefits that stretched the boundaries of amateurism. Games between rivals, such as the annual contest pitting UCLA against its crosstown rival the University of Southern California (USC) Trojans, added to the spectacle surrounding top-level intercollegiate football in the United States. The Bruins' fandom extended beyond the UCLA campus to include Pasadena and helped to feed a culture that valued sports and talented athletes at the high school level. In Pasadena, that sports culture captured Robinson and provided him with valuable experience at playing with white teammates in a segregated society.

Robinson's sports career began in Pasadena and in the shadow of the successes his older brother Mack achieved in his own athletic career. At John Muir Technical High School, Jackie earned varsity letters in four sports—football, track, basketball, and baseball. Since he did not receive any scholarship offers from four-year programs, Jackie decided to attend Pasadena Junior College (PJC) alongside Mack. Through Mack, Jackie witnessed both the promises and the limitations present to black athletes. Mack made the 1936 Olympic team that competed in Berlin, Germany, and he won the silver medal in the men's two-hundred-meter final behind his teammate Jesse Owens. While Owens pursued a professional career after the Olympics, Mack returned to Pasadena and held on to his amateur status. He competed in several track-and-field disciplines for PJC before continuing his collegiate career at the University of Oregon. After using his eligibility at Oregon, Mack returned again to Pasadena and supported himself by working as a street sweeper. Mack often wore the Olympic sweatshirt that identified him as a member of Team USA while he worked at his street sweeper job. Jackie looked up to his older brother, and he also became aware of the bitterness his brother felt at the way his country seemed to forget about him as his Olympic success faded. It took nearly seventy years for the city of Pasadena and the University of Oregon to recognize Mack's success. In the meantime, Mack's frustration left an impression upon Jackie and served as a reminder of the fragility of athletic success for African Americans.

During his two years at PJC, Jackie moved out of Mack's shadow and demonstrated his multifaceted athletic skills. As he did in high school, Jackie played at the varsity level in four sports—football, baseball, basketball, and track-and-field. On the baseball diamond, Robinson played at shortstop and displayed some of the skills that would later excite fans in Major League stadiums. He stole bases, showed off his fielding range, scored runs, and maintained a high batting average. While he wowed fans on the baseball diamond, he simultaneously competed in track-and-field and surpassed his brother's national junior college mark in the long jump. Robinson also started playing for the varsity basketball team, and after recovering from a broken ankle, he earned accolades as the star running back for PJC's varsity football team. He frequently made plays that brought thousands of fans to their feet and garnered mention in local newspapers. For example, in a game played in San Francisco, Robinson ran for a 75-yard touchdown on his first carry. He followed up that play with a 55-yard touchdown and two touchdown passes. Later, at a game held in the Rose Bowl, Robinson ran for 85 yards on one play and helped his team rout a rival from Glendale. In his final game with PJC's football team, Robinson ran the length of the field for a 104-yard touchdown. He won multiple awards for his athletic prowess in football, including a Most Valuable Player award from a local fraternal order.

In addition to showcasing his athletic talents, Robinson's two years at PJC exposed him to the racism he would encounter later in his professional career. Robinson's first year with the PJC football team coincided with the first season for the head coach, Tom Mallory, who had previously coached for a high school in Oklahoma City. Mallory brought some of his players from Oklahoma City with him, and a few of those players refused to play alongside Robinson and the other African American players. Mallory quelled the rebellion, and Robinson earned the respect of his white teammates by excelling at the running back position. On the basketball court, opposing players frequently fouled Robinson, but white referees rarely blew their whistles. Robinson took matters into his own hands and delivered his own hard fouls to ensure that the mistreatment stopped. The disrespect from his teammates and opposing players did not deter Robinson on the field or on the court. In 1938, he ranked as the second-highest scorer in PJC's basketball conference, and he scored seventeen touchdowns while rushing for over one thousand yards for the football team. In his other two sports, he maintained a .417 batting average and surpassed his brother's record for the long jump.

As a result of his athletic successes, Robinson received multiple athletic scholarship offers from four-year programs. Robinson also received enticements that stretched the boundaries of the rules governing intercollegiate athletics. For example, Fresno State University tried to entice Robinson by promising to provide him with new tires for his old car. Mack encouraged Jackie to attend the University of Oregon, but Jackie decided to remain close to home and attend UCLA. Attending UCLA made the most sense for Jackie; he could attend without paying any tuition and would actually play on the football team. Jackie doubted that all the teams that tried to recruit him would actually give him an opportunity to play competitive football. Furthermore, Jackie thought that the youthfulness of the UCLA football program provided him with a good opportunity to make an immediate impression and continue the athletic career he had built at PJC.

A VARSITY STAR AT UCLA

If not for the gentlemen's agreement barring black players, Robinson likely would have never attended UCLA and would have joined a Major League organization after his days at PJC ended. While Robinson ranked as the star of PJC's football program, he also displayed amazing skills on PJC's baseball team. In addition to his .417 batting average, he scored forty-three runs, stole twenty-five bases, and helped his team win a division title. At one point, Robinson joined a team composed of young players who faced the Chicago White Sox while the Major League club went through Spring Training in Pasadena. Against Major League players, Robinson got hits, stole second base, and displayed his defensive range as an infielder. According to a local reporter, White Sox field manager Jimmy Dykes declared that he would sign Robinson if Robinson had been white. For Robinson, however, that option did not exist and, at the time, did not appear likely to exist in the foreseeable future.

Prior to taking the field for the UCLA Bruins, Robinson suffered a devastating blow when his older brother Frank died as a result of injuries he sustained in a traffic accident. His motorcycle collided with a car that had turned into his path; the impact sent Frank flying into a parked car and left him with several fractures, including a fractured skull. He died a few hours after sustaining those injuries, and his funeral took place in July. Frank had helped Jackie make the decision to attend UCLA, and Jackie had a difficult time dealing with his brother's passing. He channeled his grief into his athletics and looked forward to the start of the Bruins' football season. Robinson also pursued other sports, including tennis and golf, as a way to cope with his brother's death before the football season provided him with a steady way to release his anger and grief.

Robinson entered UCLA at a changing time for the university, the top-level college football, and the rest of the world. Nazi Germany invaded Poland on September 1, 1939, around the time that UCLA's football season opened. In the late 1930s, less than one hundred African American players participated in top-level college football programs, and only a few of those players started for their teams. To avoid boycotts, African American players rarely took the field against teams from the South. At the same time, however, institutions such as UCLA recruited black athletes because they wanted successful football teams and black athletes represented an untapped pool of talent. UCLA in particular wanted to assert its place in the world of top-level college football. Both the UCLA football program and Robinson turned twenty in 1939, and the program evolved as the university evolved from a two-year teachers' school to a four-year modern university. For UCLA administrators, a thriving top-level football program served as an advertisement for the university and symbolized the university's new status. They also hoped that the football program would help UCLA escape from the shadow of its crosstown rival, USC. Perhaps for those reasons, UCLA made the bold decision to carry four African American athletes on its 1939 football roster and to include three of those players among the starters—Robinson, Woody Strode, Kenny Washington, and Ray Bartlett. With his three black teammates, Robinson stood poised to make history when he joined UCLA's football team in 1939 and to help the Bruins cement their place as a top-level program.

Perhaps aided by their experiences on UCLA's football team, Robinson and his three black teammates all left important legacies in American society. Robinson arguably remained the most famous of the four men due to his role in reintegrating Major League Baseball. Strode and Washington, however, integrated another league, the National Football League, one year before Robinson debuted with the Brooklyn Dodgers. Strode and Washington were seniors in 1939 when Robinson and Bartlett began their first season for the Bruins. Bartlett, who had played alongside Robinson at PJC, did not pursue a career in professional sports. Instead, after graduating from UCLA in 1944, Bartlett served his Pasadena community through organizations such as the Young Men's Christian Association (YMCA). All four men contributed to the Bruins football team in 1939 and shared the experiences of life for UCLA's black students in a society that still did not regard them as equals.

While the UCLA administration wanted black players on the football team, and UCLA fans cheered Robinson and his teammates on the field, neither the administration nor others at UCLA treated nonwhite students as full members of the university community. The part of the UCLA campus located in the Westwood section of Los Angeles remained off-limits to black students. White students excluded their black and other nonwhite peers, including Jewish students, from campus social life, such as parties. Black students could not find jobs on UCLA's campus, and the university did not employ any black professors. Progress for black students arrived slowly over the next decade, and the black athletes on UCLA's football team served as a harbinger of that progress. Robinson left campus before that progress began, but he again did not let the discrimination surrounding him deter him from achieving success on the playing field.

As he did in high school and junior college, Robinson played multiple sports for the UCLA Bruins. The cancelation of the 1940 Olympics due to World War II (1939–45) ended his dream of competing for the country's track-and-field team, so he devoted his energy to playing the same four sports he had played prior to joining the Bruins. For the Bruins' track-and-field team, Robinson competed in two disciplines and won the 1940 National Collegiate Athletic Association (NCAA) championship in the long jump. He also spent two seasons on the Bruins' lackluster basketball team, although Robinson earned accolades for his play on the basketball court. Ironically, he struggled the most on the baseball team and came to consider baseball his worst sport. By far, Robinson's greatest success came on the football field. In 1939, he played a key role in helping the team earn a winning record and in holding the USC Trojans to a tie in a contest held in front of the then-largest crowd to witness a football game in the Los Angeles Memorial Coliseum (USC's home field). In the 1940 season, Robinson again excelled at the running back position, though the team failed to repeat its success from the previous year. Despite the Bruins' poor performance, both local and national newspapers lauded Robinson as one of the top running backs in the nation. Robinson's success made him the first UCLA Bruin to earn varsity letters in four sports and cemented his legacy as one of the greatest athletes to don a Bruins jersey.

In the midst of those athletic achievements, Robinson met the woman who would become his most important ally—Rachel Isum. Robinson met the then-seventeen-year-old Rachel near the start of UCLA's 1940–41 academic year. Born in 1922, Rachel came from a family that had its roots in the American Southwest and that emphasized the importance of hard work as well as high standards. She helped take care of her father, Charles, a World War I veteran who needed constant care because of a gas attack he suffered during the war. Rachel's mother, Zellee, owned a catering business, and Rachel helped her with the business. Zellee relied upon Rachel to take care of the family's house while also taking care of Charles, and she impressed upon her the importance of a good education as well as good behavior in public. The two developed a close mother-daughter bond that included a shared love of cooking and music. Rachel enrolled at UCLA in 1940 to pursue a degree in nursing, and she formally met Robinson through his friend Bartlett. She had known Robinson through his playing days with PJC's football team, but the two had not formally met before Bartlett introduced them on UCLA's campus in the fall of 1940. In the months following their first meeting, Rachel and Robinson met each other's families and enjoyed their first date while Robinson had his first taste of athletic fame with the Bruins' disappointing 1940 football team. The relationship Robinson and Rachel established in the fall of 1940 laid the foundation for their stressful yet successful marriage. It also introduced Rachel to her role as a supporter of Robinson's athletic pursuits and as a sounding board for the choices he would make in his life.

As UCLA's disappointing football season proceeded, Robinson confided in Rachel about his decision to leave the university and pursue a job as an athletic director. Rachel, along with Mallie and few others, tried to dissuade Robinson since he had almost earned all the credits he needed to graduate from the university. Robinson, however, remained determined to pursue his career and to earn enough money to help ease the financial burden on his mother. He withdrew from UCLA in March 1941 and started his new job one month later, fully believing that his athletic career had ended and his only path ahead involved helping others excel at athletics. Robinson's sudden decision meant that he faced the possible end of his playing days. Neither Major League Baseball nor the NFL wanted Robinson due to their bans on black players, and neither of the two professional basketball leagues then in existence employed black players. Few opportunities existed for black professional track-and-field athletes, and the cancelation of the Olympic Games left him with no other avenue to pursue that sport. Without any apparent opportunities to pursue a professional sports career, Robinson set his sights on working as an athletic director for young athletes.

WORLD WAR II

Robinson arrived at his new job at the California Polytechnic Institute in April 1941, one month after leaving UCLA. At the CPI campus in San Luis Obispo, Robinson joined the National Youth Administration (NYA), a New Deal program launched in 1935. Like other New Deal programs, the NYA targeted young Americans and provided them with job training, jobs, and other forms of relief as ways to mitigate the impact of the Great Depression. With the NYA, Robinson worked as an athletic director and developed recreational programs while also playing shortstop for the organization's baseball team. Within a few months of Robinson's arrival, however, the NYA disbanded, and his career as an athletic director effectively ended. President Franklin D. Roosevelt no longer saw the need for the NYA; though the United States had not yet entered World War II, Roosevelt had signed the Selective Service and Training Act to ensure that the country had military-ready men should the country join the war. Instead of providing young men with job training, the federal government sought to prepare young men for fighting against Nazi Germany and Japan.

World War II began during Robinson's first year with UCLA and formed an important part of the backdrop for him and other young men as they sought to begin their adult lives. Under the leadership of Adolf Hitler and the Nazi Party, Germany pursued an aggressive foreign policy in the late 1930s and triggered the start of another global conflict with its invasion of Poland in September 1939. The United Kingdom and France sought to contain Germany's conquests in Europe, but their efforts largely failed in the war's early stages. Germany launched an offensive against Western Europe in the spring of 1940 and quickly occupied and conquered multiple countries—including Norway, Belgium, and France. Germany formed an alliance with other expansion-minded dictatorships—Italy and Japan—and launched an ill-advised invasion of the Soviet Union in July 1941. President Roosevelt declared America's neutrality, but he also sought to provide as much aid as possible to the United Kingdom and later the Soviet Union. Around the time that the NYA disbanded, Roosevelt met with UK prime minister Winston Churchill and developed a shared vision, known as the Atlantic Charter, for the postwar world. Though the war had not yet come to the United States in the summer of 1941, the war loomed as a threat that would upend the plans of men such as Robinson and ensnare them in yet another global conflict.

As that threat loomed over the horizon, Robinson returned to the football field and reached the limits of what he could accomplish playing football at a professional level in 1941. He first played in a charity game in Chicago that the *Tribune* sponsored and showcased the Chicago Bears against a team composed of top college players. In the game, Robinson played alongside athletes who had won the top awards in intercollegiate football and held their own against the Bears for three quarters. Robinson's talents again attracted attention, including from some of the Bears' players and from the nearly one hundred thousand fans who packed into Soldier Field. Following the game, Robinson played one game of professional football in Los Angeles, playing for a team not involved with the NFL, before heading for Hawaii and a semi-professional league known as the Hawaii Senior Football League. The opportunity provided Robinson with a salary for playing for the Honolulu Bears and for working in construction at a site near Pearl Harbor. Robinson's record at UCLA followed him to Hawaii, and he again made an impression with his football skills. Robinson, however, strongly disliked his construction job and reinjured the ankle that he had previously broken during his first year at PJC. Once the season ended, Robinson returned to his home in Pasadena. He set sail from Hawaii on December 5 and remained at sea on December 7 when he and his shipmates received news about Japan's attack on Pearl Harbor. The attack brought the United States into World War II and forced Robinson to focus all his energies on the war effort, not on sports.

When Robinson returned to Los Angeles, he tried to pursue a normal life as he awaited news from his local draft board. He lived with his mother and a collection of other relatives who resided in his mother's houses on Pepper Street. Robinson helped to support his mother by working at a factory for Lockheed Aircraft in Burbank. He also deepened his relationship with Rachel; her father's death in March 1941 brought them closer together, and Robinson sent her a bracelet as a sign of his commitment to their relationship. His attempts to appeal for an exemption from the draft failed, and he received his order to report for induction into the United States Army in March 1942. Robinson dutifully reported for induction on April 3 at a station near Los Angeles. After passing his physical examination, Robinson traveled to Fort Riley, Kansas, for his basic training. Similarly to many other men of his generation, Robinson discovered that the demands of World War II would not allow him to pursue a normal life. Though he wanted to stay in Los Angeles and support his mother, his country had other plans for him, and he lacked any means of resisting those plans.

When Robinson arrived at Fort Riley, he entered a world akin to the one he and his family had left behind in Georgia. Like other branches of the U.S. military, the army practiced segregation and relegated black men in its ranks to segregated units. The army also barred any of its few black officers from leading black units; army leaders based their actions upon the assumptions of white supremacy and black inferiority. Robinson personally faced those practices when the army rejected his application for Officer Candidate School and instead assigned him to the horse stables. The army's segregation practices also denied Robinson a spot on Fort Riley's baseball team. While Robinson had faced segregation earlier in his life, his initial experiences at Fort Riley magnified the reality that his government and many of his fellow citizens regarded him as inferior and a second-class citizen. That reality also highlighted the hypocrisy of the government and Americans who supported segregation while fighting against regimes based upon racism overseas.

After facing those initial attempts to relegate him to a subordinate place within the army, Robinson and other black enlistees at Fort Riley received relief from an unlikely source—former heavyweight boxing champion Joe Louis (1914–81). Louis rose to fame in the 1930s by twice facing the

German Max Schmeling in fights that symbolized the advance of Nazism and the democracy-led resistance against that ideology. Schmeling upset Louis in the first fight held in 1936; two years later, Louis stunned Schmeling with a first-round knockout. Louis's victory over Schmeling, and his rise to the top of the heavyweight class, made him a hero among African Americans. Articles about Louis splashed across the pages of black newspapers throughout the country as fans followed his training cycles and eagerly anticipated his next fight against a top-level opponent. Instead of continuing his boxing career, Louis volunteered to join the army in January 1942, and fate brought him to Fort Riley at the same time as Robinson started his training. Louis used his fame and connections to civil rights organizations to push for Robinson and other black enlistees to receive acceptance to the Officer Candidate School. His entreaties worked, and Robinson joined the Officer Candidate School in November 1942.

Overall, Robinson's time in the army provided him with experiences he could draw upon later in his life when he became a Major League Baseball player and an advocate for civil rights. Louis provided Robinson with an example of how a star athlete could use his fame to push for advancement in areas outside of the sports world. As one of the first black men admitted into Fort Riley's Officer Candidate School, Robinson gained experience in the process of integrating a formerly segregated institution. He successfully went through the thirteen-week training program and, on January 28, 1943, received his commission as a second lieutenant in the United States Army Calvary.

Robinson's commission put him in charge of a truck battalion at Fort Riley and as the morale officer for men under his command. In that position, Robinson dealt with the complaints about the lack of respect shown toward the black enlistees, such as the lack of sufficient seats for black soldiers at the fort's post exchange. Robinson tried to resolve the issue through a phone conversation with the fort's provost marshal, but he lost his temper when the provost marshal made a comment about the propriety of black men sitting near white women. Even though he yelled at the provost marshal, who was unaware that Robinson was African American, Robinson's efforts succeeded in providing for more seats for black soldiers at the post exchange. Robinson endured further frustration when he received a two weeks' leave right at the time when the fort's football team opened its season. He had practiced with the team and seemed likely to play, and he angrily resigned his place on the team when he returned from leave.

Robinson's decision presaged his departure from Fort Riley for Fort Sam Houston in San Antonio, Texas. After receiving treatment for his right ankle at Fort Sam Houston's Brooke General Hospital, Robinson and other black officers from Fort Riley were transferred to Camp Hood in Kileen, Texas, in 1944. Once again, Robinson and his fellow black officers faced the biting reality of segregation as they prepared to risk their lives for their country. Robinson gained even more experience in the arduous process of integration and in confronting people who sought to deny him basic rights.

In July 1944, Robinson became embroiled in a prolonged controversy that threatened to undermine his accomplishments in the army and bring his army career to an inglorious conclusion. While returning to Camp Hood on a bus operated by the base, Robinson refused the driver's orders to move to the back of the bus and away from a female passenger the driver mistakenly identified as white. Robinson knew the passenger and knew about army rules outlawing segregated seating on buses it operated. When the bus reached the camp's station, the driver, Milton Renegar, ordered the dispatcher to summon the military police. The military police who investigated the incident accused Robinson of disobeying orders, disrespecting his superiors, and engaging in behavior unbecoming of officers in the United States Army. Robinson disputed their claims and argued that the investigators did not follow proper procedures, nor did they provide him with equal opportunities to share his side of the incident. The military police soon placed Robinson under arrest, and Robinson faced the prospect of a court martial.

Even though the jurors in his court martial trial voted in favor of his acquittal, the trial effectively marked the end of his army career. In the trial, Robinson faced two charges that he violated the Articles of War by disrespecting a senior officer and by disobeying a lawful command. Robinson's defense successfully persuaded enough of the nine jurors that his actions did not constitute violations of Articles of War; Robinson himself took the stand in his own defense and issued forceful denials of the prosecution's version of events. Following his acquittal, Robinson returned to Camp Hood, but the battalion he had led had already departed for Europe. Robinson would have joined them as a morale officer if not for his court martial trial. The battalion he had helped train distinguished itself in Europe as it joined other American forces fighting across Western Europe and pushing into German territory. In August, Robinson appealed directly to the Adjutant General for his retirement from active service in the army and for his placement in the army reserves. After receiving a transfer to another military camp in Georgia, Robinson finally received his honorable discharge from the army in November 1944. His discharge finally gave him the freedom to leave behind his obligations to the army and resume the life he had left behind when he reported for duty in 1942.

As World War II reached its conclusion in the early months of 1945, Robinson began to write the next chapter in his life. Prior to returning home, Robinson and Rachel had ended their relationship over Rachel's determination to join the Nurse Cadet Corps. Robinson saw the corps as a way for enlisted men to take advantage of the young nurses, while Rachel saw the corps as an opportunity to support her country while earning some money. Once Robinson left the army, the couple resolved their differences and resumed their engagement. In addition to making plans for his personal life, Robinson decided to forge a new career path in professional baseball by joining the Negro Leagues. While serving in the army, Robinson had met Ted Alexander, formerly of the Negro American League's Kansas City Monarchs, and learned about the opportunities available to him in black professional baseball. In the spring of 1945, Robinson again headed to Texas, this time to join the Kansas City Monarchs as they started their spring training exercises. Robinson's decision brought him into the world of black professional baseball and put him in a position to catch the attention of scouts seeking the ideal man to reintegrate Major League Baseball.

2

The Negro Leagues

When Jackie Robinson joined the Kansas City Monarchs in 1945, he entered a league that reflected the United States' racial history, with its roots in the nineteenth century. A few baseball teams first appeared in the northeastern United States prior to the Civil War, and the first professional team debuted four years after the war's conclusion. Similarly to the rest of the country, professional baseball grappled with the outcome of the Civil War. Leagues that served as the Major Leagues initially welcomed black players, such as Bud Fowler, before instituting an agreement that barred team officials from signing any black players. Additionally, leagues rejected the applications of all-black teams, leaving those teams to fend for themselves and to never enjoy the benefits of organized league structures. The experiences of black players and black teams in the nineteenth century established a critical foundation for the creation of separate Negro Leagues in the twentieth century and for the alignment forces that resisted efforts toward the reintegration of Major League baseball.

In the late nineteenth and early twentieth centuries, sports promoters such as A. G. Spalding and A. G. Mills helped to perpetuate the myth that Abner Doubleday invented the game of baseball in 1839. Spalding and Mills engaged in this subterfuge in order to obscure the non-American roots of baseball and to promote the game as a distinctly American pastime. Doubleday, who fought for the Union in the American Civil War, spent 1839 as a cadet at West Point and, therefore, did not invent the game of baseball near Cooperstown, New York. On the contrary, the game evolved from ball games played in the colonies, games likely derived from the English sports rounders and cricket. Amateur clubs that played early versions of baseball first appeared in the northeastern United States prior to 1839. Those clubs helped to establish the shape of the baseball infield, the length between bases, the number of players on each team, and other rules associated with baseball. The most famous of those clubs, the New York Knickerbockers, played a leading role in developing those rules and may have participated in the first baseball game played in the United States. In 1857, amateur clubs formed the first league, the National Association of Base Ball Players (NABBP), that continued to govern the sport until the development of professional teams and leagues. The Civil War interrupted the evolution of baseball as men who could spend their leisure time playing sports needed to devote their attention to the war effort. At the same time, however, the Civil War provided a critical means of furthering the growth of baseball since it brought together men from different parts of the country and exposed them to a sport previously confined to Northeastern states.

The Civil War raged from April 1861 to April 1865 and helped to shape the society and culture from which professional baseball emerged. By winning the Civil War, the Union ensured the abolition of slavery and the ending of the Confederacy's dream of slavery as a perpetual as well as natural institution. To emphasize that outcome, the states ratified three Constitutional amendments that sought to undo slavery and make African Americans full citizens. The Thirteenth Amendment abolished slavery, the Fourteenth Amendment granted citizenship to all people born in the country, and the Fifteenth Amendment removed race as a reason to deny someone the ability to vote. Many white southerners, however, refused to accept the outcome of the Civil War and sought to recreate the society that existed under slavery. A sign of white Southerners' intransigence appeared when former Confederate states such as Mississippi sought to implement Black Codes. Those Black Codes kept power in the hands of white Americans and severely limited the freedoms of African Americans. Intervention from Radical Republicans in Congress squashed those Black Codes, but the Republicans could not squash the sentiment behind the measures. Within a decade after the Civil War ended, a spirit of reconciliation had emerged within the country and dispelled any lingering feelings about using federal power to enforce the outcome of the Civil War. Once freed from strict federal oversight, Mississippi and other states passed laws that implemented a system of legalized racial segregation. Those laws led to the creation of separate public facilitates or accommodations, limited opportunities available to African Americans, and restricted the ability of African Americans to exercise their voting rights. State and local authorities viciously lynched African Americans who advocated for civil rights or who engaged in behavior those authorities deemed undesirable.

Such developments, along with the nationwide industrial growth of the late nineteenth century, happened at the same time as the game of baseball resumed its growth. Professional teams appeared a few years after the Civil War's conclusion, and those teams soon formed into professional leagues. In the years after the Civil War, baseball emerged as the national pastime, an honor not bestowed upon the other popular sports that evolved during that same time period. As the national pastime, baseball adopted a special cultural place in the United States and absorbed as well as reflected many of the issues flowing through American society. Those issues included tensions between workers and their employers and between white and black Americans. Baseball could not escape the racial segregation that appeared in the late nineteenth century, and that racial segregation shaped the sports world that Jackie Robinson entered in the 1930s and 1940s.

THE BEGINNINGS OF PROFESSIONAL BASEBALL

As white baseball teams developed in the 1860s, black teams also appeared in cities such as Philadelphia. The year 1867 witnessed the first contest between two black teams—the Philadelphia Excelsiors and the Brooklyn Uniques—a game the Excelsiors won by the score of 42–37. Earlier in 1867, a fraternal organization in Philadelphia, the Knights of Pythias, formed a baseball club called the Philadelphia Pythians. The Pythians attracted support from Philadelphia's elite black population; some supporters had actively participated in the abolitionist movement and in the Underground Railroad. Octavius V. Catto, who served as the Pythians' captain, had a well-earned reputation as a leader and as someone who challenged racial barriers. Catto worked as a teacher at the Institute for Colored Youth and successfully pressed for black Pennsylvanians to join the Union Army during the Civil War. He also joined the Pennsylvania National Guard and served as the corresponding secretary for the Pennsylvania State Equal Rights League. In his capacity as the corresponding secretary, Catto led a successful effort to pressure the state legislature to outlaw segregation on Philadelphia's streetcars. Catto's efforts demonstrated his passion and his advocacy for civil rights, qualities that he continued to demonstrate when he served as the captain for the Philadelphia Pythians.

Under Catto's leadership, the Philadelphia Pythians emerged as the first all-black baseball team that forced the sport to decide if it would follow the path of integration or segregation. The Pythians enjoyed a successful 1867 season while playing against black teams. In 1868, Catto sought to expand the Pythians' schedule by petitioning for the team to join a new all-white organization, the Pennsylvania Convention of Baseball Clubs (PCBC). Catto turned to the Pythians' vice president, Raymond Burr, to travel to a PCBC meeting in Harrisburg and press directly for the club's membership in the organization. Some of the PCBC delegates supported the Pythians' petition, but Burr learned that a majority of the delegates did not want an all-black team to join the league. The PCBC's credential committee repeatedly ignored the Pythians' petition, thereby forcing Burr to withdraw the club's application for membership. Catto himself met a similar fate when he unsuccessfully petitioned for the Pythians to join the National Association of Base Ball Players (NABBP), an early national organization for professional baseball. The actions of the PCBC and the NABBP foreshadowed the broader societal rejection of integration as well as the "gentlemen's agreement" that would govern Major League baseball in the decades prior to Jackie Robinson's debut with the Dodgers.

Despite the rejection from the PCBC and NABBP, the Pythians did play against white teams during the 1869 season. A rumored game between the Pythians and one of the city's top white teams, the Philadelphia Athletics, never materialized. In September, the Pythians gained national attention by playing against the Olympic Club, another one of the city's top white teams, at the Olympics' home grounds. The Pythians lost the game, but they won a game against another white team, the City Items, demonstrating that a black team could compete against a white team. The Pythians' success, however, ended in 1871 with Catto's untimely death. Catto died on Election Day because he sought to exercise his right to vote, a right granted to him by the then recently ratified Fifteenth Amendment. White Philadelphians attempted to prevent him and other black men from exercising their voting rights. A white man named Frank Kelly approached Catto as he walked to his local polling place; Kelly shot Catto three times, and Catto died instantly. Catto's murder and the Pythians' rejections from white teams demonstrated the peril encountered by black teams and men associated with those teams who sought to assert racial equality. Similarly to the rest of American society, black baseball teams and officials faced hostility from whites, and they had few opportunities to prove that they could compete on equal footing with white organizations.

The disappointment that the Pythians' endured came at the same time as baseball evolved from an amateur to a professional sport. In 1869, the Cincinnati Red Stockings, a formerly amateur club that had formed a few years earlier, fielded salaried players and became the first fully professional baseball club in the United States. The Red Stockings initially operated as members of the NABBP, but it and other professional teams left the amateur organization to form the first professional league, the National Association of Professional Base Ball Players (NAPBBP), in 1872. Professional teams such as the Red Stockings benefited from the features of an industrializing country—the extensive railroad system, the expansion of newspapers, the growth of telegraph lines, and the surge in urban populations. Those features helped to further the spread of professional baseball, publicize the game and its players, and provide teams with fanbases as well as potential players. Soon, professional franchises appeared in other cities across the Northeast and Midwest—cities such as Boston, New York, Philadelphia, Pittsburgh, Chicago, and Cleveland. Professional baseball, in other words, followed American geographical patterns, a feature of the game that would continue through the twentieth century.

Professional baseball's appearance in the years following the Civil War paralleled the growth of other amateur and professional sports in the United States. Intercollegiate athletics, which existed in a very primitive form prior to the Civil War, experienced a growth spurt starting in the 1860s. By the end of the century, intercollegiate football emerged as a big-time athletic endeavor and as a defining feature of elite universities across the country. Americans also started patronizing tennis matches, cycling events, horse races, and some of the earliest basketball games. Professional boxing also emerged as a major sport in the late nineteenth century. The sport adopted new rules, such as timed rounds and the requirement for all boxers to wear gloves, that moved boxing past its bare-knuckle roots and tried to control the violence inherent in all boxing matches. Successful professional boxers became symbols of white American masculinity and national celebrities. Sports such as baseball, therefore, became an embedded feature of industrializing American society in the late nineteenth century. Stories about baseball, boxing, intercollegiate football, and other sports filled the pages of newspapers and provided entertainment for thousands of spectators.

While other sports dotted the American landscape in the late nineteenth century, baseball emerged as the only sport that represented the American pastime. Spalding's efforts to hide baseball's actual roots in an American mythology tied to a Civil War veteran took place in the late nineteenth century. That mythology helped to cement baseball's place as a truly American sport, one whose rhythms and traditions matched American society. Writers composed lyrical poems and stories, such as "Casey at the Bat," that cemented baseball's place in American popular culture as well as in its sporting culture. Intercollegiate football offered Americans a spectacle, professional boxing shaped American views on masculinity, and horse racing gave Americans an outlet for excitement as well as gambling. Baseball filled a space in American culture that none of those other sports filled. Baseball seemed like a truly American sport, one grown from American soil and shaped by American ingenuity.

As a truly American sport, baseball experienced some of the same issues that arose in American society in the late nineteenth century. Some of those issues reflected the battles between laborers and business owners that arose as those two groups sought to define how much power each had within the industrializing American economy. In 1876, officials from a group of professional teams founded the National League of Professional Base Ball Clubs—the modern-day National League—as a way to centralize their authority. The National League replaced the NAPBBP; the older professional league disbanded, and the National League attracted some of the teams from the defunct organization. Within a few years, the National League faced competition from rival leagues, including the American Association formed in 1882 and the International League formed in 1884. Professional baseball players sought to have as much control as possible over their careers, while the owner of teams sought to accumulate power and ensure that they made money from their investments. Ultimately, the owners won those battles, and players lacked the ability to form unions that could give them some measure of control over their salaries and other related issues. A sign of the owners' power came in the insertion of reserve clauses into players' contracts—those clauses gave the owners power to "reserve" the services of players every season. With those reserve clauses, players had little leverage to agitate for higher salaries and for shares in the profits owners made from their franchises.

ANDREW CARNEGIE

The rapid industrialization of the late nineteenth century made men such as Andrew Carnegie both very famous and very powerful. Carnegie made his fortune first through the railroad industry in Pennsylvania and then through the steel industry. He used his platform to write *The Gospel of Wealth*, an essay in which Carnegie recognized the gap between wealthy men like himself and millions of others who lived in poverty. In that essay, Carnegie argued against any government intervention to redistribute his wealth through taxes and to provide direct assistance to poor Americans. Instead, Carnegie argued that men like himself should remain free to redistribute their wealth as they best saw fit and to act as caretakers for poor Americans. Carnegie, in other words, argued for a *laissez-faire* style of capitalism that left as much money and power in the hands of men like himself, John D. Rockefeller, and other wealthy industrialists.

Due to the absence of laws governing labor, Carnegie and other industrialists enforced rules upon their workers that severely limited their workers' freedoms. Workers faced twelve-hour workdays six days a week, unsafe working conditions, low wages, and no insurance or guarantees for injuries sustained while on the job. Some industrialists also created company towns in which they housed their workers and exerted even more control over their workers' lives as both their employers and landlords.

Not surprisingly, many workers resented these conditions and formed unions as a means of expanding their collective power over their employers. Those unions included the American Federation of Labor, the Knights of Labor, and the United Mine Workers. Both the American Federation of Labor and the Knights of Labor appeared around the same time as the Cincinnati Red Stockings and the National League. With the backing of labor unions, workers participated in strikes; one strike involving the railroad industry spread across the country. Carnegie faced a strike at his steelworks in Homestead, Pennsylvania, in 1892. Like other industrialists, Carnegie relied upon the police and the National Guard to violently suppress the strike. Such battles dominated headlines in the late nineteenth century and led to tensions between ballplayers and franchise owners in professional baseball.

In addition to experiencing those tensions between team owners and players, baseball experienced another issue that swept across American society in the late nineteenth century—legalized racial segregation. The story of the Philadelphia Pythians showed that professional baseball leagues would not accept all-black teams, but some white teams did accept one or more black players. At the time, leagues such as the National League, the American Association, and the International League constituted the "major" leagues in professional baseball. Under those classifications, African Americans played in "major" league baseball. African Americans also played on predominantly white teams that participated in leagues classified as "minor" leagues. Similarly to what happened in American society, professional baseball adopted an unwritten color barrier, a practice of racial segregation, that lasted well into the twentieth century. The stories of some of the black players who played in the Major and Minor Leagues provide insight into the attitudes governing professional baseball in the late nineteenth century. Their stories also provide insight into the history and culture Jackie Robinson faced when he joined the Dodgers organization.

JIM CROW IN PROFESSIONAL BASEBALL

Bud Fowler's journey through various "minor" leagues in the 1870s and 1880s illustrated some of the struggles that black professional baseball players endured. His career began with an integrated amateur team in Chelsea, Massachusetts, in 1878. Over the next several seasons, Fowler moved frequently in search of opportunities to play amateur, semipro, and professional baseball. His search for work took him to various teams in Ontario, Minnesota, Iowa, Louisiana, Colorado, and Kansas. In 1887,

Fowler thought he had landed a good opportunity by signing with the Binghamton Bingoes, an integrated club that belonged to the International Association. Fowler's arrival, however, coincided with the growth of racial tensions within the league. Several teams in the league had black players, and the presence of those players led some of the white ballplayers to demand their releases from their contracts. Though Fowler compiled impressive stats with the Bingoes, he and his black teammates lacked support from their white teammates. Faced with massive insubordination from white players, officials from the Bingoes and other teams in the International Association also backed away from providing support to their black players. Fowler left the Bingoes in the middle of the season; in a note to a local newspaper, he went along with the cover story that he had left to pursue a more lucrative opportunity with the all-black Cuban Giants. He never played for the Giants because such an offer never existed; instead, Fowler sought to extend his career by again traveling across the country and looking for any opportunity. His efforts resulted in him facing more racial hostility as the color line in professional baseball hardened and as the leagues expelled all remaining black players.

Within the nineteenth-century Major Leagues, the experiences of Moses Fleetwood Walker best illustrated the perils facing black players at the highest level of professional baseball. Born in Mount Pleasant, Ohio, in 1856, Walker joined the Toledo Blue Stockings in 1883 when the team played in the Northwestern League. Walker's presence led to a failed attempt from a rival team to bar all black players from the league. Later in the same season, Walker's presence led to a confrontation with Cap Anson of the Chicago White Stockings. The White Stockings had arrived in Toledo for a scheduled exhibition game against the Blue Stockings, and Anson announced that he would not play in the game because he refused to play against a black player. The Blue Stockings supported Walker, and the game went ahead as scheduled. In the following season, Walker and the Blue Stockings joined the American Association, one of the recognized Major Leagues of the nineteenth century. During that season, Walker faced a constant stream of hostility from fans and from opposing players. He also faced hostility from his teammates, in particular the pitchers. Walker, who played catcher for the Blue Stockings, worked with pitchers who did not want to throw to a black catcher and who ignored his signs. As a result, the pitchers threw what they wanted at Walker, and Walker had to play his position without the location or the type of pitches he would receive from his battery mate.

The abuse that Walker faced culminated in September 1884. Prior to a scheduled game against a team from Richmond, Virginia, the Blue Stockings' manager Charlie Morton received a letter that threatened to harm Walker if he participated in the game. The letter ominously referred to seventy-five men who had pledged to attack Walker, and it warned Morton that he alone could prevent the bloodshed. In contrast to the situation in the previous season, the Blue Stockings chose not to support Walker in the face of racial hostility from an opponent. Walker did not participate in the game in Richmond. Injuries had limited Walker to playing in only forty-two games during the season, and the Blue Stockings released him on September 22. Walker's departure from the Blue Stockings marked the end of the Major Leagues' brief experiment with integration.

Three years after his forced departure from the Blue Stockings, Walker again played a part in the hardening color line in professional baseball. In the 1887 season, Walker played for the Newark Little Giants of the International League, a Minor League. Walker again played catcher, and he enjoyed a good rapport with George Stovey, a pitcher and another black player on the team. On July 19, Anson's Chicago White Stockings arrived to play against the Little Giants, and Anson reiterated his refusal to take the field against black players. Anson had emerged as one of the top players in professional baseball; his presence guaranteed high attendance at games and lucrative profits for owners. Since the Little Giants did not want to miss an opportunity to make money, they accommodated Anson's request, and neither Stovey nor Walker appeared in the game against the White Stockings. The Little Giants' actions led to the International League's decision to implement a written rule barring all black players. The legalized segregation that characterized other areas of American society had entered professional baseball and would remain in place until the 1940s. An African American would not appear on a roster for a Major League team until April 15, 1947.

In the years following the expulsion of black players, Major League baseball continued to organize itself and to take on the structure familiar to modern-day baseball fans. The National League withstood the fluctuations of professional baseball in the late nineteenth century and finally got a stable rival in 1901 with the emergence of the American League. In 1903, the champions of both leagues staged the first World Series, a tradition that has happened every year with the exception of 1904 and 1994. Each league carried eight franchises; some cities, such as Philadelphia, supported teams in both leagues. New York City supported three teams—the New York Yankees, the New York Giants, and the Brooklyn Dodgers. The Yankees played in the American League, while the Giants and the Dodgers played in the National League. Some of the franchises played under different nicknames. The Dodgers, for example, played under the nicknames of "Superbas" and "Robins" before settling into the nickname they used when Robinson joined them in 1945. The cities featuring Major League teams, however, remained stable until the 1950s. Those cities included Boston,

New York, Philadelphia, Pittsburgh, Cincinnati, Cleveland, Detroit, Chicago, and St. Louis.

CREATING THE RULES OF THE GAME

During the first two decades of the twentieth century, the rules governing Major League Baseball also took shape. The owners of teams in the two leagues agreed to respect the contracts of each other's players and inserted reserve clauses into those contracts. Those reserve clauses effectively granted the owners' near-total control over the players since they gave the owners the freedom to "reserve" a player's services every season. Rules concerning players' behavior came into sharper focus in the aftermath of the 1919 World Series in which members of the Chicago White Sox conspired with gamblers to deliberately lose to the Cincinnati Reds. The players, dubbed the Black Sox, engaged in that behavior because of their disgust with the low salaries that team owner Charlie Comiskey paid them. Once news of their actions emerged, the eight players faced a trial in Chicago, and the jury acquitted them of all charges. Within the Major Leagues, however, the players' actions led to the creation of a commissioner who sought to restore and protect the organization's image. The first commissioner, Kenesaw Mountain Landis, issued lifetime bans against the eight Black Sox and enforced new regulations barring players from associating with gamblers or with gambling.

In the 1920s, concerns about the Black Sox and the integrity of Major League Baseball faded away as George Herman "Babe" Ruth revolutionized the game. Prior to Ruth's ascendance with the Yankees, the home run represented an irregular feature of Major League games. Most of the action took place in the infield, and the dimensions of ballparks reflected that reality. Old ballparks concentrated the fan seating along the infield and had expansive outfields with little to no seating sections. Ruth's talent in hitting home runs altered those dynamics; he hit more home runs than any other American League team in the 1920 season. Fans flocked to ballparks to see Ruth play, and team officials ensured that the dimensions of the original Yankee Stadium accommodated Ruth's home run prowess. In addition to revolutionizing his sport, Ruth also established new standards for athletes in the entertainment world. His outsized personality complemented his home run prowess and helped him emerge as a national celebrity. Ruth appeared in advertisements and movies; newsreels and radio broadcasts showcased Yankees' games and further heightened his celebrity status. He retired in 1935 with a then-record 714 home runs; his record stood until the Atlanta Braves' Henry Aaron hit his 715th career home run in April 1974.

As Major League Baseball developed its written rules and recognized how the spectacle of the home run appealed to fans, the organization never established a written rule prohibiting black players. On the contrary, the owners of the sixteen Major League franchises operated according to a "gentlemen's agreement," an unwritten rule whereby they would not add a black player to their franchise. On a few occasions, an organization would attempt to "pass" a black player as Native American or Latino, but those efforts failed. Ruth and other Major League players from his era never competed against black players except for infrequent barnstorming contests held outside of the regular season. Prior to the 1930s, few people questioned the "gentlemen's agreement" or the exclusion of black players from Major League Baseball. Their exclusion created the conditions for a separate world housing black professional baseball, a world that Robinson entered when he joined the Kansas City Monarchs for the 1945 season.

At the same time as professional baseball implemented a color line, all-black professional teams appeared and provided black players opportunities unavailable to them in the late nineteenth-century Major and Minor Leagues. The Cuban Giants, the team used in the story to explain Fowler's departure from his Major League team, represented the first all-black professional team. Formed in Long Island in 1885, the Giants followed a schedule common for black professional baseball teams in the late nineteenth and early twentieth centuries. They traveled to multiple cities each week to play at least one game on each day; they occasionally played doubleheaders and faced a mixture of amateur as well as professional teams. Ten years after the Giants appeared, Fowler and Grant "Home Run" Johnson, another talented black ballplayer, formed the Page Fence Giants in Adrian, Michigan. The Page Fence Giants carried some notable players, including Charlie Grant and Sol White, who elevated the team as the top black professional baseball team of the 1890s. They battled for that honor against the Cuban X-Giants, a team composed of players who formerly played for the original Cuban Giants.

In addition to the establishment of all-black professional teams, the late nineteenth century also witnessed the first attempts to establish all-black baseball leagues. In 1887, Walter S. Brown of the *Cleveland Gazette* led an effort to create an eight-team organization called the League of Colored Baseball Clubs. The eight entrants included the Philadelphia Pythians, Pittsburgh Keystones, Boston Resolutes, New York Gorshams, Lord Baltimores, Washington Capital Cities, Cincinnati Browns, and the Louisville Falls Citys. Even though the teams appeared to begin their schedules, the league folded after one week due to financial problems. A few years later, financial problems also hobbled an attempt to build an all-black professional league composed of teams from midwestern cities. The proposed league never took the field, and black professional baseball entered a new century without the structure and security that benefited teams in the Major Leagues.

EXPANDING AND ORGANIZING

During the first two decades of the twentieth century, the world of black professional baseball continued to witness the creation of more teams and failed attempts to build formal league structures. Sol White, who translated his successful career as a player into a career as a writer and chronicler of early black baseball, formed a partnership with Walter Schlichter, the white sports editor for the *Philadelphia Item*, to form the Philadelphia Giants, one of the top teams of the early twentieth century. White's and Schlichter's interracial partnership and the means they used to advertise their games established a pattern for other black professional teams. They billed the Philadelphia Giants as the "World's Colored Champions" and attracted challenges from other teams, most notably the Cuban X-Giants, for that claim. White published a baseball guide; his guide, along with Schlichter's columns in the *Philadelphia Item*, promoted the Giants and helped boost their popularity among black baseball fans. They also recruited some of the top players—including Andrew "Rube" Foster, "Home Run" Johnson, John Henry "Pop" Lloyd, and Charlie Grant. The 1906 season represented the peak of the Philadelphia Giants' existence; the team joined the short-lived International League of Professional Base Ball Clubs, another failed attempt to provide a structure for black professional baseball. Though the Giants won the league's championship, it faced a revolt from the players due to the low salaries. Foster and eight members of the Giants' roster left after the 1906 season and sought more lucrative opportunities with midwestern teams. Those departures presaged the demise of the Giants; the league did not field any clubs in the 1907 season.

A few years later, two key events happened that shaped the course of black professional baseball for the rest of its existence. Former Philadelphia Giant Foster found success as a player and baseball entrepreneur in the Midwest. He formed the Chicago American Giants in 1910 and helped to transform the franchise into one of the top black professional teams in the country. Most importantly, Foster's American Giants would give him the foundation to build the first successful league for black professional baseball. One year after Foster formed the American Giants, an amateur team known as the Hilldale Daisies invited Ed Bolden to keep score of one of their games. Hilldale played in Darby, a suburb of Philadelphia, and Bolden stood as a respected member of the community. Bolden soon took control of the amateur team and worked to transform them into one of the most fearsome black professional teams in the country. With Hilldale, Bolden laid the foundation to make the Philadelphia region the center of black professional baseball in the east and a means to challenge Foster with his own league of black professional teams.

To build their respective franchises, Foster and Bolden developed strong relationships with the local black newspapers and used those newspapers to advertise their teams. Foster worked to ensure that the *Chicago Defender*, one of the most prominent black newspapers in the country, promoted the Chicago American Giants. Foster also used the pages of the *Chicago Defender* to engage in a battle with C. I. Taylor of the Indianapolis ABCs, the top threat to the Chicago American Giants' prowess in the Midwest. Similarly, Bolden used the *Philadelphia Tribune*, the region's oldest black newspaper, to promote Hilldale and to rebut criticism of his management of the team. As the 1917 season dawned, Bolden made his first significant venture involving Hilldale—he made the franchise a fully professional team through the agency of the Hilldale Base Ball and Exposition Company. Bolden served as the company's president, and other African American men joined him as the company's shareholders. To signify Hilldale's new professional status, Bolden aggressively targeted top professional talent such as Otto Briggs and pitcher Frank "Doc" Sykes. Briggs had played for Taylor's Indianapolis ABCs and had a connection to the *Philadelphia Tribune* that Bolden fully exploited to promote Hilldale. Over the next few seasons, Bolden kept Hilldale competitive by signing other top players such as Dick Lundy, Louis Santop, Phil Cockrell, and William Julius "Judy" Johnson. With Foster's American Giants dominating the Midwest and Bolden's Hilldale dominating the East, black professional baseball had solid foundations for building leagues that could mimic the Major Leagues and bring some stability to black professional baseball.

Outside of baseball, developments in American society helped to make possible the establishment of a successful professional baseball league. Legalized segregation created a need for black-owned businesses and enterprises, such as baseball teams, that catered to black clienteles. Those black-owned businesses and enterprises created entrepreneurs and a class of black Americans who had the capital to build and support black baseball teams. In 1917, the same year in which Bolden made Hilldale a professional franchise, America's entry into World War I helped to create additional conditions conducive to the growth of black professional baseball. While the war effort took some black players away from their teams, the war effort also encouraged the migration of African Americans from southern to northern cities such as Chicago and Philadelphia. African Americans who took part in that migration, known as the Great Migration, sought better opportunities and an escape from the Jim Crow South. Their presence in northern cities provided teams such as the Chicago American

Giants and Hilldale with large fanbases and hope to entrepreneurs that those fans could support a league structure.

Through a series of five articles published in the *Chicago Defender* in December 1919 and January 1920, Foster detailed his vision and reasoning for an organized league in black professional baseball. In those articles, Foster outlined his plans for a league that would include teams in both the East and Midwest, an organization similar to the one in Major League Baseball. He insisted that a league structure would protect the financial investments that owners made in their teams and their players by eliminating the threat of raids on rosters by competing owners. Foster's articles also discussed the importance of leadership within the new league. Not surprisingly, he touted himself as the person who possessed the needed qualities for leading the league and for keeping black professional baseball out of the hands of white booking agents. Some owners of independent teams had formed partnerships with white booking agents because those agents could schedule games at ballparks they controlled and could help set the terms of how each team would earn profits from the gate receipts. Foster insisted that a formal league structure would put black professional baseball on a firm financial foundation and would discourage partnerships with white booking agents.

In February 1920, shortly after Jackie Robinson celebrated his first birthday, Foster formally established the Negro National League (NNL) at a meeting of the new league's owners in Kansas City, Missouri. The inaugural members of the NNL included Taylor's Indianapolis ABCs, Foster's Chicago American Giants, and Robinson's future team, the Kansas City Monarchs. Foster served as the NNL's president, and *Chicago Defender* sports editor Cary B. Lewis as the new league's secretary. Lewis's role as NNL secretary and editor for the *Chicago Defender* reflected the close relationship between black baseball and the black press, an enduring feature of the NNL and subsequent Negro Leagues. The NNL's first meeting in February 1920 included a handful of black sportswriters, who provided coverage of the event in their newspapers. Black sportswriters also helped to write the NNL's constitution. While the NNL included teams only in midwestern cities, Foster incorporated the league in several eastern states, including Pennsylvania, because he aspired to build a second division of eastern teams. Foster also extended his reach into the East because of another enduring feature of the Negro Leagues, a fierce rivalry with another owner. In this specific instance, the fierce rivalry involved Foster and Bolden and set the stage for the progress of the Negro Leagues in the 1920s.

The root of the animosity between Foster and Bolden stemmed from Bolden's signing of three American Giants' players after the 1919 season ended. Unlike teams in the Major Leagues, teams in black professional baseball did not insert reserve clauses into their players' contracts. Bolden, therefore, felt that he had a right to sign those players since their contracts ended with the conclusion of 1919 season. Foster disagreed and actively supported two teams, the Madison Stars and the Bacharach Giants, who played in Philadelphia. He struck a deeper blow against Bolden when he enticed the Bacharach Giants to join the NNL as an associate member. With that associate membership, the Bacharach Giants pledged to not raid the rosters of NNL teams, but no such regulation prevented them from raiding the rosters of non-NNL teams such as Hilldale. The Bacharach Giants proceeded to sign three players under contract with Hilldale. A furious Bolden tried to get a court-ordered injunction against the signing of his three players, but his effort failed, and the players remained with the Bacharach Giants.

Despite that animosity, both Hilldale and the NNL enjoyed a successful 1920 season and joined forces at the conclusion of the season. Bolden took the same path that the Bacharach Giants took—Hilldale joined the NNL as an associate member for the 1921 season. Though Hilldale did not need the financial support of the NNL's teams, Bolden needed the protection from player raids that came with membership in the league. At the league meeting in December 1920, all signs of animosity between Foster and Bolden disappeared. The two men seemed committed to making the league successful and profitable.

Over the next two seasons, Hilldale continued to enjoy success, but Foster's NNL showed signs of decline. The NNL's finances suffered due to lower attendance numbers, and one franchise, the Cleveland Buckeyes, disbanded. Additionally, the NNL teams did not play all of the games on their schedules. The uneven records created some confusion about which team won the championship; Foster claimed the title for his American Giants. Foster defended his leadership in articles for the *Chicago Defender* and blamed owners for lacking the acumen necessary to run successful teams. He also assigned blame for the declining attendance to the players and the black umpires who worked the NNL's games. To Foster, the players' poor conduct and the umpires' failures to understand baseball's rules undermined the quality of the games. Bolden briefly considered leaving the NNL after the 1921 season, but he decided to stay after Foster issued threats of raids on Hilldale's roster and the denial of any games with league teams. In the 1922 season, the NNL showed additional signs of decay as three franchises folded, as attendance figures continued to decline, and as teams incurred debts. The NNL's troubles caused owners such as Bolden to chafe at Foster's leadership and at the ways he allegedly favored his Chicago American Giants above the interests of the NNL. Those issues, combined with the seeming failure of the NNL, led Bolden to create his own league composed of teams based in eastern cities.

Bolden's Mutual Association of Eastern Colored Baseball Clubs, or the Eastern Colored League (ECL), officially launched in December 1922. Five teams joined Hilldale as charter members of the ECL, and the league's first meeting included white booking agents such as Nat Strong. Though Foster had spoken against the use of white booking agents, he worked closely with white businessman John Schorling who owned the American Giants' home ballpark. The presence of white booking agents and businessmen represented a necessary feature of the Negro Leagues since most teams did not own their home ballparks. Black teams, therefore, needed to work with white booking agents in order to gain access to schedule both home and away games and collect their portions of the gate receipts. The Negro Leagues' reliance upon white booking agents helped keep those leagues in business, but it hurt the leagues' reputation when officials such as Branch Rickey initiated his plan to include black players. Those booking agents, combined with the lack of reserve clauses in players' contracts, led Rickey to regard the Negro Leagues as a racket and as not entitled to compensation for any players lost to the Major Leagues. The Negro Leagues of the 1920s, therefore, contained the seeds of their own eventual downfall in a world with an integrated Major Leagues.

With the ECL, Bolden and Hilldale enjoyed unrivaled prowess in the East. Hilldale easily won the ECL's first championship in 1923; Bolden served as the ECL's president and happily presided over the addition of two new franchises following the 1923 season. In contrast, Foster, the American Giants, and the NNL seemed to enter a state of irreversible decline. Two more NNL franchises folded, and Foster's American Giants no longer represented an unstoppable force within the league. The Kansas City Monarchs surpassed the American Giants and captured the NNL's championship in 1923. Animosity between Foster and Bolden prevented the two Negro Leagues from establishing a postseason championship modeled after the Major Leagues' World Series. In 1924, however, enough time had passed that Foster and Bolden could work through their bad feelings for each other and could help establish the plans for the first World Series between the winners of the NNL and the ECL. Both Foster and Bolden joined a National Commission that worked to plan the World Series in a way that benefited both leagues. The plan the Commission developed took the eight-game World Series through four cities, two with teams belonging to the ECL and two with teams belonging to the NNL. Other plans outlined the share of gate receipts the two World Series teams would receive as well as the amount that would go to those who sat on the Commission.

THE GREAT DEPRESSION IN BLACK BASEBALL

The 1924 World Series featuring the Kansas City Monarchs and Hilldale produced some mixed results that spoke to persistent troubles for the Negro Leagues. Since the Monarchs and Hilldale played to a tie in Game

Three, the World Series added a ninth game. The Monarchs prevailed, winning five games of the nine games. Both teams played well throughout the series, but the games failed to attract large crowds. The overall attendance figure for the nine games stood at 45,000 fans. A Sunday game in Kansas City drew the largest audience, 8,865 fans, during the series; a Monday game in Baltimore drew the smallest audience, 584 fans. The attendance figures translated into low financial returns for the players, the teams, and the other interests who had stakes in the series' gate receipts. The World Series generated only $52,114; a healthy portion of that amount went to travel and other expenses, leaving $23,463,44 for the rest of the parties involved in the contests. The winning share for the entire Monarchs' roster stood at $4,927.32; $3,284.88 went to the players on Hilldale's roster. Foster, Bolden, and other league officials also took disappointing returns from the gate receipts. Five years after pledging that a league organization would improve the financial standing of black professional baseball, Foster had failed to deliver on his promise. The financial foundation of the Negro Leagues remained unsteady, and it imperiled his dream for an organization that resembled the Major Leagues.

At the end of the 1925 season, the Monarchs and Hilldale met in a rematch of the 1924 World Series, and Hilldale prevailed in the six-game series. Hilldale dominated the Monarchs in the series, capturing five of the six games. While Bolden and Hilldale basked in their accomplishment, the World Series again offered ominous signs for the Negro Leagues' future. A shorter series, six games as opposed to nine games, and poor weather led to lower attendance numbers at the series' games. Total attendance for the six-game series stood at only 20,067, a sharp decline from the total attendance from the 1924 series. Those lower attendance numbers translated into much lower profits for the leagues and the players. The series grossed only $21,044.60 in receipts. Hilldale's winning players split less money, only $1,233.11, than they had earned by losing the previous year's World Series. Even worse, the Monarchs' players split only $822.08. The financial problems plaguing the Negro Leagues had grown more acute. While the 1920s ushered in a new era of success and popularity for the Major Leagues, the decade appeared to highlight the limits of the Negro Leagues and to raise doubts about the viability of league-based organization in black professional baseball.

Following the 1925 season, both Foster and Bolden faced increasing criticism as their respective leagues seemed to crumble. The use of white umpires and the open lack of respect accorded to black umpires sparked a round of controversy that also touched upon some sensitive race-related issues with the Negro Leagues. For the World Series contests, the National Commission hired white umpires to cover all of the games. During the 1925 season, the normally supportive *Philadelphia Tribune* published a

cartoon depicting the ECL as an Uncle Tom because of the league's decision to hire a white man, Bill Dallas, to manage the umpiring crew. Bolden
used the newspaper to publicly defend Dallas's hiring, and he praised Dallas as the best person to manage the ECL's umpires. Foster took a different
approach by releasing most the NNL's umpires and used the *Chicago
Defender* to launch a diatribe against umpires he deemed as unintelligent
and lacking in the skills needed to perform their jobs.

In the midst of those outbursts, several incidents happened during a
Hilldale game that helped to illustrate the reasons for declining attendance
at that year's World Series. During a game between Hilldale and the Harrisburg Giants, fights erupted on the field and in the stands. According to
well-regarded black newspaper columnist W. Rollo Wilson, the fights that
marred the Hilldale-Harrisburg game represented the norm at ECL games.
At one point, according to Wilson, the umpire seemed to display an obvious bias toward Hilldale by calling a time-out and grabbing a drink of
water. To Wilson and perhaps others at the game, the umpire's actions
appeared to help the Hilldale pitcher. In that same game, a player protested
the umpire's call by throwing dirt on the umpire's face, but the umpire did
not punish the player. As Wilson correctly noted, the umpire's actions
undermined the integrity of ECL games, and if fans did not believe in the
integrity of ECL games, then they would not attend those games. Since the
ECL depended heavily upon gate receipts, declining attendance could
erode the league's finances and lead some franchises to dissolve.

In addition to causing attendance declines at Negro League games, the
controversies involving umpires raised uncomfortable questions about
respect for black umpires and the message conveyed by the use of white
umpires. Bert Gholston, one of the NNL umpires whom Foster dismissed,
asserted that teams openly disrespected black umpires and planned physical attacks against them. Both Foster and Bolden seemed to believe in the
practice of self-help for African Americans. Bolden had established an all-
African American corporation to support Hilldale, and Foster cited the
principle as one of the reasons for his decision to launch the NNL. White
umpires at black baseball games, however, gave the ugly impression that
the players and the field managers would only respect the authority of
white men. The treatment accorded black umpires gave the ugly impression that African Americans could not manage their own affairs. Both of
those impressions undermined the principles guiding the Negro Leagues
and had the potential to seriously injure the leagues' claims to represent
legitimate organizations.

With problems mounting in the NNL and the ECL, both Foster and
Bolden faced threats to their leadership of their respective leagues. For
Foster, the end of his career began in 1925 after he announced that he
would no longer offer financial assistance to the other NNL owners. On

the heels of that announcement, Foster nearly died from a gas leak at his boarding house in Indianapolis. He made a quick recovery and returned to Chicago to rejoin his team. One year later, Foster suffered a complete and very public mental breakdown. At one point, Foster tried to catch imaginary fly balls in Chicago's streets; he also locked himself in his office's bathroom. Chicago police arrested Foster, and Foster entered psychiatric care. He died in 1930 while still undergoing treatment for his mental breakdown. In his absence, both the Chicago American Giants and the NNL moved on to different leaders, but the league continued to suffer problems both on and off the field. Within the ECL, Bolden faced a revolt from other owners since problems concerning umpires, uneven schedules among league teams, and finances remained unresolved. Prior to the 1927 season, the other ECL owners selected a new league president, attorney Isaac Nutter from Atlantic City. In September, Bolden suffered his own mental breakdown, a less severe breakdown than the one Foster had suffered in the previous year. Bolden's breakdown took him away from running Hilldale, giving other members of the corporation an opportunity to run the franchise.

Bolden returned to work in 1928 with a fierce attitude and proceeded to make decisions that helped to usher in the second era of Negro League baseball. He promptly ended the attempted coup within the Hilldale corporation, forcing those who had attempted to oust him to tender their resignations. Bolden also replaced the recently hired field manager with one of his loyalists from the Corporation and withdrew Hilldale from the ECL. Two other franchises, the Brooklyn Royal Giants and the Harrisburg Giants, also withdrew from the ECL, leaving the league on perilous ground. To explain his actions, Bolden reasoned that Hilldale had more opportunities to make money as an independent franchise rather than as a franchise tied to a league. Bolden also publicly raised doubts about the viability of an organized league structure within black professional baseball, and the ECL seemed to confirm his doubts by folding in the middle of the 1928 season.

Despite his earlier disparagement of league-based baseball, Bolden helmed the American Negro League (ANL) in the 1929 season. In addition to Hilldale, several other former ECL teams joined the new organization. Bolden and the other owners established regulations designed to avoid the problems that had plagued the ECL and the NNL. Bolden and the other owners, however, lacked the willpower to enforce those regulations, and the same problems that engulfed the ECL and the NNL swiftly engulfed the ANL. Players engaged in fights, attacked umpires, and occasionally failed to respect their contracts. One of the owners, Cumberland Posey of the Homestead Grays, sparked a conflict with the teetering NNL by signing players under contract with NNL teams. Bolden again faced criticism for his use of white umpires in the ANL and at Hilldale's games. In the

Philadelphia Tribune, sportswriter Randy Dixon made an important connection between the use of white umpires and efforts in Philadelphia to promote African Americans into leadership positions. To Dixon, the fact that an African American corporation and one of the Negro Leagues used white umpires undermined efforts to promote racial equality in other areas of American society. He even made a comparison to slavery and alleged that Bolden suffered from a sense of racial inferiority.

In October 1929, the crash of the stock market sent a chill through the American economy and dampened the prospects for successful Negro Leagues. The ANL folded in 1930, and the NNL followed suit in 1931. More significantly, Bolden, one of the pillars of the Negro Leagues in the 1920s, faced expulsion from both Hilldale and black professional baseball. After meeting with other ANL owners to dissolve the league, Bolden took steps to dissolve the Hilldale corporation and move the franchise to a field West Philadelphia under the control of white businessman Harry Passon. Other members of the Hilldale corporation blocked Bolden's plans, renewed the lease on the ballpark in Darby, and ousted Bolden from the corporation. Faced with that reality, Bolden spent the 1930 season in the wilderness.

ED BOLDEN

Ed Bolden represents the kind of entrepreneur who faced the struggles common within the Negro Leagues and whose work reflected the limited options available to Jackie Robinson as he pursued a professional career. Born in 1881, Bolden spent almost his entire adult life in the Negro Leagues though he never played baseball at a professional level. Bolden displayed strong business acumen when he ran the Hilldale franchise. His team and the leagues he ran, however, frequently ran into financial problems because of the limited amount of capital available to African American businessmen. That limited capital created competition among other Negro League franchise owners, who often undermined the league structure by seeking the best options for themselves and for their franchises.

After his ugly departure from Hilldale, Bolden reemerged in 1933 as the owner of the Philadelphia Stars, one of the teams still in existence when Robinson joined the Kansas City Monarchs in 1945. Unlike the Monarchs, the Stars did not have a glorious or successful existence. The Stars won a title in 1934, giving Bolden the rare accomplishment of leading two teams in two different leagues to their respective championships. Despite his team's struggles, Bolden remained in the middle of the Negro Leagues' operations in the 1930s and 1940s and stood out as one of the rare owners who did not express concern over the reintegration of the Major Leagues. Bolden felt that reintegration had the potential to strengthen the Negro Leagues by making them a feeder system for teams seeking black ballplayers.

Bolden did not fully grasp the change on the horizon that would come when players like Robinson joined Major League franchises. At the same time, Bolden's career symbolizes the limits of what Robinson faced when he joined the Monarchs in 1945. Robinson joined an organization that had frequently operated at the brink of nonexistence. Seemingly every year, Bolden and others sought means to keep their franchises viable in the face of increasing obstacles. Had Robinson stayed in the Negro Leagues, he never would have enjoyed the fame or financial success he enjoyed after joining the Brooklyn Dodgers. Bolden and many others involved in the Negro Leagues operated in the shadows of racial segregation. They never had the opportunity to assert themselves or display their skills at the top levels of the Major Leagues.

As black professional baseball headed into the 1930s, the dream of building stable Negro Leagues modeled after the Major Leagues appeared dead. The Great Depression, which began in earnest in 1930, made the prospects of sustaining successful franchises and leagues daunting. With Foster's death and Bolden's expulsion, black professional baseball lost the two figures who had attempted to build leagues in the 1920s and who had shouldered the burden of running those leagues. Their absence from black professional baseball created opportunities for new leaders to emerge and to create the Negro League structure that greeted Jackie Robinson when he joined the Kansas City Monarchs in 1945. The next decade would also provide opportunities for a new sportswriter to emerge, Wendell Smith, who dared to breach a subject not found in coverage of the Negro Leagues in the 1920s—integration.

3

The Negro Leagues and the Opening Act of Reintegration

During the 1930s, as Jackie Robinson emerged as a star athlete in high school and at UCLA, ambitious individuals such as William Augustus "Gus" Greenlee, Cumberland Posey, J. L. Wilkinson, Ed Bolden, Ed Gottlieb, and Effa Manley kept the Negro Leagues alive. The two new Negro Leagues—a new version of the NNL and the Negro American League (NAL)—suffered from many of the same problems that undermined the Negro Leagues of the 1920s. The NNL and the NAL, however, did help to raise the profile of black baseball players and served as a base from which black sportswriters could call for the reintegration of Major League Baseball. While black newspapers continued to represent the primary way in which Negro League teams advertised their games, black sportswriters felt they had an obligation to openly discuss reintegration and to press Major League executives to sign black players. Their efforts made little progress in the 1930s, but the Double Victory campaign associated with America's involvement in World War II gave the reintegration effort a critical boost. Those developments—the creation of two new Negro Leagues and the newspaper-led reintegration campaign—predated Robinson's involvement with the Kansas City Monarchs. Those developments, however, help to explain how Robinson emerged as the best candidate to reintegrate the Major Leagues and how his debut with the Brooklyn Dodgers contributed to the disappearance of the Negro Leagues.

WILLIAM AUGUSTUS "GUS" GREENLEE'S LEGACY

For most of the 1930s, William Augustus "Gus" Greenlee of Pittsburgh represented the dominant force in the Negro Leagues. In 1931, Greenlee formed the Pittsburgh Crawfords, one of the decade's most successful franchises. He named the franchise after a business he owned, the Crawford Grill. In addition to owning that business, Greenlee served as a promotor for several professional boxers, most notably John Henry Lewis, the first black light heavyweight champion. Greenlee also made money from running a numbers lottery, a popular enterprise among African Americans that provided runners such as Greenlee to make large sums of money. With his riches, Greenlee took the extraordinary step of building and owning a ballpark, Greenlee Field, for his Crawfords. No other eastern black professional baseball team owned their own ballpark in the 1930s; they remained dependent upon white-owned ballparks and white booking agents. Greenlee Field gave the Crawfords an advantage over their rivals and spoke to its namesake's ambitions for black professional baseball. One of those ambitions included reviving Andrew Foster's dream of building a league with teams in both the East and Midwest. Greenlee fulfilled that dream by launching a new NNL in early 1933 with teams that stretched from Pittsburgh to Baltimore and to Chicago. He served as the NNL's president and tried to implement regulations designed to make the league structure viable.

In his capacity as the NNL's president, Greenlee established two key innovations that helped raise the profile of black baseball players and demonstrated a key way that the Negro Leagues supported their communities. Under his tutelage, NNL teams played in four-team doubleheaders in Major League ballparks, such as Yankee Stadium. A portion of the profits for those games went to specific charities or to organizations housed in local communities. Those games not only provided Negro League teams with opportunities to demonstrate their civic-mindedness but also exposed black baseball players to large audiences. Games featuring Negro League teams in Major League ballparks often attracted both black and white fans, whereas games held in Negro League ballparks attracted few white fans. Another Greenlee innovation—the annual East-West Game—provided another opportunity to showcase the Negro Leagues and the talented players to a wide interracial audience. Held at Commiskey Park in Chicago, the home of the White Sox, the annual East-West Game served as the Negro League version of the Major League All-Star Game. Greenlee launched the first East-West Game in 1933, the same year as the first Major League All-Star Game, and black newspapers helped to hype the contest by publishing the ballots for fans to use to vote for members of both teams. Players from NNL teams located in eastern cities filled the East squad, while players from NNL located in midwestern cities filled the West squad. After the formation of the NAL, players from that league filled the West squad, and players from the NNL filled the East squad.

Alongside Greenlee, other key figures in the NNL in the 1930s included Cumberland Posey of the Homestead Grays and Ed Bolden of the new Philadelphia Stars. Like the Crawfords, the Homestead Grays played in Pittsburgh. Posey joined the Grays as a player in 1910 and led the franchise for the remainder of his life. He worked with Greenlee to help establish the East-West Game, regularly published columns in the *Pittsburgh Courier,* and remained an active member of his native Pittsburgh community. Bolden's Philadelphia Stars marked his triumphant return to black professional baseball. His old Hilldale franchise folded in 1932, providing him the opportunity he needed to relaunch his baseball career. The Stars played their first season in 1933, but they did not join the NNL until 1934. Bolden never reached the heights of power he had reached with the ECL and the ANL, but he held several leadership positions within the NNL. Most importantly, Bolden had a partnership with Ed Gottlieb, a white booking agent based in Philadelphia who controlled many of the ballparks that NNL teams used in eastern cities.

The presence of Gottlieb spoke to an issue that hurt the Negro Leagues' reputation in the coming effort to reintegrate the Major Leagues. Greenlee officially announced the formation of the NNL in Gottlieb's office in Philadelphia, a sign of how Greenlee needed Gottlieb's support in order to make the NNL a successful venture. While Greenlee owned his own ballpark, none of the other NNL teams enjoyed that luxury. NNL teams, therefore, depended upon booking agents such as Gottlieb for access to ballparks and for their league schedules. Gottlieb also assisted in the scheduling of four-team doubleheaders in Yankee Stadium and collected a portion of the gate receipts from the games he scheduled. Since Major League teams did not depend upon booking agents, the dependence upon booking agents in the Negro Leagues made those leagues seem inferior. The practice also made the Negro Leagues vulnerable to criticism and occasionally caused friction among owners who quibbled over the receipts from their games.

In addition to associating with white booking agents, the NNL also associated with people involved in the illegal gambling world. Greenlee himself operated a numbers lottery; Posey turned to another person involved in Pittsburgh's illegal numbers lottery, Rufus "Sonnyman" Jackson, to bankroll the Grays. Those men occasionally ran afoul of Pittsburgh's police force, but Greenlee formed relationships with local politicians to help shield his illegal enterprises. Alejandro "Alex" Pompez, who brought his New York Cubans into the NNL in 1935, made his riches in New York City's illegal gambling world. Like Greenlee and Jackson, Pompez would make thousands of dollars per day through the illegal numbers lottery, a lottery whereby participants could wager money on a winning combination of numbers. Additionally, like Greenlee and Jackson, Pompez occasionally found himself in legal trouble because of his illegal enterprises. In October 1935, Pompez fled the country following the murder of a rival who had taken over his gambling business. That murder prompted an investigation by Thomas Dewey, a special prosecutor in New York City, and a raid on Pompez's businesses, which revealed the extent of his wealth from those enterprises. Authorities captured Pompez in Mexico in 1937, and Dewey prevailed in obtaining an extradition to force Pompez to return to New York City. Pompez avoided a jail sentence by testifying against a corrupt politician and pleading guilty to the crime of conspiracy. Once his legal travails ended, Pompez revived the New York Cubans and returned to the NNL for the 1939 season. No one in the NNL shunned Pompez because of his legal travails. On the contrary, other NNL owners voted to make Pompez the league vice president starting in 1940.

Even though Pompez and Greenlee dabbled in illegal enterprises, they both possessed a determination to make their teams successful. Prior to his legal troubles, Pompez enjoyed exclusive access to Dyckman Oval, a field located outside of Harlem, as the home field for his franchise. As the son of Cuban immigrants, Pompez also served as a critical link between the Negro Leagues and Latin American ballplayers who could not play in the Major Leagues because of the color of their skin. Greenlee freely spent his money to attract the top talent to play for the Crawfords. At one point, the Crawfords' roster included notable players such as Leroy "Satchel" Paige, Josh Gibson, Oscar Charleston, Sam Bankhead, Judy Johnson, and James "Cool Papa" Bell. The Crawfords dominated their competition during the NNL's first four seasons, winning the 1935 league championship in a seven-game series against the New York Cubans. Greenlee took pride in the success of his Crawfords, but their success did not translate into success for the rest of the NNL.

From the outset, Greenlee's NNL demonstrated signs of instability. In the middle of the NNL's inaugural season, the league suspended Posey's Homestead Grays because of a dispute over two players Posey had signed. According to the owner of the Detroit Stars, Posey had violated the NNL's rules by signing two players under contract with the Detroit team. Posey refused to return the players, thereby leading the other NNL owners to suspend the Grays for the remainder of the 1933 season. At that same meeting, Tom Wilson of the Nashville Elite Giants issued his own protest against Bolden and the Philadelphia Stars. Wilson accused Bolden of signing a player he had signed for the Elite Giants. As a sign of solidarity with Wilson, the NNL owners agreed to avoid all games with Bolden's Stars until he returned the disputed player.

JOSH GIBSON

Similarly to Ed Bolden, Josh Gibson represents a different fate that would have awaited Jackie Robinson if he never had the opportunity to join the Brooklyn Dodgers. Like Robinson, Gibson was a native of Georgia; he was born in Buena Vista, Georgia, on December 21, 1911. Like Robinson, Gibson's father worked as a sharecropper. In 1926, Gibson and the rest of his family joined his father in Pittsburgh; his father had moved there three years earlier and had finally made enough money to support his family in the steel city. Gibson dropped out of school as a teenager so that he could contribute to his family's finances, and he joined his first organized baseball team at the age of sixteen. Gibson played for amateur teams in Negro Greater Pittsburgh Industrial League until he joined the Homestead Grays in the 1930 season. Two years later, Greenlee traded for Gibson and added him to a potent Crawfords' team. He remained with the Crawfords until Greenlee ran into money problems and had to trade him back to the Grays. He remained with the Grays for the rest of his career in the Negro Leagues.

In an effort to maximize on his potential earnings, Gibson frequently played for teams outside of the United States. Regardless of where he played, Gibson dazzled spectators and amazed his teammates as well as opposing players. According to one legend, Gibson hit a home run that cleared the rooftop of old Yankee Stadium. Other legends claim that Gibson hit home runs that hit train tracks and other items located outside of ballparks. None of those legends can be substantiated due to the lack of any game broadcasts and the unreliability of stories that often appeared in newspapers. Team officials often served as ghostwriters for those stories and had incentives to exaggerate the accomplishments of their star players.

Despite his athletic prowess, Gibson's name rarely appeared in white newspapers, and his official baseball stats remain unknown. He suffered from poor health in the 1940s, and he developed drug and alcohol addictions. Gibson never had the opportunity to play in the Major Leagues, and he died shortly before Robinson played in his first game for the Dodgers. Gibson may have hit more home runs than anyone in Major League Baseball's history, yet his games did not get the same attention as Major League games. Gibson, like Bolden, operated in the shadows of segregation. Robinson would have faced the same situation, a career in relative obscurity, had he not enjoyed the good fortune of coming to the attention of Branch Rickey and of playing in the Major Leagues.

Posey did not go away quietly, and the dispute played out across the pages of the *Pittsburgh Courier*. John Clark, an ally of Greenlee and the NNL secretary, wrote a lengthy column that effectively declared war on the Grays and invited NNL teams to raid the Grays' roster. He also accused Posey of inflating the Grays' record against non-NNL teams, of holding back his players' development by facing inferior opponents, and of not meeting his financial obligations to the NNL. Posey fired back in one of his regular columns and accused Clark of engaging in a bad faith attack against the Grays. He also defended the Grays' importance to the NNL by pointing out the high attendance figures at games featuring his team. Posey, furthermore, openly questioned Greenlee's ability to place the NNL's interests ahead of the interests of the Crawfords. He also insinuated that Greenlee attacked the Grays because it represented a way he could hide his poor management of the NNL.

In addition to those nasty public spats between owners, the NNL often struggled to complete full seasons, award undisputed championships, and produce a quality product for its fans. To help determine a champion, the NNL teams agreed to play a split-season schedule; the first half ran from April to July and the second half ran from July through September. The respective winners of those split-seasons, or half-seasons, would meet in a postseason series to determine the league championship. In 1933, the NNL teams did not complete the second half of the schedule, leading Greenlee to claim the league championship for his Crawfords. One year later, the championship series between Bolden's Stars and the Chicago American Giants, owned by Robert Cole, reawakened concerns about player conduct and respect for umpires. In Game Six of the series, two Stars players remained in the game after attacking umpires, and the Stars won the game to tie the series. The American Giants' manager filed a protest with NNL commissioner W. Rollo Wilson, but Wilson declined the protest under pressure from Bolden and Gottlieb. Game Seven ended in a tie and featured another physical altercation between a player and the umpire. In that incident, the umpire removed the offending American Giants' player from the game. The Stars won Game Eight, which featured more protests from both teams as well as a crowd of only two thousand fans. Two years later, disputes over which team won the half-season titles prevented the staging of a postseason championship, and Greenlee again simply claimed the title for his Crawfords.

Greenlee's and the Crawfords' reigns came to an end in 1937 due to another sign of instability within the NNL—contract jumping. Throughout the history of the Negro Leagues, players frequently jumped their contracts, meaning they left their teams, in pursuit of more lucrative opportunities. In 1937, a particularly dire threat came from Rafael Trujillo, the dictator of the Dominican Republic. Trujillo sought to capitalize on the popularity of baseball in the Dominican Republic and to build a powerful baseball team that would also enhance his own popularity. Trujillo reached out to Satchel Paige, arguably the best pitcher in the NNL, to recruit Negro League talent for the team he decided to name Ciudad Trujillo. Both Major League and Negro League players had participated in winter leagues in the Dominican Republic as well as other areas of the

Caribbean. Baseball fans in the Dominican Republican knew those players, and Trujillo bet that a team composed of the best Negro League players would attract large audiences across the country. Major League players
faced lifetime bans for jumping their contracts, but Negro League players
did not face such restrictions. Paige recruited several of his fellow
Crawfords—including Gibson, Bankhead, and Bell—as well as a collection
of top players from other NNL teams. The Crawfords lost the most players
and, therefore, suffered the most from the contract jumping that plagued
the 1937 season. Greenlee sold the franchise in 1939, and the Crawfords
played in Toledo and Indianapolis before dissolving in the early 1940s.
With the loss of his Crawfords, Greenlee lost his leadership position within
the league he founded and spent several seasons away from the Negro
Leagues.

The rise of the threat from the Dominican Republic came at the same
time as the NNL faced the threat of a rival league, the Negro American
League (NAL). Greenlee's dream of having an NNL with franchises in both
the Midwest and East died when franchises such as the Chicago American
Giants withdrew. Those American Giants—along with the Kansas City
Monarchs, the Detroit Stars, the Memphis Red Sox, the Cincinnati
Tigers, the Indianapolis Athletics, and the Birmingham Black Barons—
formed the new NAL. The NAL suffered from many of the same issues that
plagued the NNL—contract jumping, uneven schedules, reliance upon
white booking agents to schedule games, and conflicts among owners. The
formation of the NAL established the geographic pattern of the two dominant Negro Leagues from the late 1930s to the late 1940s. The NAL incorporated teams in the Midwest and South, whereas the NNL incorporated
teams in the East. In addition to the Stars, the Grays, and the Cubans,
other long-term members of the NNL included the Newark Eagles, the
New York Black Yankees, and an Elite Giants franchise that played in both
Nashville and Baltimore. Abe and Effa Manley operated the Eagles, and
Effa Manley emerged as a key figure in the NNL's leadership in the years
leading to and leading from Greenlee's departure.

For both the NNL and the NAL, the Ciudad Trujillo team represented a
threat the leagues' leaders needed to confront because the team's success
could entice more players to jump their contracts. The NNL owners initially acted in a decisive manner and banned the players on Ciudad Trujillo
from playing in the league. Undaunted, the Ciudad Trujillo players returned
to the United States after capturing the Dominican Republic's championship and played as an independent traveling team. Faced with the popularity of the contract jumpers and dwindling attendance at NNL games, the
owners did not enforce the bans. Gottlieb even scheduled a game between
the Stars and the "outlawed" players at the Stars' home ballpark, and the
contest drew a near-capacity crowd. The actions of the owners ensured

that players would continue to jump their contracts, usually for teams in the Caribbean or in Mexico. Those leagues offered black baseball players perks not available in the Negro Leagues. Owners of teams in those leagues paid the players higher salaries than those available in the Negro Leagues and often offered bonuses for on-field feats such as home runs or amazing catches. The players also enjoyed better playing conditions, better living accommodations, and, most importantly, freedom from the discrimination that existed in the United States. With those conditions in rival leagues, the Negro Leagues faced a daunting future as the 1930s transitioned into the 1940s.

THE BLACK PRESS AND THE PUSH FOR REINTEGRATION

In the 1930s, the sports pages of black newspapers contained stories that covered another, at that time distant, threat to the Negro Leagues—the reintegration of the Major Leagues. Ironically, a front-page story in the *Pittsburgh Courier* about Greenlee's launch of the new NNL appeared above a story on white sportswriter Heywood Broun's denunciation of the Major Leagues' color line. Broun made that denunciation the hallmark of a speech he delivered at the annual meeting of the Baseball Writers' Association Dinner. In his speech, Broun openly questioned why the color line existed, and he argued that the presence of black athletes on the 1932 Olympic team proved that black athletes could compete with white athletes. At that same dinner, *New York Daily News* sportswriter Jimmy Powers took an informal poll of six people in attendance and found that the majority supported Broun's views. Earlier, Powers had written an editorial in favor of adding black players to the Major Leagues. Like Broun, Powers pointed to the success of black athletes in other sports, particularly college football and track and field, in which they competed against white athletes. Powers also expressed his confidence that black players would inevitably join the Major Leagues, likely in the near future, and that they would receive acceptance from their white teammates.

On the heels of that article, the newspaper conducted a four-month-long "Big League Symposium" in which it published interviews with Major League executives on the issue of the sport's color line. Chester Washington, the *Courier's* sports editor who also wrote a regular column, spearheaded the effort. One week after the article on Broun and Powers, the *Courier* published an article that contained the views of National League president John Heydler. In a telegram to the newspaper, Heydler denied that a color line existed in the Major Leagues. He insisted that the Major Leagues did not and had never barred a player solely because of his race. Heydler further insisted players' character and abilities served as the only requirements determining whether or not they could play in the National or American League. Heydler's comments did not comport with the facts of history; leagues in the nineteenth century actively rejected players solely because of their race, not because of their character or abilities. While Heydler's comments showed his ignorance or his denial of baseball's history, they generated headlines in the newspaper and set the tone for the *Courier's* "Symposium."

In that same edition of the *Courier*, William G. Nunn published a column in which he expressed hope and optimism about the impending addition of black players to the Major Leagues. Nunn sense budding momentum on the heels of Broun's speech and Powers' editorial. He also expressed confidence that the attention given to the issue of adding black players to the Major Leagues would help to boost the newly launched NNL. Similarly to Broun and Powers, Nunn reminded his readers about the prevalence and popularity of black athletes in other sports, most notably college football and professional boxing. Nunn also reminded readers about the recent 1932 Olympics and the laudatory stories about black athletes who competed for Team USA. Nunn concluded his column by listing great black baseball players from previous years as well as current black baseball players who could compete at the Major League level. Some of the players he mentioned included Oscar Charleston, Webster MacDonald, Willie Wells, Duck Lundy, James "Cool Papa" Bell, Raleigh "Biz" Mackey, Judy Johnson, and Ted Page.

On the heels of those articles, W. Rollo Wilson wrote about Gerry Nugent's views on black players in the Major Leagues. Nugent owned the Philadelphia Phillies, and similarly to others interviewed on the subject, he did not acknowledge that a racial barrier existed in either the National or American League. Nugent, however, seemed less optimistic about the prospect of a black player joining a Major League in the immediate future. To Nugent, the Negro Leagues did not provide black players with the kind of competition and development opportunities that white players experienced in the Minor Leagues. He likened the Negro Leagues to sandlot teams and noted that white players did not make a jump from sandlot leagues to the Major Leagues. Nugent's response touched upon a common argument against signing black players—a skills deficit in comparison to white players. He did not deny the talent of black players, but he regarded white players as more talented and more prepared to play in the Major Leagues. By focusing on talent, Nugent could deflect attention away from race and from the "gentlemen's agreement" that kept black players out of the Major Leagues.

A few weeks later, the *Courier* published yet another article that contained the views of Major League officials on the signing of black players. Leslie O'Connor, who worked in Commissioner's office, flatly denied that a formal racial barrier existed and insisted that league officials had never discussed signing black players. J. Louis Comiskey, the Chicago White Sox's president, slightly contradicted O'Connor when he hinted that the "gentlemen's agreement" represented the only reason he had not signed black players. Chester Washington, who wrote the column, noted the contradiction in his commentary accompanying the interviews. Washington chose to remain optimistic by noting that many of the people interviewed expressed support for signing black players.

Subsequent interviews with white sportswriters and other Major League officials repeated the same themes. Team officials expressed an openness to signing black players and insisted that talent, not race, represented the barrier to playing in the Major Leagues. Sportswriters as well voiced support for adding black players. When Washington ended the "Symposium," he maintained his optimism about the impending addition of black players to the Major Leagues. While none of the Major League officials revealed a specific plan to scout and sign black players, their expressed determination to sign the most talented players provided some hope that a black player would join a Major League team in the near future. Washington also took his cues from the musings of the manager of the Buffalo franchise in the International League, a Minor League. That manager predicted an impending decline in the Minor Leagues due to a lack of talent and resources for Minor League franchises. To Washington, such a decline would inevitably lead Major League officials to scout for Negro League players. Washington stopped short of predicting that a Major League team would sign a black player in the near future. Instead, he spoke glowingly about awakening Major League officials to the potential talent awaiting them in the Negro Leagues and about encouraging black players to raise their level of play. To Washington, both of those things demonstrated the success of the *Courier*'s "Symposium."

Contrary to Washington's hopes, the "Symposium" did not move any Major League team to actively scout and sign a black player, nor did it have its desired effect upon the Negro Leagues. Major League baseball remained stubbornly segregated, and the Negro Leagues remained unstable. The "Symposium," however, did put the newspaper at the forefront of the effort to entice Major League teams to sign black players. In October 1937, Washington transformed his regular column to an open letter to Horace Stoneham, the president of the New York Giants. The Giants had recently lost the World Series to the Yankees, and Washington suggested to Stoneham that the Giants would have won if he had signed black players. Washington proceeded to conduct a position-by-position overview of the Negro League talent available to the Giants—talent such as Paige, Gibson, Norman "Turkey" Stearns, Jud Wilson, and Vic Harris. He jokingly told Stoneham that the players he mentioned could finally help the Giants overcome the Yankees and win the World Series.

More significantly, the *Courier*'s "Symposium" established a foundation that Wendell Smith used to successfully push for the reintegration of the Major Leagues. Smith joined the *Courier* in 1938, and he wrote a regular column called "Smitty Sports Spurts." In his first column on segregation in baseball, Smith adopted a harsher and more critical tone than the one Washington and Nunn had used in their earlier articles on the topic. Smith spoke directly to black baseball fans in Pittsburgh and asked them why they patronized the Pirates and other Major League teams since the Major Leagues clearly did not want black players. He chastised them for not patronizing the Negro Leagues, whose teams and players needed the support and encouragement of black baseball fans. Additionally, Smith insinuated that the white players would not appreciate the support they received from black fans. On the contrary, Smith argued, white players likely regarded black Americans as inferior. Through his column, Smith wanted to nudge his readers to take pride in those leagues and to question their support of Major League teams that had not taken any steps to sign black players. To Smith, pride in the Negro Leagues represented a necessary corollary to any effort to push the Major Leagues to add black players. Neither Smith nor other sportswriters intended for their efforts to result in the demise of the Negro Leagues. They valued the Negro Leagues, but they wanted black baseball players to have the same opportunities that were available to white baseball players.

During the remainder of 1938, two events demonstrated the promise as well as the peril of adding black players on Major League teams. Jimmy Powers of the *New York Daily News* again provided hope by asserting that if they could pick players for the New York Giants, he would immediately select seven black players. Powers asserted that those players would transform the Giants into the National League's pennant winner in the 1939 season. He later assembled a "jury" of former Major League players that selected Negro League players who they believed could compete at the Major League level. An incident involving Jake Powell, however, offered a different perspective about the likelihood of adding black players to Major League teams. Powell played for the New York Yankees; while in Chicago for a game against the White Sox, he gave a controversial interview with the WGN radio station. In response to a question about his off-season activities, Powell said that he kept in shape by working as a police officer in Dayton, Ohio, and hitting African Americans on the head with his nightstick. Powell used a racial slur when referring to African Americans; his interview sparked widespread outrage. A group of African American leaders in Chicago, where Landis had his office, met with the commissioner to demand a lifetime ban for Powell. Landis suspended Powell for ten days. Powell blamed the interviewer for the comments, and officials with the Yankees organization seemed unwilling to hold Powell to any consequences for his comments.

Instead, they noted how well they treated black employees at Yankee Stadium and how they had accommodated both black teams and black fans at the ballpark. The ugly incident stood in stark contrast to the openness Major League officials had expressed in the *Courier*'s "Symposium" and raised the specter that other players harbored prejudices against black players.

In his first column for 1939, Smith reflected on the episode involving Powell and offered an idea for how black baseball fans could press for the addition of black players to the Major Leagues. To Smith, the Powell suspension represented another instance of the Major Leagues' emptiness when it came to race relations and to the treatment accorded black baseball fans. As he did in his first column, Smith called upon his readers to stop supporting Major League baseball and to organize in support of black baseball players. He envisioned an organization akin to the NAACP, but he focused solely on the singular issue of pressuring Major League teams into signing black players. Smith believed that black baseball fans, acting collectively and in an organized manner, could create the kind of pressure needed to get the Major Leagues to take some real action and not simply make empty gestures. At the end of his column, Smith invited readers to contact him if they had any interest in forming and supporting such an organization.

Smith's column established the tone for the *Courier*'s continued advocacy over the next several years. In his next regular column, Chester Washington noted that more white sportswriters had joined Powers in pressing the Major Leagues to add black players. Those sportswriters included Sam Lacey of the *Washington Tribune* and Warren Brown of the *Chicago Herald-Examiner*. Washington also published a letter from a white baseball fan, Alan Meyers, to the Pittsburgh Pirates' president, William Benswanger. In the letter, Meyers noted the Pirates' recent attempts to improve their roster and suggested that the organization try a thus-far untapped talent pool—Negro League players. Meyers noted the absurdity of the bar against black players since black athletes had proven their talents in other sports, such as professional boxing and track and field. He anticipated an argument against the signing of black players, that it would cause drops in attendance, by noting that fights involving black boxers drew large audiences. To Meyers, baseball fans would continue to attend Pirates games since the addition of black players would improve the team and, therefore, provide more entertainment for the city's baseball fans. Meyers also suggested that adding black players would draw more of the city's black residents to Forbes Field and would make the franchise a leader in a movement that would spread throughout both the American and National Leagues.

On the heels of Washington's column, Smith published a lengthy interview with National League president Ford Frick in which Frick denied that National League teams did not want to sign black players. On the contrary, Frick insisted that teams wanted black players, but team officials did not sign such players because of the views of the fanbases supporting those teams. Frick, in other words, blamed public opinion, and not an unwritten "gentlemen's agreement" or bias among team officials and players, for the lack of black players on National League teams. In addition to blaming public opinion, Frick cited other factors that inhibited National League teams from signing black players. He noted that teams held spring training exercises in the South, an area of the country that followed strict segregation laws. Due to those laws, black players could not stay in the same hotels or use the same public accommodations as their white teammates, and that arrangement would undermine cohesion and morale on integrated teams. Frick insisted that black players could compete at the same level as white players and that National League teams would welcome black players in the near future. He also urged Smith and other African Americans to continue to press for the signing of black players, since that pressure could change public opinion and make it possible for National League teams to sign black players.

Following his interview with Frick, Smith continued to devote his columns to pressing for the inclusion of black players in the Major Leagues. He rejected Frick's claims about unfavorable public opinion by noting that fans paid money to watch black athletes, such as heavyweight champion Joe Louis, compete in their sports. Smith also sarcastically noted that Major League Baseball supposedly represented the national pastime in the land of the "free" United States, yet it actively excluded black players. He further rejected claims that biased white players would reject their black teammates particularly since they would risk losing their salaries by taking such action. Smith focused his ire on what he regarded as the true reason for the lack of black players in the Major Leagues—the lack of willingness among the owners to sign black players. For that reason, Smith's campaign remained focused on pressuring owners, both directly and indirectly, to offer tryouts to talented black players and to add them to their franchises.

Smith's reference to Joe Louis raised an important point about American sports in the 1930s—black athletes competed with and against white athletes in many venues. Both the 1932 and 1936 Olympic teams included black athletes. The Summer 1936 Olympics, held in Berlin, featured Jesse Owens, who undermined Adolf Hitler's claims about Aryan supremacy in front of the dictator who wanted to use the games to showcase the Third Reich to the rest of the world. During his career, Louis had two memorable fights against Germany's Max Schmeling. Many fans and sportswriters regarded those fights as proxy battles between the ideology of the United States and the ideology of Nazi Germany. Louis's triumph over Schmeling in 1938 received widespread praise across the United States and helped to make him a national celebrity. Black college athletes, particularly football players, also attracted widespread attention and praise for their skills. The earliest stories in the *Courier* on Jackie Robinson came when he played for the UCLA Bruins alongside Kenny Washington and Woody Strode. Their exploits, along with those of Louis and Owens, helped Smith to make the case that white sports fans would patronize integrated Major League teams and that black athletes could compete with white athletes.

Despite that seemingly favorable atmosphere for adding black players to the Major Leagues, none of the owners took the steps of even holding tryouts for black players. Additionally, the Negro Leagues remained embarrassingly disorganized, a factor that drew Smith's ire in many of his columns. Smith often complained about the lack of published information, such as standings and batting averages, offered by the Negro Leagues. His columns occasionally prompted a public response from Tom Wilson, the NNL's president, who defended the actions of his fellow owners and his own actions in running the league. Smith also encouraged the NNL and the NAL to engage in more charity games once World War II began and pushed them to utilize a commissioner modeled after Kenesaw Mountain Landis. Additionally, Smith praised the NNL and the NAL for staging popular East-West Games every year and for ensuring that those games remained showcases for the leagues' talented players.

While he covered and nudged the Negro Leagues, Smith never lost his focus on his crusade to add black players to the Major Leagues, an action that would lead to the end of the Negro Leagues. He spent several months in 1939 publishing interviews that he conducted of forty Major League players and eight field managers. In his first article on the interviews, Smith provided readers with insight into his reasons for launching such a project in 1939. To Smith, the exclusion of black players represented a stain on the national pastime, particularly during a year in which that pastime celebrated its one hundredth birthday. Smith, furthermore, argued that the exclusion of black players from the national pastime undermined the ideals of the United States, ideals reflected in symbols such as the Statue of Liberty. He also referred to the growing war clouds in Europe, and he drew a parallel between those clouds and the racial prejudice that hovered over the game of baseball in the United States. Additionally, Smith reminded his readers about Frick's comments and made it clear he had launched his interview project as a way to refute Frick's reasoning for not adding black players to the National League.

WENDELL SMITH AND THE PITTSBURGH COURIER

For his massive project, "Are Negro Ball Players Good Enough to 'Crash' the Majors?" Smith interviewed players and the managers from all eight National League franchises—the Cincinnati Reds, New York Giants, Philadelphia Phillies, Brooklyn Dodgers, Chicago Cubs, St. Louis Cardinals, Boston Braves, and Pittsburgh Pirates. With the exception of Giants manager "Memphis Bill" Terry, the players and managers who were interviewed expressed support for adding black players to their teams. Before announcing that he opposed the addition of black players, Terry noted that many current Negro League players had the talents necessary to compete in the Major Leagues. He cited some of the same reasons that Frick had cited in his earlier interview with Smith—segregation laws that would prevent black and white teammates from using the same public accommodations. Even when pressed by Smith, Terry remained adamant and suggested that black players should play in an improved Negro League, but he offered few details about how that improved singular Negro League would operate. Other players on the Giants did not appear to share their manager's views and mentioned black players, such as Paige and Gibson, had Major League–ready skills.

Overall, Smith's interview project confirmed his conclusions about Frick and the real obstacles to signing black players. Reds' manager, Bill McKechnie, lauded Negro League players and expressed an openness to adding black players to his team. Phillies' manager, Thompson Prothro, said he would use black players if the team's owner and other National League officials permitted that action. Leo Durocher, manager of the Brooklyn Dodgers, also asserted that he would use black players and rattled off a list of the great Negro League players he had faced in barnstorming games. Leo "Gabby" Hartnett, the player-manager of the Chicago Cubs, also said he would add black players if allowed and predicted that teams would race to sign Negro League players once the Major Leagues lifted the ban. Cardinals' manager, Ray Blades, seemed to take Frick's views that public opinion needed to change before any Major League team would sign a black player, but he never directly said he would not use black players on his team. Casey Stengel, manager of the Boston Braves, put the onus squarely on the owners and did not foresee the addition of any black players in the near future. The Pirates' Pie Traynor, whose interview concluded Smith's project, followed the same line as many of his fellow managers and said he would use black players if permitted. He too put the onus on the owners and said that those owners would need to address the issue in the near future.

Smith's exhaustive project demonstrated his journalism skills and his determination to maintain pressure on the owners of Major League clubs. His project served as a rebuke to Frick and revealed an openness among players and most managers in the National League to using black players. His project, most importantly, revealed that players and managers assumed a bar against using black players existed and that only the owners, along with the commissioner, could remove that barrier. Since Smith's project focused on the National League, the views of American League managers and players remained unknown. Additionally, due to the project's focus, Smith never took time to consider the role of the existing Negro Leagues once Major League teams signed black players. In a column following the project's conclusion, Smith finally addressed that issue. Smith chose to address the issue because many letters that he received asked him if the dissolution of the existing Negro Leagues represented part of his vision for the inclusion of black players in the Major Leagues. Smith asserted that adding black players to Major League clubs would boost the existing Negro Leagues because those leagues held exclusive rights to black players. The Negro Leagues' owners, therefore, would hold leverage over Major League owners and would extract large sums of money for their best players. The owners would then take that money and reinvest the profits in their franchises. To prepare for that situation, Smith urged the Negro Leagues' owners to develop an agreement with the Major Leagues akin to the agreements that existed between the Minor Leagues and the Major Leagues. He firmly did not believe that the inclusion of black players in the Major Leagues would automatically lead to the dissolution of the NNL and the NAL.

WORLD WAR II AND THE PUSH FOR REINTEGRATION

The next two years, 1940 and 1941, saw little progress in the campaign to add black players to the Major Leagues. Smith did not follow up his interview project with additional interviews or direct appeals to owners, and none of the Major League clubs offered tryouts to any black players. Smith's interview project did lead the New York Trade Union Athletic Association to launch a petition drive aimed at ending the color barrier in the Major Leagues. The Association also staged protests on two consecutive Sundays—June 30 and July 7, 1940—at the grounds that housed the 1939 World Fair. Those protests aimed to bring the area's labor unions into the movement to end the color barrier in the Major Leagues and to put pressure on owners of the local teams to sign black players. Civic leaders in

Philadelphia also called for an end to the Major Leagues' color barrier. Larry MacPhail, the Brooklyn Dodgers' president, faced another direct appeal to sign black players from Dave Farrell, a sportswriter from *The Daily Worker.* Farrell wrote that he targeted MacPhail because he regarded him as the smartest executive in the Major Leagues and because he shared MacPhail's belief that teams needed to act to spark renewed interest in the sport. He mentioned two players whom MacPhail should sign to bring a spark to the Dodgers' organization—Kenny Washington and Jackie Robinson. Farrell briefly outlined the accomplishments of both players and urged MacPhail to sign both of them before another organization added them to its system.

Farrell's letter marked the first time that someone suggested Robinson as one of the players who could break the Major Leagues' color barrier. Nothing immediately happened as a result of Farrell's letter, but in 1942, Robinson surfaced again as a possible contender to play in the Major Leagues. In March of that year, Robinson and another player, pitcher Nate Moreland, asked the Chicago White Sox for tryouts at the team's spring training site in Pasadena. Jimmy Dykes, the White Sox's field manager, said he would welcome black players on the White Sox and surmised that his fellow managers in both the American League and National League shared his views. Neither Dykes nor the White Sox management, however, allowed Robinson and Moreland to stage a tryout for the team. Both Robinson and Moreland left the White Sox's spring training grounds without incident, and Robinson soon left behind his athletic career for his service in the United States Army.

The denied tryouts for Robinson and Moreland marked the beginning of the next phase of the push for black players in the Major Leagues, a phase that coincided with and gained momentum because of the United States' entry into World War II. Among African Americans, a "Double Victory" campaign emerged that tied the defeat of racial ideologies overseas to the defeat of legalized segregation and racism on the home front. In their columns, both Smith and Washington used the war to put increased pressure on the Major Leagues to add black players. Washington used one of his columns in 1942 to write an open letter to Landis and urged him to consider the recent actions of the United States Navy to create more opportunities for its black enlistees. He also reminded Landis about Smith's interview project, dismissed any arguments against the signing of black players, and insisted that black players would attract large audiences at ballparks. Smith adopted a similar focus in his columns that nudged Major League owners to sign black players. He pointed out the hypocrisy of the national pastime barring black players at a time when black soldiers, pilots, and other service members risked their lives for the United States. To Smith, signing black players represented the most logical solution for

DOUBLE VICTORY CAMPAIGN

In addition to its role in pushing for the reintegration of the Major Leagues, the *Pittsburgh Courier* stood at the forefront of the Double Victory campaign. The *Pittsburgh Courier* launched the Double Victory campaign on February 7, 1942, a mere two months after Japan's attack on Pearl Harbor. In its announcement of the Double Victory campaign, the newspaper explicitly tied an American victory over its foes in Europe and Asia to African Americans' victory over racism within the United States. The campaign, furthermore, explicitly tied the patriotism of many African Americans to their determination to press for equal rights as American citizens. As the newspaper noted, many African Americans would join the calls to enlist in the U.S. military and to fight on foreign battlefields. That demonstrated not only their patriotism but also their determination to fight against racism wherever it appeared in the world.

The Double Victory campaign appeared in some of the propaganda posters that appeared on the American home front during World War II. The campaign's name played on the phrase "V for Victory," so many of Double Victory campaign posters featured two letter "Vs" stacked on top of each other. Other images in the posters included white and black factory workers working alongside each other as well as images of African Americans in military uniforms. The posters also featured the phrase "Democracy At Home-Abroad," the phrase that served as the central tenet of the campaign.

With its focus on connecting the international American war effort to the ongoing domestic quest for equal rights, the Double Victory campaign emphasized how many African Americans saw an opportunity during World War II. They recognized the hypocrisy of a country fighting to eliminate race-based totalitarian regimes on two continents while still maintaining a system of racial segregation that treated African Americans as second-class citizens. Many African Americans did enlist in the armed forces, and many engaged in civil rights activism on the home front. The World War II era, with the Double Victory campaign, provided a critical boost to civil rights in the United States and helped to bring the movement to reintegrate the Major Leagues to a successful conclusion.

Major League teams looking to boost morale on the home front, win games, and replace players lost to the armed forces.

REINTEGRATION GAINS STEAM

Overall, the year 1942 witnessed some significant progress in the push for black players in the Major Leagues. Two more unions, the National Maritime Union and the International Workers' Order, threw their collective weight behind the movement and wrote letters to Landis, urging him to direct owners to sign black players. Leo Durocher, the Dodgers' longtime field manager, also put additional pressure on Landis by stating that the commissioner opposed the addition of black players to Major League teams. In response, Landis declared that no formal ban against black players existed in the Major Leagues' rules. Both Washington and Smith celebrated Landis's admission in their columns, and they correctly noted that Landis in effect put a spotlight on the owners. Smith urged the NAACP, the Urban League, and other black fraternal organizations to maintain the pressure by organizing nationwide campaigns until at least one franchise signed a black player. On the heels of Landis's statement, a report surfaced that Pirates' president Benswanger had agreed to give tryouts to three black players whom Smith had selected. That prompted National League president Frick to assert he would not deny an owner's request to sign one or more black players since no rules prohibited owners from signing black players. Those tryouts never happened, but other developments in 1942 seemed to make the reintegration of the Major Leagues a real possibility in the not-so-distant future.

The progress toward adding black players to the Major Leagues came at a time when the NNL and the NAL faced strong obstacles to their continued survival. Similarly to the situation in the Major Leagues, teams in both the NNL and the NAL lost players to the armed services. Those losses left owners scrambling to fill their rosters and raised questions as to whether the leagues could operate during the duration of World War II. Gas rationing and restrictions on using buses for travel further hampered the ability of Negro League teams to operate regular schedules. Despite those obstacles, the leagues continued to operate throughout World War II and continued to hold the annual East-West Classic. As they did before the war, the owners squabbled over player contracts; they also staged more charity games and raised money for war-related efforts. The teams also used more Major League ballparks, such as Shibe Park in Philadelphia, which exposed them to larger audiences while making them more dependent upon the Major Leagues. Even though the issue of adding black players to the Major Leagues dominated black newspapers, NNL owners avoided addressing the topic at their meetings. J. B. Martin, the NAL's president, said that the owners in his league did not oppose the addition of black players to the Major Leagues. Martin, however, cautioned that the owners expected fair treatment and compensation from any official in the Major Leagues who wanted a player under contract to any NAL team. The mixed responses reflected the tough position facing owners in the NNL and NAL. They could not block any of their players from going to the Major Leagues, but they also could not afford to lose their players without financial compensation. They needed the respect of Major League franchises; otherwise, they faced the possibility of obsolescence when black players joined Major League teams.

While the NNL and NAL owners continued to operate their teams, the progress toward adding black players to the Major Leagues continued without their involvement. In 1943, much of the focus shifted from the Major Leagues to the Pacific Coast League (PCL), a significant Minor League that frequently sent players to Major League franchises. The PCL captured attention because of the promise, followed quickly by the denial, of tryouts to black players. In response, Los Angeles's City Council and Los Angeles County's Board of Supervisors issued their opposition to the actions of the PCL. Art Cohn of the *Oakland Tribune* added his voice to the controversy by urging the PCL's Oakland franchise to sign black players. He argued that black boxers saved professional boxing in the United States and that black baseball players would do the same for Oakland's baseball club. Civic leaders in Los Angeles worked to create a Committee for Equal Participation in Organized Baseball. More unions joined the effort to push for black players in the PCL and the Major Leagues, and pro-integration demonstrators greeted fans who came to watch a Minor League baseball game at Los Angeles Park. The PCL remained off-limits to black players, but the actions in Los Angeles demonstrated that the movement for integrated baseball remained viable and had captured the attention of more people.

After the end of the 1943 season, Landis sent mixed messages about his true views on the addition of black players to the Major Leagues. For many years, black and white players had faced each other in barnstorming tours, tours of exhibition games, and in winter league contests. Those contests gave black players opportunities to mingle with Major League stars and to demonstrate that they could compete with the country's best white baseball players. Landis had clamped down on barnstorming tours involving Major League players, and in 1943, he prohibited them from competing in winter league contests held in southern California. He threatened to fine players who did not heed his edict, but his edict did not stop white and black players from competing against each other in the 1943 winter league season. Soon after issuing that edict, Landis met with Smith and other members of the Negro Newspaper Association and asserted that he did not oppose the addition of black players to the Major Leagues. The meeting also included officials from Major League franchises, such as the Dodgers' Branch Rickey and Paul Robeson, an African American athlete, artist, and activist. Ira F. Lewis, the *Courier*'s president, delivered a lengthy speech in which he eloquently advocated for the inclusion of black players in the Major Leagues by trying to take advantage of the owners' sense of patriotism. While Landis expressed his support for adding black players, he could not predict if and when a team would take that step. As he had done in the past, Landis put the onus on individual teams, and not the commissioner's office, for bringing black players into the Major Leagues.

Despite Landis's proclamation, the status quo reigned for the 1944 season. None of the Major League franchises offered tryouts to black players, nor did they seem interested in scouting the Negro Leagues for potential talent. Instead of placing their leagues on firmer foundations, the NNL and NAL owners continued to engage in internal battles, and NAL president Martin never followed through on his promise to stage a charity game whose profits would go to war-related organizations. After the season ended, Smith reported on a rumor of a new Negro League launching in 1945, and he remarked that the new league could put both the NNL and the NAL out of business. The biggest development in regards to the reintegration of the Major Leagues came in November when Landis died at the age of seventy-eight. Though Landis publicly insisted that he did not oppose the inclusion of black players in the Major Leagues, he did not exert any pressure on individual owners to take that step. In early 1945, the owners made Albert "Happy" Chandler the new commissioner. Landis's death and Chandler's arrival opened the possibility that the commissioner's office would not hinder the effort of any franchise to sign black players.

As the year 1945 dawned, the conditions did not appear ripe for any Major League franchise to sign one or more black players. World War II continued to rage in both Europe and in the Pacific, and no one could confidently predict when the conflict would end. Major League owners seemed more focused on selecting a new commissioner and on planning for another wartime season than they did on scouting the Negro Leagues for untapped sources of talent. NNL and NAL owners seemed content to operate as they had done in past seasons and avoided making any plans in case the Major Leagues sought their best players. Despite those realities, the campaign to add black players to the Major Leagues had made progress and had left an indelible imprint on American society. More civic leaders and politicians would join the campaign in 1945, and they put increased pressure on Major League franchises to sign black players. What Smith and the *Courier* started in the 1930s had grown into a nationwide movement that would achieve victory by the time the year ended. Smith himself would play a central role in the final act of reintegration and would continue to play a central role as the process of reintegration proceeded.

All those factors—the instability of the NNL and the NAL, the public campaigns in the *Courier* and other newspapers, and the pressure on Major League teams to sign black players—shaped the world that Robinson entered when he joined the Kansas City Monarchs for spring training in early 1945. Robinson too would soon play a central role in the final act of the reintegration of the Major Leagues. Though he had not played professional baseball prior to 1945, Robinson possessed the qualities that made him the ideal candidate to become the first black player on a Major League team in the twentieth century. Robinson had the talent and the qualities, and Smith had the platform needed to advocate for black players. Their fortunes collided in 1945 and put them in a position to take advantage of the ambition of Branch Rickey, who had a grand plan to transform the Dodgers from the "bums" to World Series champions.

4

The Beginning of a New Era in Baseball

In the year 1945, the ambitions of Wendell Smith, Branch Rickey, and Jackie Robinson collided and transformed American society. During the early months of 1945, Smith grew bolder in his attempts to pressure Major League owners to sign black players and arranged a tryout for three players with the Boston Red Sox. Robinson participated in that tryout, which indirectly brought him to Rickey's attention. Rickey emerged as a prominent voice in the debate over adding black players because of his prominent place within the National League and his involvement with a new Negro League, the United States League (USL). For Rickey, the USL merely served as a cover for him to fulfill his long-held intention to sign black players and put those players on his team's Major League roster. Robinson's journey to the Brooklyn Dodgers' organization, first through the Minor League with the Dodger's top farm club, took place at a time when more politicians and civic organizations put pressure on Rickey and other executives to add black players to their all-white rosters. Rickey, though, did not want to appear as if he signed black players in response to political and civic pressure. As a result, he accelerated his plans to sign multiple players and went ahead and signed Robinson to a contract in October 1945. The contract made Robinson a member of the Brooklyn Dodgers' organization, and it represented the first time that a Major League organization had a black player since the 1890s. The contract also represented the culmination of the long-term effort to reintegrate the Major Leagues and to break the unwritten color barrier blocking black players from competing at the highest levels of professional baseball.

A PIONEER AMONG THE MONARCHS

When Robinson joined the Kansas City Monarchs in the spring of 1945, he joined one of the most successful franchises in the history of the Negro Leagues. J. L. Wilkinson, the only white owner in the Negro Leagues, had owned the team since its inaugural season in 1920 and had the reputation as one of the best owners in the Negro Leagues. He paid his players good salaries and helped to bring nighttime baseball to the Negro Leagues by using a portable lighting system at Monarchs' games. During his time as the Monarchs' owner, the franchise won ten league titles—three titles in the old NNL and seven in the NAL. The Monarchs also appeared in four World Series, including the first two World Series played in the 1920s and two more played in the 1940s after the NNL and the NAL reinstituted the annual contest. In those four World Series, the Monarchs won two titles, the last one coming over the Homestead Grays in 1942. Wilkinson ensured his teams' continued success by signing some of the best players in the Negro Leagues—players such as Satchel Paige, Norman "Turkey" Stearns, Charles Willard "Bullet" Rogan, Hilton Smith, and Willard Brown. Robinson quickly joined that pantheon of talented Monarchs, finishing the season with the best batting average on the team. The Monarchs did not win the NAL title, but they did compile a winning record and finished in second place.

Though Robinson played for one of the best franchises and enjoyed a successful season, he disliked the time he spent with the Monarchs. His contract guaranteed him $400 a month, good money for him at that stage of his life, and he appreciated the salary he earned playing baseball. Robinson, however, abhorred the long road trips that started in spring training and continued through the regular season. The Monarchs' schedule took them on extended road trips to eastern cities, playing doubleheaders and games in different cities on different days of the week. While on those extended trips, Robinson and his teammates had few choices for finding good meals since many places refused to serve black customers. Robinson also seemed like an outcast among his teammates and players on other teams in the Negro Leagues. While many players enjoyed parties, drinking, and fraternizing with women, Robinson did not drink and remained faithful to his fiancée, Rachel. Robinson remained committed to living a life that adhered to his religious faith, the same faith that he believed had helped to save him during his teenage years in Pasadena, California. Those factors, along with the seeming lack of stability in the management of many Negro Leagues franchises, led Robinson to reconsider his choice of pursuing a career in professional baseball. Fortunately, Robinson stuck with the Monarchs throughout the season and even earned a coveted position on the West team in the annual East-West Classic. Unbeknownst to Robinson, his impressive play for the Monarchs and his decision to stick with the team kept him in a position to remain the focus of a scout, Clyde Sukeforth, who focused on the twenty-six-year-old rookie at the behest of his boss Branch Rickey.

BRANCH RICKEY'S GREAT EXPECTATIONS

By 1945, Rickey had compiled an impressive record as an executive in the Major Leagues. He had an undistinguished career as a player and a field manager; he lost his job as the St. Louis Cardinals' field manager in 1925, but he remained the team's general manager. As the Cardinals' general manager, Rickey made the franchise a perennial contender in the National League and transformed how the franchise fostered talent. By selecting and investing in Minor League franchises, Rickey created a farm system for the Cardinals and used that system to develop talented players. Through his efforts, the Cardinals won three National League pennants and two World Series in the 1930s; they won their third World Series title in 1942, Rickey's last season with the club. The players that Rickey's farm system developed included multiple Hall of Famers—most notably Enos Slaughter, Stan Musial, Jay Hanna "Dizzy" Dean, Joe Medwick, and Johnny Mise. Other Major League franchises followed Rickey's lead and created their own farm systems of Minor League clubs. Rickey left the Cardinals after the 1942 season to become the president and general manager of the Brooklyn Dodgers, a franchise that lacked the Cardinals' history of sustained success. The Dodgers carried the appropriate nickname of "the Bums," winning only two National League pennants and zero World Series titles. With the Dodgers, Rickey had another opportunity to bring more innovative ideas to Major League baseball and enact yet another plan that would revolutionize baseball.

At some point in his long career, Rickey decided that he would break the Major Leagues' color barrier by signing black players. Later in his life, Rickey cited an experience he had while coaching Ohio Wesleyan University's baseball team in 1906. During a road trip to South Bend, Indiana, the hotel denied a room to the baseball team's only black player, catcher Charles Thomas. Rickey intervened and said that Thomas could sleep on a cot in his hotel room, and the hotel accommodated his request. While sharing the room with Thomas, Rickey recalled seeing his catcher cry and bemoan the color of his skin. Rickey said that he tried to console Thomas and claimed that the scene haunted him for many years. For Rickey, that experience marked the beginning of his determination to fight against racial discrimination, and his role with the Brooklyn Dodgers gave him the ideal position to live out that promise.

While Rickey had noble reasons for adding black players to the Dodgers, he also had other baseball-related reasons for taking that action. After winning the National League pennant in 1941 and winning over one hundred games in 1942, the Dodgers had slipped down the league's standings over the next two years. The Dodgers finished in third place in 1943 and in seventh place in 1944 before rebounding for another third place finish in 1945. Rickey took control of a team that had some good players, such as Eddie Stanky and Dixie Walker, but needed an infusion of talent. The team also needed the players, such as Pee Wee Reese, who left for the armed forces to return and hopefully continue to play at their prewar levels. To build a foundation for a successful Dodgers team, Rickey crafted a player development system akin to the one he developed with the Cardinals. He signed players throughout the wartime years and assigned them to Minor League teams where they could gain experience while remaining under the Dodgers' control. The Dodgers also faced fierce competition from the two other Major League franchises that operated within New York City— the New York Yankees and the New York Giants. Signing black players would bring the Dodgers much-needed attention in the city's tabloids, bring fans to aging Ebbets Field in Brooklyn, and give them an edge over other teams in the National League.

As he developed his plans to sign black players for the Brooklyn Dodgers, Rickey proceeded with caution and sought players who had a particular combination of specific qualities. Rickey knew that the first black player in the Major Leagues in the twentieth century needed more than athletic talent; he needed the strength to withstand abuse from fans, opposing teams, and perhaps even his own teammates without fighting back. Additionally, the player who officially broke the color barrier needed to possess good moral character, something that Rickey valued and saw as important for his plan to succeed. Rickey himself possessed a deep religious faith, leading to one of his nicknames of "the Mahatma," and that faith also shaped his decision to sign black players for his Dodgers. Even though Major League clubs had faced pressure for nearly a decade to sign black players, the actual signing of one or more black players remained a very controversial move for Rickey. When he revealed his plans to his family, they all opposed him. Rickey, therefore, could not openly send out his scouts to look for black players for the Brooklyn Dodgers. He needed a cover story, and that cover story appeared in the formation of a new Negro League in early 1945.

After spending several years in the wilderness, Gus Greenlee returned to the world of black professional baseball in January 1945 with the formation of the United States League (USL). The USL initially included six franchises—the Pittsburgh Crawfords, Philadelphia Hilldales, Toldeo Rays, Chicago Brown Bombers, Detroit Giants, and the Brooklyn Brown Dodgers. Neither the Crawfords nor the Hilldales possessed any ties to the franchises that previously carried those names. Rickey himself seemed to represent the main force in organizing the Brown Dodgers, and the franchise would share Ebbets Field with the Dodgers. During a press conference called to announce the formation of the Brooklyn Brown Dodgers, Rickey revealed his contempt for the existing Negro Leagues, particularly the NNL. In response to questions shouted at him by the Newark Eagles' Effa Manley, Rickey ominously asserted that a true organized league did not exist in the world of black professional baseball. Rickey went further and denounced the owners for associating with gamblers and for engaging in business practices below the standards expected of organized leagues. He expressed faith that the USL would provide black professional baseball with the organized league structure it needed and expressed hope that it could become affiliated in some way with Major League Baseball. With the existence of the Brown Dodgers, the USL provided Rickey cover to actively scout black players and gave him a platform to chide the NNL and the NAL. The Brown Dodgers and the USL also gave Rickey the platform to deflect questions as to his intentions about the Dodgers and black players. Rickey faced those questions because of rapid developments that happened in the early months of 1945.

UNDER PRESSURE

As the 1945 baseball season dawned, Rickey and other Major League executives faced increasing pressure to sign black players. That pressure came from activists who picketed outside Major League ballparks as well as from politicians in northern cities who sought to cultivate voters by pushing for integration in the Major Leagues. In Boston, city councilman Isadore H. Y. Muchnick threatened to bar both the Red Sox and the Braves from playing on Sundays unless they permitted at least one black player to try out for their clubs. In New York, the state legislature passed the Ives-Quinn Bill, which established a State Commission Against Discrimination. That commission placed all three of the state's Major League franchises under investigation since none of them employed black players. Within New York City, Mayor Fiorello LaGuardia and other politicians, most notably Charles Evan Hughes Jr., added additional pressure to the Dodgers, Giants, and Yankees. Hughes had served as leading voice in favor of the Ives-Quinn Bill, and he formed a Committee of Unity to investigate the ban on black players in the Major Leagues. Both Rickey and his counterpart on the

New York Yankees, Larry MacPhail, served on that committee. A few months later, LaGuardia appointed his own committee, composed of both black and white members, to make specific recommendations to the Major Leagues. Rickey personally received additional pressure from a member of the New York State Assembly, Philip J. Schupler, who wrote a letter directly to the Dodgers' general manager. In the letter, Schupler outlined his support for the Dodgers and his sincere belief that adding black players would bring fans to Ebbets Field and would elevate the teams' status in the National League. Schupler closed his letter with a not-so-subtle reference to the Ives-Quinn Bill and by stating that Rickey could show his support for that measure by signing black players.

The increased pressure that Major League franchises faced came in an atmosphere of other changes in American society. In April of 1945, President Franklin Roosevelt died suddenly; he had served since 1933 and had started his fourth term in January. With his death, Harry Truman assumed the presidency and had to help steer the nation and the world toward the successful completion of World War II. With its conclusion, the American home front started the transition from a wartime to a peacetime society. People who had served overseas for several years headed home; those people included prominent baseball players such as Joe DiMaggio and Ted Williams. The conclusion of World War II also added to the momentum to bring black players into the Major Leagues. The United States had played a leading role in a war that conquered racist regimes in Europe and in the Pacific, and black servicemen had helped achieve that victory. Surely, if black servicemen could risk their lives for their country, then they could play alongside white players in the Major Leagues.

ROOSEVELT AND TRUMAN

Until 1940, all presidents who won a second term observed the tradition established by George Washington and retired at the conclusion of that second term. Franklin Roosevelt easily won reelection in 1936 and faced the same questions that his two-term predecessors faced as the 1940 election approached. Due to the onset of World War II in 1939, Roosevelt decided to break the two-term tradition and run for an unprecedented third term in 1940 as a means of providing stability and continuity in a world at war. Roosevelt easily dispatched his Republican opponent, Wendell Willkie, and immediately worked to position the United States as the "great arsenal of democracy." He also spent his third term planning for American victory in World War II and for American leadership in the postwar world.

In 1944, Roosevelt launched his fourth and final campaign for the presidency. Henry Wallace had served as his vice president since 1941, but the Democratic Party maneuvered to have Roosevelt select Senator Harry Truman of Missouri as his running mate in the 1944 election. Party leaders convinced Roosevelt to make that change because they disliked Wallace's views and saw him as an unfit option for president. Roosevelt suffered from ill health in 1944; if Roosevelt died in office, the vice president would become the president and serve the remainder of his term. The ticket of Roosevelt and Truman defeated the ticket of Thomas Dewey and John Bricker, and Roosevelt took the Oath of Office for the fourth time on January 20, 1945.

Truman served as the vice president for eleven weeks. He had Secret Service protection, an honor not accorded his predecessors, and he fulfilled the few duties allocated to the vice president. On April 12, 1945, Truman remained in Washington, D.C., while Roosevelt spent time in Warm Springs, Georgia. He had built a resort in Warm Springs in the hope that the naturally warm water would help cure polio, the disease that had afflicted him since 1921. Around noon, Roosevelt suffered a fatal stroke. The news of Roosevelt's passing stunned Americans and people around the world. When the news reached Truman, he recalled that he felt as if the entire universe had suddenly fallen on his shoulders. He immediately stepped into the presidency and faced the prospect of not only ending the war but also implementing the plans Roosevelt had developed with other Allied leaders. Truman admirably did both and showed that Democratic Party leaders had made a wise decision at the 1944 convention.

In that atmosphere, Smith and other black sportswriters did not back down from their long-term efforts to get black players into the Major Leagues. Jimmy Smith, another sportswriter for the *Courier*, and Joe Bostie of *The People's Voice*, a paper based in New York City, successfully arranged for a tryout for Terry McDuffie and Dave Thomas with the Dodgers. McDuffie, a pitcher, played for the Philadelphia Stars, while Thomas played at first base for the New York Cubans. Rickey did not want to feel pressured into giving the players a tryout, so McDuffie and Thomas did not receive an immediate invitation to join the Dodgers' practice. On the following day, however, the players donned Dodgers uniforms and joined the rest of the squad for their practices at West Point's baseball field. Neither player received an invitation to join the team, but Wendell Smith praised the event as a sign of progress toward adding black players to at least one Major League franchise. Smith did not see either player as a Major League prospect, but he praised his fellow sportswriters for taking the two players to the Dodgers and getting each of them a tryout. He also praised Rickey for his baseball acumen and confidently predicted that better players would partake in the next tryout for the Dodgers, players whom Rickey could not refuse to add to the Dodgers' system.

Following that tryout with the Dodgers, Smith adopted a harder edge in pressing forward with his campaign. Each year during America's involvement in World War II, President Roosevelt urged the Major League teams to continue operations as a morale booster for the American home front. He did that for the final time shortly before his death, and Smith wrote a very pointed column in response to the president's plea. As he had done in the past, Smith noted the hypocrisy of baseball's place as "America's pastime," though the sport maintained a color barrier that seemed to violate the country's founding ideals. In his column in March 1945, Smith drew a direct comparison between the Major Leagues' color barrier and Adolf Hitler's actions in Germany and in the countries Germany occupied. He also pointed out that Major League teams had signed white players with physical disabilities instead of black players. Smith called upon President Roosevelt to require the Major Leagues to adopt a fair employment practice policy, similar to the Fair Employment Practices Commission (FEPC) he had authorized by executive order in 1941. The FEPC barred discriminatory hiring practices in industries engaged in wartime service, so, to Smith, it represented a natural basis on which to form a similar commission for the Major Leagues.

On the heels of writing that column, Smith took advantage of the missive Muchnick delivered to the Boston Red Sox and Braves. Working with Muchnick, Smith selected three players to travel to Boston for tryouts—Sam Jethroe, Marvin Williams, and Robinson. At first, Muchnick's and Smith's efforts to reach officials from the Red Sox and the Braves failed, leading Muchnick to grow more indignant at the actions of the two clubs. Finally, on April 16, the Red Sox conceded to holding a tryout for the three players at Fenway Park. While the players demonstrated their considerable baseball skills, Red Sox officials never contacted the players once they returned to their Negro League teams. Smith remained defiant, even using the analogy of Paul Revere's ride in 1775 to assert that he and others would not back down from their crusade. Even though the tryouts failed, they brought together Smith and Robinson, whom Smith recognized as having the talent to compete in the Major Leagues. The timing of the tryouts also proved fortuitous since they came immediately prior to Rickey's press conference on the USL. Smith attended that press conference and mentioned Robinson as a player whom Rickey should watch if he wanted to sign black players. Following that conversation, Rickey sent Sukeforth and other scouts to follow Robinson and report on the rookie's performance with the Monarchs.

While Rickey engaged in his subterfuge, the regular season proceeded for both the Major Leagues and the Negro Leagues. The Detroit Tigers won the American League pennant, while the Chicago Cubs captured the team's final National League pennant of the twentieth century. In the World Series, the Tigers prevailed over the Cubs in a seven-game series, leaving the Cubs without a title since 1908. The NNL and the NAL staged their fourth World Series; the Cleveland Buckeyes swept the Homestead

Grays in a low-scoring series that featured two shutouts. While the NNL and the NAL staged a successful World Series, the leagues remained unstable and seemed to confirm Rickey's criticisms that they did not meet the high standards for "organized" professional baseball. In one game at the Cubs' Wrigley Field, Memphis Red Sox third baseman Jim Ford physically attacked an umpire, leading to a brawl on the field. Ford's teammates supported him and threatened the other umpire on the field, while the field manager Larry Brown joined in the fray. The fracas happened in front of NAL president J. B. Martin, who did nothing to intervene and restore order on the field. After the game, he issued a meek fine of $50 on Ford, but he took no other action against the other Red Sox players or the field manager. As a result of the incident, Cubs' management effectively shut the door to all future games involving Negro League teams at Wrigley Field by implementing a rental fee of $5,000. Since teams in the Negro Leagues lacked the funds to pay the rental fee, they could no longer use the ballpark to stage their contests.

The incident at Wrigley Field did not represent an isolated incident for the Negro Leagues in the 1945 season. In a game against the Philadelphia Stars, the New York Black Yankees walked off the field in the fifth inning due to a dispute with an umpire. The same Black Yankees also forfeited a game against the Newark Eagles due to a dispute with yet another umpire. Those incidents drew strong rebukes in black newspapers and doomed the slim chances that the NNL and the NAL had to compete alongside the Major Leagues. Those incidents also raised the possibility that other Major League teams would follow the Cubs' lead and effectively bar Negro League teams from competing in their ballparks. Such bars would hurt the Negro Leagues' finances, and the ugly on-field incidents could hurt the push to get black players into the Major Leagues. Despite warnings from Rickey, Smith, and other black sportswriters, the owners in the NNL and the NAL made little attempts to change the ways they operated.

Despite those issues, Comiskey Park in Chicago remained open to both the NNL and the NAL teams. The leagues successfully staged their annual East-West Game at the ballpark before over thirty-seven thousand fans. In the game, the West team defeated the East team by a score of 9–6. Robinson started at shortstop for the West team and scored one of the runs that put the game out of reach for the East team. About one month later, Robinson returned to Comiskey Park, this time with his Monarchs for a doubleheader against the Chicago American Giants. Robinson had hurt his shoulder, so he did not intend to play in the contests while his shoulder recovered. He did, however, go onto the field before the game with the rest of his teammates. While on the field, he had a conversation with a white scout that would change his life and the rest of American society.

ENDGAME

By the end of August 1945, Rickey had decided to put the final parts of his plan to sign black players into motion. He sent Sukeforth to Comiskey Park and contact Robinson, and Sukeforth complied. When Sukeforth approached Robinson at Comiskey Park, he said that Rickey wanted to talk to him about joining the Brown Dodgers. Robinson responded that he could not play in the doubleheader because of his injured shoulder, but that news did not deter Sukeforth. He asked Robinson to visit him at his hotel after the doubleheader ended. At first, Robinson regarded the meeting as a waste of his time, but he went to see Sukeforth in his hotel room. Thanks to a bribe from Sukeforth, the hotel's management allowed Robinson to use the passenger elevator that usually remained off-limits for black guests. At the meeting, Sukeforth again pressed Robinson that Rickey wanted him for his USL team and wanted him to come to Brooklyn for an in-person meeting. Robinson again hesitated since he had a contract with the Monarchs and did not want to violate that contract. Sukeforth persuaded Robinson to make the journey by noting that his shoulder would anyway keep him out of any games he would miss while visiting Brooklyn. Robinson agreed; Sukeforth left to scout another player in Toldeo, and Robinson joined so that they could travel together by train to New York City. On August 28, Sukeforth and Robinson finally walked into Rickey's office for a meeting that Robinson believed would focus on the Brooklyn Brown Dodgers.

Rickey's office on the fourth floor of a building located on 215 Montague Street served as the setting for one of the most important meetings in baseball's history. The office featured dark panels and a portrait of the Dodgers' current field manager, Leo Durocher. Another portrait on the wall featured Abraham Lincoln, a president Rickey admired and who helped set in motion the meeting held on August 28. Other features in Rickey's office included a blackboard with the names of every player within the Dodgers' extensive organization. That feature attested to Rickey's investment in the farm system and his tendency to trade away good players knowing that a cheaper prospect could take their place on the Major League roster. For the meeting, Rickey sat behind his desk while Robinson sat in an overstuffed chair. Sukeforth provided a quick introduction, and then Rickey took over the meeting.

As a first question, Rickey asked Robinson if he had a girl, and the question surprised Robinson. He replied that he had a girlfriend, Rachel, but that the long distance and travel had kept them apart for a long time. Rickey encouraged Robinson to marry Rachel because he believed that a woman could provide support for ballplayers during tough times in their lives. The response also surprised Robinson; Rickey pressed on and asked

Robinson if he knew the reasons for the meeting in Brooklyn. Robinson responded with the information Sukeforth had supplied to him—Rickey wanted him on the Brown Dodgers' USL team. Rickey then shared with Robinson his true intentions: Rickey wanted Robinson for the Brooklyn Dodgers, not the Brooklyn Brown Dodgers. Rickey's Brown Dodgers franchise and his interest in the USL served as his cover to scout Robinson and other Negro League players.

Sukeforth and Rickey talked about his skills as a baseball player while Robinson contemplated what he had learned. Rickey asked him directly if he believed he could play for the Dodgers, and after hesitating, Robinson finally responded with a yes. Rickey then impressed upon Robinson the grander importance of adding a black player to the Major Leagues. He revealed that he had investigated Robinson's life and knew about his time at UCLA and his experiences in the United States Army that led to the court martial. While Rickey admired Robinson, he cautioned the ballplayer about the reality facing him in the Major Leagues. Rickey painted a dire portrait of all the people who would oppose Robinson's inclusion on the Dodgers' roster and intoned that Robinson's performance alone would not convince other teams to sign black players. Robinson, Rickey intoned, would need to control his emotions. Robinson asked him if he wanted a player too scared to fight back against those who questioned him and hurled abuse at him. Rickey responded that he wanted a player with the strength to not fight back against the abuse. For at least the first few seasons, the first player to break the color barrier would need to adopt a stance of nonviolence toward that abuse. To Rickey, the success of his plan depended upon persuading those who opposed adding black players to Major League rosters, and that persuasion would fail if the first player developed a bad reputation. Fighting back would give critics the opening they needed to argue that all black players lacked the stamina and the personality to play in the Major Leagues alongside white players.

To test Robinson, Rickey spent the next part of the meeting acting out the different scenarios Robinson could face once he joined the Dodgers. Those scenarios included people who refused to serve him in restaurants, hotels, and other public spaces that served his white teammates. Other scenarios included hecklers in ballparks who hurled racial epithets at Robinson and insulted his family, ballplayers who spiked Robinson while sliding into bases, and ballplayers who joined in the racial epithets coming from the crowd. As Rickey went through those scenarios, Robinson remained in his seat and thought about the larger stakes involved if he joined the Dodgers' organization. He remained transfixed by Rickey, by his earnestness in wanting to add not just one but multiple black players to his franchise. Robinson was aware of his temper, of how he had reacted in the past to racial abuse he received while playing sports and while serving in the army. Robinson, though, also realized that he needed to take advantage of this opportunity and that he did possess the strength to not fight back against the abuse he would receive.

The monumental meeting in Rickey's office lasted approximately two hours. By the time Robinson left, he had agreed to a contract, signed at a later date, to play for the Dodgers' top-level farm team, the Montreal Royals. He would earn $600 a month on top of a signing bonus of $3,500. After leaving Rickey's office, Robinson returned to the Monarchs and continued to play the remainder of the games on the team's schedule. He could not share any news of what had happened in Rickey's office with his teammates or the Monarchs' management, nor could he share the news with his mother Mallie or with Rachel. When he spoke to them, he could only drop hints about what had happened. In September, Robinson's time with the Monarchs ended abruptly once he left the team to return to his home in Pasadena. The Monarchs' management expressed their displeasure with his decision as well as his secretive meeting in Brooklyn with Rickey. The management threatened to kick Robinson off the team and warned him that he would not find a job in any NNL or NAL team if he left the Monarchs. Knowing that his days in the Negro Leagues had already ended, Robinson did not bow to those threats and returned to Pasadena.

As Robinson played out his final games with the Monarchs, Smith broke the story of his meeting with Rickey in the *Courier*. Smith reported most of the details surrounding the meeting—the contact between Sukeforth and Robinson in Chicago, the location of the meeting, and the meeting's length. Smith also published some quotes he had received from Rickey about the nature of the meeting. Rickey innocently claimed that he met with Robinson to discuss the situation in black baseball, not to discuss his addition to the Dodgers' organization. As he had done in the past, Rickey asserted that a true organization did not exist in black baseball and that he wanted black baseball to have a legitimate league. Smith expressed skepticism since Robinson had spent only one season with the Monarchs and, therefore, did not possess the expertise to advise Rickey on the best ways to organize black baseball. He reasoned that if Rickey really wanted advice on black baseball, the Dodgers' general manager would have asked a veteran of the Negro Leagues. Smith also raised the issue of player tampering since Robinson remained under contract with the Monarchs. He wondered how Rickey would approach players he wanted for the Brown Dodgers and whether he would approach the owners who had those players under contract. Smith asserted that Rickey had an obligation to go through the NNL and NAL owners if he wanted any players in those leagues to join the Brown Dodgers.

Smith's column raised key issues that would come to bedevil the NNL and the NAL in the near future. Robinson had a contract with the

Monarchs, a contract that lasted through the 1945 season. He had that contract when Sukeforth approached him in Comiskey Park, and he had that contract when he met with Rickey on August 28. At no point, however, did Rickey approach Wilkinson or other executives with the Monarchs to inquire about Robinson's availability or negotiate an amount he would pay in compensation to the Monarchs. On the contrary, Rickey acted as if Robinson did not possess a valid contract and could freely sign with the Dodgers' organization. He asked Robinson to remain quiet and delayed the official signing of his contract with the Dodgers' organization because he planned to sign more black players. Rickey did not delay his announcement because he respected the contract Robinson had with the Monarchs. His actions represented the logical extension of the negative views of the NNL and the NAL he had aired earlier in the season. Due to those negative views, Rickey had no intention of sending compensation to Wilkinson for Robinson or to any other owner for any black player he wanted for the Dodgers. Since the NNL and the NAL had never developed a plan with the Major Leagues for their players, Rickey's actions had the potential to establish a pattern that would doom the Negro Leagues and leave them with no recourse to demand compensation.

In the meantime, Robinson returned to Pasadena and reunited with Rachel. He also participated on a traveling black barnstorming team that played under the name the Kansas City Royals. Other Negro League players joined him on the Royals, and their games in southern California drew overflowing crowds. After their brief reunion, Rachel left with a friend for New York City, her first time visiting the city. Robinson joined them a short time later on his way to Venezuela with the rest of his Royals team for more barnstorming contests. His stay in New York City lasted longer than planned due to a delay in the start of the barnstorming tour in Venezuela. Robinson used the delay to spend time with Rachel, who tried to find work as a nurse while also shopping for items for her upcoming wedding. Rachel bought her wedding dress, veil, and shoes from Saks Fifth Avenue. Together, they explored the city that would eventually become their home. Another factor kept Robinson in New York City longer than he had planned—he received a phone call that ordered him to go to Montreal for the formal signing of his Dodgers' contract.

The formal public announcement of Robinson's signing happened because of events beyond Rickey's and Robinson's control. Rickey initially wanted to announce the signing on November 1, but he later decided to push the date back to January 1, 1946. He made that change because he wanted to give himself more time to sign additional black players and to make them part of the announcement. LaGuardia, however, forced Rickey to change his plans because of a promise the mayor had made near the end of his reelection campaign. To ensure that the city's black residents voted for him, LaGuardia announced that he would push the city's three Major League teams to formally pledge to uphold the Ives-Quinn law by signing black players. Rickey did not want to appear as if he signed Robinson due to the mayor's threat, so he moved quickly to announce the signing before Election Day. For that reason, he contacted Robinson and scheduled a press conference in Montreal. He chose Montreal because Robinson would join the Dodgers' farm team based in the city, the Montreal Royals, in the 1946 season. The Royals served as the highest farm team in the Dodgers' system, and players who joined the team had a high likelihood of playing for the Dodgers.

A New Era

The mounting public pressure on Branch Rickey and other Major League officials came at a time when Americans celebrated the end of World War II. May 8, 1945, marked Victory in Europe Day, and celebrations commenced across the country and around the world. The war in the Pacific theater continued until August 1945. On August 6 and August 9, Harry Truman made the tough decision to drop atomic bombs on the Japanese cities of Hiroshima and Nagasaki. Truman made that decision based upon information that the Japanese government intended to continue the war and that an invasion of Japan would cost many American lives. Japanese Emperor Hirohito announced Japan's surrender on August 15, and Japanese officials formally signed their surrender documents on the USS *Missouri* on September 2. Across the United States, Japan's surrender sparked another round of celebrations and a sense of relief that the long World War II had finally ended in victory.

Robinson's historic meeting with Rickey came in between the announcement of Japan's surrender and the formal surrender ceremony on the USS *Missouri*. Stories about those events, therefore, splashed across newspapers alongside stories about pressure campaigns on Major League Baseball officials. The ending of World War II in America's favor also meant that one half of the Double Victory campaign had ended in success. With that half of the Double Victory secured, activists could turn their attention toward the second half of that Double Victory. Bringing a black player to the Major Leagues for the first time since the 1880s appeared as the ideal place to bring the Double Victory to fruition.

Branch Rickey intended to bring multiple black players into the Dodgers' organization regardless of the calls from Fiorello LaGuardia and other politicians. He acted in October 1945, less than two months after Japan's formal surrender, before any politician could claim credit for his plan. Robinson's signing, therefore, came at a time when the entire country embarked upon a new era, the post–World War II era in which the country emerged as an international superpower. The signing served as a symbol of that new era; change was coming to baseball, to the United States, and to the rest of the world.

On October 23, Robinson signed the contract that officially made him part of the Dodgers' organization and the first black player linked to a Major League organization in the twentieth century. The contract officially made him a member of the Montreal Royals, and it contained the salary terms discussed during the meeting in August. In addition to Robinson and Rickey, Branch Rickey Jr., who served as the head of the Dodgers' farm system, and Hector Racine, the president of the Montreal Royals, attended the meeting. The sportswriters assembled in the room seemed shocked by the signing. Robinson spoke briefly to express his happiness at the signing and pledge his determination to succeed in this new venture. Rickey Jr. also spoke and acknowledged that signing Robinson might cost the Dodgers' some supporters and perhaps even some white players on the roster. He said that the loss of support and players would not deter the Dodgers from keeping Robinson and from signing other black players.

The surprising news of Robinson's signing splashed across the front pages and sports pages of black newspapers. Black sportswriters unanimously praised Rickey and expressed cautious hope that Robinson could succeed against high-level Minor League and Major League talent. The *Courier* published a column from Robinson, likely ghostwritten by Smith, that outlined his thoughts and feelings on joining the Dodgers' organization. Robinson said that he had a childhood dream of playing in the big leagues and that he deeply appreciated the opportunity to actually play for a big league team. He also expressed his gratitude to Rickey and Racine for their courage in signing a black player in the face of enormous pressure. Robinson, furthermore, stated his steadfast determination to work hard to ensure that he served as a good model for all African Americans and prove that Rickey had made a good decision. To reassure his readers, Robinson insisted that his signing represented more than an empty gesture of goodwill from Rickey. He explained the reasons for the secrecy, and he outlined his experiences playing on integrated teams that included southerners. Those experiences, plus his impending marriage to Rachel, made him both qualified and prepared to assume the responsibility of breaking baseball's color barrier.

In that same edition of the *Courier*, Smith devoted one of his columns to publishing an extensive interview that Rickey gave to sportswriters. Smith presented Rickey as a devoutly religious man whose faith compelled him to despise the color barrier in the Major Leagues and to decide that he needed to break that barrier. Rickey took care to note the scouting reports he had received on Robinson to display his sincerity about signing him and about judging ballplayers on their talents, not on the color of their skin. Smith added that Rickey intended to scout other black players and to add Robinson to the Dodgers' roster if he succeeded with the Royals. A quote from Rickey promising to add Robinson to the Dodgers' roster supported

Smith's assertions. Rickey also referred to letters of support he had received from different areas of the country, and he dispelled the idea that he had signed Robinson due to pressure from politicians and the Ives-Quinn legislation. He insisted that his plan to sign black players predated the legislation and issued a warning to other owners in the Major Leagues. To those owners, Rickey cautioned them that the time had come to sign black players and that they could not, and should not, stop that movement. Smith pressed Rickey on an issue that had arisen as a reason against signing black players—segregation in southern cities that hosted spring training sites. Rickey said that the Dodgers' organization would obey southern laws and would find accommodations for Robinson if he could not stay in the same places as his white teammates.

As the interview continued, it ventured into other potential obstacles that could hurt Robinson and the greater cause of bringing black players to the Major Leagues. Smith asked him about the reactions of players from the South and mentioned the alleged negative reaction to Robinson's signing from Dixie Walker, a key member of the Dodgers' roster. Without directly addressing Walker's alleged comments, Rickey confidently declared that he did not see any reason to worry about players' reactions to Robinson. He implied that such reactions amounted to criticisms of the ways he conducted his job as a general manager. To Rickey, players should simply focus on playing baseball and should accept any players, including black players, he added to the Dodgers' roster. Smith and Rickey also broached the topic of the Negro Leagues, and Rickey directed his anger at owners in the leagues who complained about the fact that he had not compensated the Monarchs for Robinson. He indignantly dismissed the NNL and the NAL as actual leagues who policed player behavior and maintained valid player contracts. Rickey claimed that Robinson did not recall signing a formal contract prior to joining the Monarchs. He also decried the practice of owners serving as league executives and claimed that he possessed no obligation to respect those leagues because of the leagues' shoddy practices. Other factors that made the NNL and the NAL illegitimate in the eyes of Rickey included the uneven number of games played by league teams and the scheduling of exhibition contests in the middle of the regular season. He remained insistent that he would not regard either the NNL or the NAL as legitimate leagues until they cleaned house and made significant changes to their operations.

Near the end of the interview, Rickey directed some invective toward Clark Griffith of the Washington Senators. Griffith, who owned the Senators, accused Rickey of conducting a contract raid in his pursuit of Robinson. Rickey challenged Griffith to prove the legitimacy of the NNL and the NAL. He also wondered why Griffith did not launch a campaign to bring those leagues into an agreement with the Major Leagues if he regarded those leagues as legitimate organizations. Rickey went further and accused Griffith of caring solely about money, not about the well-being of the Negro Leagues. Griffith had leased the Senators' ballpark to Negro League teams, and he enjoyed a comfortable relationship with the Homestead Grays since that team had moved from Pittsburgh to Washington, D.C. Those factors led Rickey to dismiss Griffith's criticisms as rooted in self-interest, not in the interest of preserving well-run leagues.

The wide-ranging interview with Rickey underscored several important items. First, the interview proved that Smith would continue to play a central role in the addition of black players to the Major Leagues. Smith had injected life into the movement in the 1930s, had pressed for tryouts for black players, and had brought Robinson to Rickey's attention. Now that his efforts had paid off, Smith would not fade into the background. He would follow Robinson's progress from the Royals to the Dodgers and would serve as a conduit between the ballplayer and the readers of the *Courier*. Second, the interview proved that Rickey would not tolerate any criticism for his actions and remained steadfast in his decision to add black players to the Dodgers. With an almost religious-like devotion, Rickey believed in the righteousness of his decision and regarded any criticism as rooted in bad faith. Third, Rickey remained aware of the obstacles facing Robinson and the success of any movement to bring black players to the Major Leagues. Since he saw the long-term nature of the movement, he would not deliberately provoke southern cities by demanding that they drop their laws for the Dodgers. Rickey, however, would not tolerate boycotts or other demands from white players who did not want to share the field with Robinson. He had no qualms about threatening those players and supporting Robinson in the face of opposition from teammates.

REACTIONS TO ROBINSON'S SIGNING

Outside of the black press, Robinson's signing produced some mixed reactions. Horace Stoneham of the Giants praised the signing and, likely as a way to deflect political pressure, pledged to scout black players in the 1946 season. He claimed that the Giants could not scout black players in the past season due to a lack of resources. Other executives within the Major Leagues praised Rickey's decision; some of them expressed skepticism that Robinson could succeed, but none outright said that they opposed the move. Bob Feller, star pitcher for the Cleveland Indians, expressed admiration for Robinson's talent, but predicted that he would not make it to the Major Leagues. He stressed that he was not biased against Robinson because of his race; rather, Feller noted that Robinson could not hit inside pitches and that he had an upper body more suited for football. Feller asserted that

Paige and Gibson ranked as the only Negro League players who could succeed in the Major Leagues. Even though he doubted Robinson's offensive abilities, Feller noted that Robinson could effectively play at second base and stood as a fine role model for his fellow African Americans.

White sportswriters also weighed in on Robinson's signing and offered a wide range of views. In newspapers across the country, white sportswriters praised Rickey for breaking a color barrier they regarded as outdated and as contrary to the founding ideals of the country. Some sportswriters, however, echoed the kind of views that Feller expressed and questioned whether Robinson could succeed in the Major Leagues. Ironically, the *New York Daily News'* Jimmy Powers emerged as a critic of Robinson's abilities. In the 1930s, Powers had pushed for the addition of black players on Major League rosters and used his columns to decry the color barrier. After Robinson's signing, however, Powers took a dim view of his chances of appearing on the Dodgers' roster in 1946 or 1947. As Powers reasoned, players who had halted their careers to serve in World War II would return to Major League rosters, leaving little room for Robinson. Like Feller, Powers also seemed to doubt Robinson's baseball skills, though he did not oppose Rickey's decision to sign a black player.

Another voice in opposition to Robinson's signing came from W. G. Bramham, the commissioner of the Minor Leagues. Bramham approved the contract Robinson signed with the Montreal Royals because no law existed that prevented a black player from signing such a contract. That likely represented the only reason Bramham approved the contract. He referred to Rickey as a carpet-bagger and asserted that the Dodgers' general manager put his selfish interests ahead of the interests of Robinson and other black players. Bramham insinuated that the existing Negro Leagues negated the need for black players to play alongside white players in both the Minor and Major Leagues. He also insinuated that Robinson, like other black players, lacked the skills needed to compete against white players. Bramham clearly wanted the status quo—black players in the Negro Leagues and white players in the Minor and Major Leagues. He claimed that black players could reach out to moguls such as Rickey when they felt they could compete with white players. Until that time came, Bramham felt that the status quo best protected the interests of both black and white players.

In the immediate aftermath of Robinson's signing, the most sustained anger emanated from owners in the NNL and the NAL, in particular from Wilkinson. Wilkinson threatened to challenge the signing since Rickey never offered compensation to the Monarchs for Robinson. He dismissed claims that Robinson did not have a formal contract with the Monarchs and asserted that the player's rights still belonged to the Monarchs. Soon after making those pronouncements, however, Wilkinson relented and withdrew any threats of blocking Robinson's move to the Dodgers' organization. In an interview with Smith, Wilkinson lauded Robinson and pledged to do what he could to support the ballplayer. Wilkinson did express some bitterness toward Rickey and declared that the Monarchs and other teams needed protection against raids on their rosters. He wanted an agreement that would protect the interests of the owners and would require Major League organizations to provide compensation when signing black players.

While Wilkinson backed down from any immediate challenges to Rickey, he and other Negro Leagues owners sought other avenues to address their grievances with the Dodgers' general manager. Three days after Robinson formally signed his contract, Effa Manley sent a letter to J. B. Martin, president of the NAL, and set in motion discussions of ways to respond to Rickey's actions. Martin wanted to appeal first to the National League's president, Ford Frick, before taking a case directly to the commission Albert "Happy" Chandler. Martin held out some hope that the Monarchs could gain financial compensation from Rickey and that Frick would listen to their appeals for a formal agreement between the Major Leagues and the Negro Leagues. Discontent over Rickey's actions spilled over into a joint meeting between officials of the NNL and the NAL held in Chicago in November. At that meeting, the owners abandoned the earlier plan of appealing to Frick and instead filed a protest directly to Chandler. In the letter, the NNL and NAL officials claimed that they did not want to block Robinson from joining the Dodgers' organization. Instead, they wanted the Major Leagues to respect the legitimacy of the Negro Leagues and to provide financial compensation for any players that had contracts with Negro League teams. The owners wanted the same kind of agreement that governed decisions between the Major and Minor Leagues. Rickey used the protest to again assert that Robinson did not have a valid contract when he signed with the Montreal Royals on October 23. Chandler considered their protest, but an agreement never materialized between the Negro Leagues and the Major Leagues in regards to financial compensation for players.

While black sportswriters urged their readers to patronize the Negro Leagues, they had little sympathy for the owners themselves and for the ways they organized the leagues. Smith offered a scathing indictment of the owners in his column on the November meeting. He outlined the many steps that the owners could have followed in order to improve the organization and legitimacy of the leagues. Those steps included hiring a commissioner, blocking owners of teams from serving as league executives, establishing territorial rights by investing in their own ballparks, limiting the activities of booking agents, and adopting other rules found in the Major Leagues. He noted that the owners took some steps to improve their leagues—they agreed to adopt new constitutions and add reserve clauses to the players' contracts. Smith, however, declared that the leagues remained weak and that the longtime weak enforcement of contracts gave

Rickey the opening he needed to sign Robinson without bothering about compensation for the Monarchs. Smith, furthermore, blasted the owners' criticism of black sportswriters by pointing out that he and other sportswriters had warned the owners about the need to hire a commissioner and make other improvements to the leagues' operations. With much derision, Smith noted that two booking agents, Eddie Gottlieb and Abe Saperstein, represented two of the most vocal attendees at the meeting. Smith clearly had little sympathy for the predicament that the NNL and the NAL faced and felt that the owners had brought that predicament upon themselves.

While many debated Robinson's chances of success and while the Negro League owners made futile attempts to call for financial compensation, Robinson completed his barnstorming tour in Venezuela. His teammates included prominent Negro League stars who had long careers in those leagues and who had every reason to feel envious that a rookie had beaten them to a Major League organization. Some of the players on the tour tried to help Robinson prepare for his upcoming challenges, but Robinson largely rejected their overtures. Robinson left Venezuela in early January 1946 after playing with his barnstorming team for ten weeks. He needed to focus on another important upcoming event—his wedding.

After returning to the United States, Robinson and Rachel reunited in New York City and then made a cross-country railroad trip to Pasadena. Once they returned home, they realized that their families had already started with their wedding preparations. The small, intimate wedding that both Robinson and Rachel wanted would not materialize; their families, in particular Rachel's mother, wanted something larger and grander for the couple. Robinson and Rachel complied, and their wedding took place on February 10 in the Independent Church of Christ. Rev. Karl Downs, one of Robinson's father figures, officiated the ceremony. Those in attendance included members of their families and people Robinson knew from his time with the UCLA Bruins. Soon after the ceremony, Robinson and Rachel spent a short honeymoon in San Jose, California, before returning to Pasadena to prepare for their departure for spring training.

With the Dodgers' spring training set to begin on March 1, Robinson and Rachel departed for Los Angeles by airplane on February 28. Their trip included stops in New Orleans, Louisiana, and Pensacola, Florida, on their way to the spring training site in Daytona Beach. The newlywed couple boarded the plane and waved goodbye to their loved ones who had come to the airport to see them off on their next adventure. Sadly, the adventure would have a rough beginning and would set the stage for the obstacles Robinson would face throughout the 1946 baseball season.

5

The Montreal Royals and Jackie Robinson

When Jackie Robinson took the field wearing a Montreal Royals jersey in 1946, he became the first black player since the 1880s to play alongside white players in the Minor Leagues. Both Robinson and the Royals enjoyed spectacular seasons, but Robinson received a taste of the obstacles that confronted him as he broke the color barrier. Robinson did not represent the only black player in the Minor Leagues; Rickey had followed through on his play to sign other black players and assigned them to different farm teams. Most of the attention focused on Robinson since he represented the first black player to join the Dodgers' organization and since he played for the Dodgers' highest-level farm team. While Robinson and other black players pursued their careers in the Minor Leagues, the Negro Leagues struggled to remain relevant and viable. After receiving a strong rebuke from Commissioner Albert "Happy" Chandler, the Negro League owners focused on improving their operations in the vain hope of notching an agreement with the Major Leagues. Their efforts failed, and the leagues moved forward into 1947 unprepared to deal with the reality of one or more integrated Major League teams.

THE BEGINNING OF THE END FOR THE NEGRO LEAGUES

As NNL and NAL owners made plans for the 1946 season, they still struggled to deal with the fallout of Branch Rickey's decision to sign Robinson without compensating the Kansas City Monarchs. In January, Chandler followed the same path that Rickey had followed and demanded that the two leagues improve their operations before asking for compensation and an agreement regarding black players. Chandler left the owners with no recourse and with no other choice but to concentrate on building a better organization for black professional baseball. Before they could make those plans, the owners in both the NNL and the NAL rejected Gus Greenlee's petition for membership. Greenlee apparently wanted to bring the teams from his USL into the NNL and the NAL; the USL had struggled to complete the 1945 season and had a poor outlook for the 1946 season. With that rejection, the USL launched again with only four franchises and vainly tried to compete with the NNL and the NAL for attention. The continued existence of the USL only added to the confusion and instability that characterized the NNL and the NAL throughout the season.

A column from Cumberland Posey exposed the deep rifts within the two leagues and the challenges facing anyone who attempted to reorganize the leagues onto sounder footing. Posey opened his column by pledging that he had always worked in the best interests of the Homestead Grays, not in his personal self-interests. While Posey expressed admiration for Ed Gottlieb, he referred to bookings agents as necessary evils and bemoaned the 10 percent cut of the profits that Gottlieb took from games at Yankee Stadium. Gottlieb also served as the booking agent for the games in Shibe Park, the park the Philadelphia Stars increasingly used to stage home contests. Posey implied that Gottlieb put his own financial interests ahead of the interests of the leagues. He also expressed admiration for Tom Wilson, the longtime president of the NNL, while bemoaning that the NAL president J. B. Martin acted like a dictator who often pretended as if Wilson and the NNL did not exist. Posey closed by outlining several ideas for ways to improve operations in the Negro Leagues. Those ideas included better scheduling of games, moving the East-West Game from Chicago to other league cities, and the removal of all owners from league offices. Posey offered no details about the ways to achieve those goals, but he concurred that the Negro Leagues had no business asking for an agreement with the Major Leagues under current conditions. Posey died from lung cancer a few months after penning that column, so the task of implementing any reforms fell to other owners.

Effa Manley of the Newark Eagles represented one of the most prominent NNL officials and someone who tried to improve the leagues' operations. The Eagles enjoyed one of their best, if not their best overall, season in 1946. They dominated their competition in the NNL, winning both halves of the season, before facing the Kansas City Monarchs in the World Series. In a thrilling seven-game series, the Eagles prevailed thanks to the talents of future Major Leaguers Larry Doby and Monte Irvin. Early in the season, Manley reached out to other officials and owners in order to try to reorganize the NNL and to implement some reforms. Those efforts failed. Near the end of the regular season, Manley and Tom Baird, who co-owned the Monarchs with J. L. Wilkinson, had to start the process of scheduling the World Series. Ten days before the scheduled start of the World Series, the two sides had agreed to dates and locations for only five games

EFFA MANLEY

Effa Manley represented one of the most important officials in the Negro Leagues and one of the owners who pushed the most forcefully for compensation when Major League franchises signed her players. Born in Philadelphia in 1897, Manley married Abe Manley in 1935 and worked closely with her husband in running the Newark Eagles franchise. Under her tutelage, the Newark Eagles consistently ranked as one of the best franchises in the Negro National League. Manley also had oversight of the league's finances and remained in the center of decisions the league made about booking games, paying umpires, and sharing gate receipts. Manley, therefore, did not represent a mere figurehead. She stood as one of the most powerful owners in the league and as someone who could try to save the league from collapsing. Despite her efforts, the league could not overcome its long-term structural and financial problems. Manley understood the rough time ahead for the Eagles and the rest of black baseball, and she ceased her involvement with the franchise after the 1948 season.

In 1971, ten years before Manley's death, Major League Baseball established the first of two Special Committees on the Negro Leagues. The committee had the charge of selecting former Negro League players for induction into the Hall of Fame, regardless of whether those players had ever joined the Major Leagues. Before it disbanded in 1977, the committee selected players such as Josh Gibson, Judy Johnson, and Oscar Charleston. Thirty years after the first committee convened, a second Special Committee on the Negro Leagues convened to consider additional players overlooked by the first committee and by the Veterans Committee. Since the disbanding of the first committee, the Veterans Committee had continued the process of selecting former Negro League players and officials. The second committee's work resulted in the induction of seventeen Negro League players and officials in 2006. Manley was one of those inductees along with Cumberland Posey and J. L. Wilkerson.

With her induction in 2006, Manley became the first woman inducted into the Hall of Fame. The women who played as part of the All-American Girls Professional Baseball League in the 1940s and 1950s are part of a permanent display in Cooperstown; they are not inductees into the Hall of Fame. Like the other players and officials inducted into the Hall of Fame, Manley has a plaque and a place of immortality within the world of professional baseball.

in the series. The two sides reasoned that they could schedule a sixth and seventh game at a later date if the two teams had not completed the World Series in five games. That chaotic and incomplete scheduling spoke to the structural problems that plagued both leagues. Those structural problems meant that the two leagues could never organize and operate on terms favorable to the Major Leagues and, therefore, could never position themselves to survive alongside integrated Major League teams.

While black newspapers continued to cover the Negro Leagues, the sportswriters expressed little sympathy for the plight of owners who did not get their agreement with the Major Leagues. Wendell Smith in particular criticized the black officials in the Negro Leagues for never evincing a sense of racial pride. He claimed that both black and white officials in the Negro Leagues never cared about advancing the careers of black players; they only cared about advancing their own financial and personal interests. Smith lamented that no one ever built the NNL or the NAL into organizations that could serve as good examples of black enterprise or black leadership. Additionally, he correctly predicted that no one involved with either league had actionable ideas for how the organizations could make the changes necessary for a formal agreement with the Major Leagues.

While Smith and other sportswriters kept their focus on the Negro Leagues, they also devoted columns to updating their readers on the progress of Robinson and other black players in the Minor Leagues. Those columns foreshadowed the kind of coverage the Negro Leagues would receive as those black players moved out of the Minor Leagues and into the Major Leagues. Smith spent time in Daytona Beach, the Dodgers' spring training site, awaiting Robinson's arrival and workouts with the Montreal Royals. In his first column on the Dodgers' spring training, Smith vowed to his readers that he would seek to cover a set of specific topics. Those topics included the reactions of white teammates to black players, the abilities of those black players, and the response of opposing teams to the black players. Additionally, Smith promised to write about the refusals of hotels and other public spaces to welcome the black players, about the ability of the players to withstand verbal abuse, and about their chances of making the Dodgers' roster. In January, Rickey had signed a second black player, Johnny Wright, to accompany Robinson in spring training. Wright, a pitcher, would briefly join Robinson on the Royals' roster before facing a demotion to a lower team in the Dodgers' farm system.

THE ROBINSONS GET A DOSE OF REALITY

The happy send-off that Robinson and Rachel received at the airport in Los Angeles represented the highlight of their cross-country trip to Daytona

Beach. Robinson and Rachel made it safely to their first destination, New Orleans, with little trouble. For Rachel, the trip marked her first time in the segregated South, meaning it marked the first time she saw water fountains and restrooms designated for "whites only" and "colored only." She defiantly drank from the "whites only" water fountain and used the "whites only" ladies room without facing any consequences. The couple's problems began a few hours after they arrived in New Orleans; they had landed at seven in the morning and had to catch their connecting flight to Pensacola four hours later. About an hour before their departure, however, the couple learned that the airline had bumped them from their flight. They stayed at the airport because the airline promised them seats on a later flight, but that flight left without them on board. None of the spaces in the airport would feed them, so they feasted on the fried chicken and hard-boiled eggs Mallie Robinson had given them before they left Los Angeles. They finally departed for New Orleans ten hours after they had arrived, but the next leg of their journey had even more obstacles for the young couple.

As soon as they landed in Pensacola, Robinson and Rachel learned that they could not continue on the flight to Daytona Beach. White passengers took their seats on the flight, and the flight continued to its final destination. Robinson received no help from anyone at the Pensacola airport until he revealed his reason for coming to Florida—to join the Dodgers at their spring training site. They tried to find a room for the couple in Pensacola, but that effort ended in failure. At that point, Robinson and Rachel abandoned their earlier plans to take a flight into Daytona Beach and chose to take a bus to Jacksonville and then take another bus to the spring training site. After initially sitting in a row with reclining seats, Robinson and Rachel moved to the last row of the bus at the insistence of the white driver. Once they arrived in Jacksonville, they spent time in a hot and crowded station waiting for their connection to Daytona Beach. When they finally arrived at spring training, they had logged thirty-six hours of travel time. Robinson arrived a day late for the start of spring training exercises, but he had phoned ahead of time to alert team officials about the multiple travel delays.

For both Robinson and Rachel, the arduous thirty-six-hour journey from Los Angeles to Daytona Beach tested their patience and their pride. The airlines' actions demonstrated clear racial bias; they bumped the couple from their paid-for seats in order to accommodate white passengers. Rachel had her first experiences of segregation, and she refused to go along with the treatment accorded African Americans in the South. She refused to eat at places that treated her rudely, and she broke down in tears during the long bus ride to Jacksonville. Robinson too felt frustrated and humiliated, but he stuck to the plan that Rickey had outlined during their meeting in the previous year. He did not fight back against the biased treatment;

he hid his anger and remained focused on the goal of joining his new teammates in Daytona Beach.

When a beleaguered Robinson and Rachel finally arrived in Daytona Beach, they received a warm welcome from the three people sent to the bus station to greet them. Those three people included two employees of the *Courier*—Smith and photographer Billy Rowe—whom Rickey had paid to accompany Robinson and Rachel during spring training. The other black player in spring training, Wright, filled out the welcoming party. The trio helped to calm Robinson down after his frustrating journey and to help him remain focused on the task at hand—making the Montreal Royals' roster. Robinson and Rachel found Daytona Beach more accommodating than the other areas of Florida they had passed through on their trip. Mayor William Perry had agreed to welcome Robinson and Wright because the relationship with the Dodgers benefited his city. Instead of staying in the same place as the white players in spring training, Robinson and Rachel stayed in the home of Joseph Harris, a black leader in Daytona Beach who had helped to ease some of the local segregation ordinances. The couple felt welcomed in Harris's house and found some peace in the room set aside for them on the second floor.

Rickey had arranged for the Robinsons to say in the Harris household, and he had arranged for the welcoming party at the bus station. Rickey also helped to prepare for Robinson's arrival by delivering a lecture to the players who had gathered in the Dodgers' camp for spring training exercises. In the lecture, Rickey called upon his players to treat Robinson and Wright in the same way they would treat two white teammates. He also warned his players that he had no tolerance for any campaigns against Robinson and Wright and that he expected everyone to behave like gentlemen around the two new black ballplayers. Rickey also claimed that he signed Robinson and Wright because he wanted to win the National League pennant, not because politicians in New York City had forced his hand. The lecture demonstrated the lengths that Rickey went to prove that he voluntarily decided to sign Robinson and Wright because he believed that the players could help the Dodgers succeed on the baseball field. He did not want to give his players the impression that he did not want either player, that he signed them simply to appease politicians. Such an admission would give the Dodgers' white players an opening to regard Robinson and Wright as unworthy of their respect and to argue that they should return to the Negro Leagues. Rickey wanted harmony on the Dodgers, and more importantly, he wanted his players to know that he had no sympathy for any qualms they may have about playing alongside black ballplayers.

Soon after arriving in Daytona Beach, Robinson and Rachel moved to nearby Sanford and stayed in another home that Rickey had pre-selected for the couple. The home belonged to David Brock, a respected black leader in Sanford; the white players stayed at a local hotel that did not welcome black guests. The Dodgers maintained a training facility in Sanford, and Robinson planned to spend a week there training with his new teammates. In Sanford, Robinson nervously took the field for the first time in a Montreal Royals uniform and fielded questions from the press corps sent to cover the momentous event. He responded in a good-natured way about how he would react if a pitcher threw at his head and whether he wanted to replace the current Dodgers' shortstop, the popular Pee Wee Reese. After that impromptu press conference, Robinson joined his new teammates in their training drills. He sought to lose weight and to find a place on the infield where he could make the Royals' roster. The Royals had a capable shortstop, the French Canadian Stanley Breard, and Robinson seemed to lack the arm strength to play at third base. Robinson also needed to battle the views of the Royals' manager, Clay Hopper, who owned a plantation in Mississippi and harbored deep biases against African Americans. Rickey had intervened to ensure that Hopper would treat Robinson with respect and would give him a fair chance to make the team.

After two days of training in Sanford, Robinson once again experienced the inhospitality of the Jim Crow South. With little warning, Robinson, Rachel, and Wright left Sanford late and night and returned to the friendlier confines of Daytona Beach. Smith helped to facilitate their quick departure from Sanford; he did so at the urgent request of Rickey, who wanted the trio out of town before white residents could cause trouble. Rickey had learned that a significant contingent of whites in Sanford had complained to their mayor about the ballplayers' presence in their town and wanted the mayor to demand that they leave. A rumor spread that angry whites had planned to march to the Brock house. With such tension rising, Rickey wanted Robinson and Wright out of harm's way and back in a place that had vowed to welcome black ballplayers.

After returning to Daytona Beach, Robinson struggled to find his form, and he suffered an injury to his throwing shoulder. While he recovered from his injury, he spent more time with Rachel, the only wife Rickey had allowed to come to spring training, and the two deepened their bond. The injury and Robinson's poor practices prior to the injury gave skeptical sportswriters an opening to question Rickey's decision to sign the player. In the *New York Daily News*, Jimmy Powers reiterated his earlier prediction that Robinson would never play in the Major Leagues. He derided Rickey for supporting Robinson and mocked his elevation as a modern-day Abraham Lincoln. Those stories weighed on Robinson and made him even more reliant upon Rachel as a pillar of support. Rickey also remained a vocal supporter of Robinson and often acted like a coach for him during the spring training drills. The support he received from Rachel and Rickey helped Robinson overcome the isolation he felt from the white players in camp. A few players—including Breard, Lou Rochelli, and Al Campanis—approached Robinson and helped him improve his performance. Most of the other players kept their distance.

Another source of constant support came from Smith, who accompanied the Robinsons in Daytona Beach while filing his columns for the *Courier*. In one of those columns, Smith took aim at Powers and Dan Parker, a writer from the *New York Daily Mirror* who also doubted Robinson's abilities and questioned Rickey's intentions in signing two black players. Smith insinuated that racial bias motivated both writers to denigrate both Robinson and Rickey, and he lambasted them for asserting that Rickey wanted to emulate Abraham Lincoln. To Smith, Powers and Parker represented the true modern-day Lincolns since their efforts to break the color barrier in the Major Leagues predated Rickey's search for black players. He also assailed the sportswriters as hypocrites whose actions resembled those of the people who supported the Confederacy during the Civil War. Smith went further and asserted that neither writer had interviewed Robinson and remained blind to the segregation that surrounded the Dodgers' spring training site in Daytona Beach. Both writers had looked for and saw signs of progress, but Smith demolished their arguments as both ignorant and naïve. With such columns, Smith demonstrated his worth to both Rickey and Robinson. He would not only keep his readers informed about Robinson's progress but also offer explanations for any negative columns that appeared in other publications. His columns complemented his role as one of Robinson's companions in Daytona Beach and as someone who would help see through Robinson's entrance into a Major League organization.

As he tried to find his form and as those stories swirled in the press, Robinson made history on Sunday, March 17, when he stepped onto the field to play in an exhibition contest against the Dodgers. Four thousand fans, a large crowd for the Royals-Dodgers exhibition contest, crowded into the City Island Park to watch the historic contest. The ballpark contained segregated seating sections, and the section reserved for black patrons could not accommodate the number of black fans who wanted to watch Robinson for the first time. As a result, the overflowing crowd stood near the right field side of the ballpark and cheered for both Robinson and Wright. Robinson played for five innings in the game; he did not get any hits, but he did reach base one time and scored a run. After the game, Dodgers' field manager Leo Durocher praised Robinson's performance and lauded him as a true ballplayer who could play well under tough circumstances. Later that same week, the commissioner Chandler gave his stamp of approval by attending another exhibition contest between the Dodgers and the Royals. He sat behind home plate next to Rickey and expressed some sympathy for Wright, who had a shaky outing in the contest.

Even though he performed well in the first exhibition contest with the Dodgers, Robinson had a rough and challenging spring training experience. He fell into a prolonged hitting slump that made him and Rachel worry about him making the Royals' roster at the end of spring training. Robinson's and Wright's presence on the Royals also led to sudden cancellations on the team's spring training schedule. On May 21, the Royals canceled a game against the Jersey City Giants, a club in the New York Giants' farms system, scheduled for Jacksonville. City ordinances prohibited competition between black and white players on the Giants' field, so the Giants asked the Royals to leave the two black players in Daytona Beach. The Royals refused; the team ultimately canceled nine games, including one held farther north in Richmond, Virginia. An incident happened in Sanford when the Royals played the St. Paul Saints. At the start of the third inning, Sanford's chief of police went to Hopper, the Royals' field manager, and demanded that he remove Robinson from the game. The chief threatened Hopper with arrest if he did not comply; Hopper complied, and Robinson sat for the remainder of the game. Smith outlined these events for his readers and lauded Rickey for refusing to bow to the demands. He also noted that the good residents of Sanford did not want him or the *Courier*'s photographer in the city.

Rather than weakening his resolve or making him second-guess his plans for the Dodgers, the reactions against Robinson and Wright only seemed to strengthen Rickey's resolve to add black players to the organization. In April, Rickey demonstrated his resolve by announcing the signing of Roy Campanella, a catcher, and Don Newcombe, a pitcher. Rickey sent both players to Nashua, a Dodgers' farm team that played in the New England League. Campanella had played for the past six seasons for the Baltimore Elite Giants, and Newcombe had pitched for the Newark Eagles. The additions of Campanella and Newcombe gave the Dodgers four black players in their development system, a clear sign of the franchise's commitment to adding black players and developing them into Major League-level talent.

THE HISTORIC 1946 SEASON

Despite their inconsistent spring training performances, both Robinson and Wright made the Royals' opening-day roster and traveled with the team to its opening contest in Jersey City, New Jersey. Robinson participated in the first game; he batted second in the lineup and played at second base. He had settled at that position after trying out at other positions in the infield during spring training. On April 18, the date of the opening-day contest, over twenty-five thousand fans crowded into Roosevelt Stadium to watch the hometown Jersey City Giants face the Royals. Pregame ceremonies to mark the start of a new season included marching bands and a parade. The real show, however, began in the top of the first inning when Robinson stepped to the plate, making him the first black player to bat in a Minor League game since the late nineteenth century. In the stands, Rachel and the thousands of black spectators watched nervously as Robinson worked a full count and then grounded out to the shortstop. Robinson took the field at second base in the bottom of the first inning, and his turn at bat came up again in the third inning. Unlike his first time at the plate, Robinson connected on a pitch and delivered it some 340 feet away into the left field stands. Parts of the crowd erupted in cheers; Robinson's teammates and the field manager greeted him warmly as he rounded the bases and returned to the dugout. For Robinson, the moment truly made him a member of the Royals' team. He felt the support and gratitude from his teammates, including those who came from the South and who had kept their distance.

Overall, both Robinson and the Royals enjoyed a productive and successful opening-day. The Royals won the game by the score of 14–1. In addition to his home run, Robinson hit three singles, including a bunt single that he legged out for an infield hit. After reaching first on that hit, Robinson easily stole second base and then reached third base on a fielder's choice. While on third base, Robinson flustered the Giants catcher and pitcher by making feints to steal home before running back to third base. On one of those feints, Robinson induced the pitcher into committing a balk, allowing Robinson to trot in from third base and score another run. Most importantly, the crowd in Jersey City reacted warmly and enthusiastically to Robinson's performance. Both black and white fans in the ballpark cheered his prowess on the base paths and seemed to treat him in the same way they treated the white players.

With the regular season underway, Smith continued his coverage of Robinson and offered an extremely positive view of his success on Opening Day. Smith's coverage included an overview of the fans' reactions to Robinson. Prior to the start of the season, Smith devoted one of his regular columns to make an appeal directly to his readers and anyone who planned to attend at least one of Robinson's games. He warned his readers that making the opening-day roster did not guarantee either Robinson or Wright a permanent spot on the Royals' roster and that they, the fans, represented one of the most important factor in determining the players' success. Specifically, he warned his readers against expressing too much enthusiasm for the players and admonished them to always remain on good behavior when attending their games. Smith reminded his readers about the amount of pressure both Robinson and Wright felt since both of them, particularly Robinson, carried the hopes and dreams of all African

Americans on their shoulders. Excessive cheering for Robinson and Wright would only add to that pressure and, therefore, had the potential to drive them out of the Royals' roster. Smith also presumed that critics of Robinson and Wright would use any instances of bad behavior from black fans to argue that adding those and other black players to the Major Leagues would cause riots at ballparks. He concluded by pleading with his readers to maintain proper public conduct at the ballparks and to not unintentionally act as hindrances for the black players.

The three-game opening series in Jersey City seemed to dispel any concerns about the addition of black players to the Major Leagues. After the first game, a chaotic scene erupted in the clubhouse as reporters jockeyed to interview Robinson and snag some quotes for their columns. Those columns generally praised Robinson's batting and fielding and noted that his success marked a personal triumph as well as a triumph for all African Americans. The Royals won the next two games, and Robinson continued his success at the plate and on the bases. Instead of experiencing a steep drop-off in attendance, the other two games of the series also drew close to twenty thousand fans to Roosevelt Stadium. The enthusiasm continued as the Royals moved through the rest of the road trip in Newark against the Newark Bears and in Syracuse against the Syracuse Chiefs. In those cities, the Royals continued to draw large crowds; a record crowd for a weekday contest greeted the Royals and the Chiefs during one of the games in Syracuse. Robinson notched fourteen hits in his first forty-two at bats, solidifying his spot in the regular lineup and at second base. He did not face any racial taunts from fans in the ballpark or from the opposing team. The opening road trip seemed to mark a tremendous success both for the Royals and for Robinson.

Unfortunately, a different reality set in once the Royals traveled to Baltimore for a series against the Orioles, a Minor League team at the time. Due to concerns about trouble in the stands, only three thousand fans attended the first game. Rachel had attended all her husband's games, and the game in Baltimore marked the first time that he faced racial taunts from the crowd. Rachel sat horrified in the stands, while Robinson tried to block out the verbal abuse. He stuck to the agreement with Rickey and focused on playing the game. The next game, a doubleheader, brought a larger crowd of twenty-five thousand fans, which meant that Robinson faced even louder verbal abuse from fans. In the midst of that abuse, however, Robinson began to fully appreciate the connection that black fans felt with him. He recognized that the large number of black fans came to the Royals games to see him and give him the support he needed as he played in the games.

After that harrowing experience in Baltimore, Robinson and the Royals finally headed to Montreal for their home opener. From the outset, the fans in Montreal warmly greeted Robinson and Wright and cheered for their hometown baseball team. The warmth that Robinson and Rachel felt at the ballpark in Montreal extended to their lives beyond the ballpark. When Rachel looked for an apartment in an exclusively French-speaking area of Montreal, she did not face any hostility from white landlords or white residents who did not want to associate with African Americans. She easily found a furnished apartment for herself and Robinson, and the young couple settled easily into their new apartment. Rachel also began making plans for the couple's first child and formed strong friendships with some nearby women who helped her buy items using the ration books still in effect in Montreal. They developed a friendship with a couple having seven children and with a Jewish couple, Sam and Belle Maltin, who introduced them to the city's cultural life. Overall, life moved pleasantly for Robinson and Rachel during their one year in Montreal. While a significant language barrier existed between them and their neighbors, they never experienced any racial animus or felt unwelcome.

While Rachel and Robinson settled into life in Montreal, the Royals struggled through the early part of their schedule and prompted a shake-up from Branch Rickey Jr., the eldest son of the Brooklyn Dodgers' general manager. The younger Rickey had oversight over the Dodgers' farm system. Robinson had a secure spot on the roster, but Wright had struggled in his appearances and earned a demotion to the Three Rivers Dodgers. Rickey Jr. replaced Wright with Roy Partlow, a pitcher he had bought from the Philadelphia Stars. Unlike his earlier acquisitions of black players, the elder Rickey had paid the Stars' co-owners, Ed Bolden and Eddie Gottlieb, for Partlow before adding him to the Royals' roster. Rickey Jr. dealt away other players, including the shortstop Breard who had befriended Robinson during their short time as teammates. Campanis replaced Breard at shortstop and formed a potent double-play duo with Robinson. With those changes, Robinson continued to excel, and in June, he rose to the top of the league leaders in batting average. The Royals also seemed to turn a corner and seemed poised to rise to the top of the league.

In June, Robinson showed the first signs of his future activism when he accepted an invitation to speak at the Abyssinian Baptist Church in Harlem. He received that invitation from the United Negro and Allied Veterans of America's (UNAVA) organizing committee. The committee also asked Robinson to serve as its chairman, an invitation he also accepted. Prominent political figures based in Harlem also sat on that committee. Those political figures included Adam Clayton Powell, a member of the U.S. House of Representatives; Hulan Jack, a member of the New York State Assembly; and Benjamin Davis Jr., a member of the New York City Council. When Rickey learned of the invitation, he directed Robinson to decline and to stay away from the Abyssinian Church on the date of his planned talk. Rickey did not approve of any of his ballplayers engaging in such activities while they played for the Dodgers or other teams in the farm system. He also likely did not want Robinson to publicly associate with political figures since such associations could taint his reputation and undermine the effort to bring him to the Dodgers.

Outside Montreal, Robinson faced abuse from opposing teams and from members of the large crowds that filled the ballparks. In one incident at Syracuse, an opposing player caused a delay when he released a black cat and yelled at Robinson, "Hey, Jackie, there's your cousin" (Robinson and Duckett 2013, 49). The umpire halted play until he had successfully corralled the frightened cat; Robinson responded with a double and by scoring on the next single to centerfield. As he passed Syracuse's dugout, Robinson delivered his own taunt back to the opposing team by telling them, "I guess my cousin's pretty happy now" (Robinson and Duckett 2013, 49). In another game at Syracuse, though, Robinson kept to his pact with Rickey and did not participate in an argument at home plate. He remained at second base and allowed Hopper and his white teammates to sort out the mess. In other games, Robinson faced pitchers who threw at his head; like other players of that era, Robinson did not wear a hard batting helmet, so throws to his head had the potential to lead to serious injuries. Opposing players also spiked Robinson when he slid into second base in an attempt to injure him and take him out of the game and perhaps the league. The other black player on the team, Partlow, quickly disappeared from the Royals' roster. Robinson lamented that Partlow did not take full advantage of the opportunity to play for the Royals. By July, Partlow had joined Wright with the Three Rivers team, leaving Robinson without a black teammate. That made him even more dependent upon Rachel for support and even more exposed to abuse from opposing teams and fans.

The abuse from opposing fans and players took an emotional toll on Robinson. He had trouble sleeping and eating, and a doctor warned him about the potential of having a nervous breakdown. The doctor recommended that he take a rest in order to avoid having that breakdown. Robinson rested for only one day before he returned to the starting lineup and more abuse from fans and players. He did not follow his doctor's orders because he did not want to give the impression that he sat out in order to protect his batting average and retain his top place in the league's standings. At the same time, Rachel experienced some pregnancy complications, which she hid from her husband in order to avoid overburdening him with more stress. Despite all those pressures, Robinson never strayed from the pact he had made with Rickey during their first meeting in August 1945. Robinson also did not turn to vices, such as drugs or alcohol, to help mitigate the pain he felt while playing for the Royals. He tried to remain focused on helping the Royals win the championship in the International

League and on proving that he had earned a promotion to the Dodgers for the 1947 season.

In addition to helping the Royals win games, Robinson helped the Royals set attendance records both at home and at away games. The Royals drew larger crowds for their home games when compared to the 1945 season, a season in which the team won the International League's championship. Additionally, road games featuring Robinson and the Royals drew over one hundred thousand more fans than those who had attended road contests featuring the Royals in the 1945 season. Those figures included twenty-eight thousand fans for a Sunday game in Baltimore and record-setting crowds for day games in other cities on the Royals' schedule. Robinson's and the Royals' success earned praise from Chandler, who lauded the ballplayer as a great role model for all African Americans. Chandler also used the opportunity to respond to a question about his authority over the Negro Leagues. He responded by noting that he lacked that authority since the leagues did not have uniform policies in regards to contracts and salaries. The record-setting crowds and Chandler's comments set an ominous tone for the future of the Negro Leagues. Fans who might have attended Negro Leagues games preferred to see Robinson, and the leagues themselves did not have a lifeline from the Major Leagues or any other organization.

Robinson's success with the Royals came at the same time as reintegration happened in another major sport, professional football. Much like the Major Leagues, the National Football League (NFL) had black players for a short time; the last remaining black player appeared in an NFL game in the 1920s. Following the 1945 season, the Cleveland Rams moved to the Los Angeles and used the Los Angeles Coliseum as their home field. Since the team used a publicly financed field, it faced immediate pressure to integrate its roster. Rams executives complied by signing two of Robinson's teammates from his days at UCLA—Kenny Washington and Woody Strode. Both players made the team's regular season roster and made contributions to the Rams, and they went on to play two more seasons with the team. Back in Cleveland, a new franchise called the Cleveland Browns joined the All-America Football Conference (AAFC), a league formed in 1944 to challenge the hegemony of the NFL. The team took its name from the last name of the head coach, Paul Brown. In addition to signing veteran players who had served overseas, Brown also signed two black players—Marion Motley and Bill Willis. Similarly to Washington and Strode, Motley and Willis contributed to the Browns' success in the 1946. Both Motley and Willis went on to have distinguished careers in both the AAFC and the NFL, the league the Browns joined after the AAFC folded. Robinson's presence with the Royals, combined with the presence of four African Americans on professional football teams, served as harbingers of

American society's future. While the process of integration occasionally moved slowly, it moved ahead and eventually made segregated sports a relic of America's history.

As those four players started their careers in the NFL and the AAFC, Robinson and the Royals wrapped up a fantastic season. The Royals won one hundred games, and Robinson's .349 batting average stood atop the International League. He earned other impressive offensive stats—including 66

FRITZ POLLARD

On August 20, 1920, representatives from several football teams gathered at the Jordan and Hupmobile car dealership in Canton, Ohio, to form the American Professional Football Conference. Two years later, that organization changed its name to the National Football League (NFL). At the time of its founding, the NFL had two African American players, the most notable one being Fritz Pollard. Pollard was born in Chicago, Illinois, on January 27, 1894, and he attended Brown University to pursue a major in chemistry. Like Jackie Robinson, Pollard played at halfback for Brown University's football team, becoming the first-ever black player on the team's roster. He helped Brown University reach the prestigious Rose Bowl, and in 1916, he became the first African American running back selected for Walter Camp's All-American team in intercollegiate football.

After leaving Brown University, Pollard served as the head football coach at Lincoln University, a historically black university in Pennsylvania. Pollard also joined the Akron Pros in 1919, the same year in which Jackie Robinson was born. In August 1920, the Akron Pros was one of the franchises that participated in the founding of the NFL. As he did at Brown University, Pollard played at halfback and led his team to success. He helped the Pros win the NFL title in 1920, and in the following year, he became the NFL's first African America head coach. He shared those duties with another head coach while also maintaining his role as the team's halfback. In addition to playing and coaching for the Pros, Pollard played and coached for other NFL franchises—the Milwaukee Badgers, the Hammond Pros, and the Providence Steam Rollers. Pollard last played in the NFL in the 1926 season; the league removed him and all black players and did not welcome another black player for twenty years. After leaving the NFL, Pollard served as the head coach for an all-black football team, Chicago Black Hawks, before embarking upon other adventures for the remainder of his life.

Pollard died in 1986 at the age of ninety-two. Nineteen years later, the National Football League honored Pollard by inducting him into the Pro Football Hall of Fame in Canton, Ohio. At the ceremony, Pollard's grandson Fritz Pollard III delivered a speech in honor of his grandfather. That induction brought new attention to Pollard's pioneering place in NFL history and to the brief period of integration that existed during the NFL's formative years.

RBIs, score of 113 runs, and 40 stolen bases. Robinson's success prompted Sam Matlin, one of Robinson's friends in Montreal and a sportswriter for *The Montreal Herald*, to write an open letter to Bob Feller. Feller had questioned Robinson's skills, and Matlin took the opportunity to point out Feller's many errors. Matlin began by recalling Feller's criticisms of Robinson's skills, specifically his offensive skills, and by noting that Robinson led the International League in batting average. He went through Robinson's other accomplishments and noted that he represented the first player from the Royals to lead the International League in batting average since 1930. Matlin then switched tactics and spoke to Feller's expertise as a pitcher and asked him to consider how the pitchers in the International League had tried to challenge Robinson. Robinson prevailed over those challenges, and he also mastered a new position in the infield. Matlin also noted how many fans paid to watch Robinson play, both at home and on the road, and emphasized the main point that Robinson had disproved all of Feller's criticisms.

THE LITTLE WORLD SERIES

With their one hundred wins, the Royals easily won the International League's pennant and faced the Louisville Colonels of the American Association for the Little World Series. The series opened with three games in Louisville, a southern city that did not greet Robinson with open arms. Team officials put a limit on the number of black spectators allowed into the ballpark, leaving many black fans standing outside without any means of watching the game. The crowd directed verbal abuse at Robinson, and Robinson responded by entering a hitting slump. During the three games in Louisville, Robinson managed to get only one hit. Robinson's failures at the plate only emboldened his verbal abusers in the stands, creating a very ugly atmosphere in the ballpark. The Royals won the first game of the series, but they dropped the next two games to the Colonels, giving the Louisville team a valuable lead in the series as the teams went to Montreal to wrap up the series.

Back in Montreal, Robinson ended his hitting slump and helped the Royals win the series. In game four, Robinson helped his team overcome a four-run deficit and got the game-winning hit in the tenth inning. In the following game, Robinson hit a triple and laid down a bunt that effectively ended any chance for the Colonels to win the game. The Royals went on to win game six by the score of 2–0 and capture the Little World Series title. Despite his slump during the series' first three games, Robinson ended with a batting average of .400, well above the batting average he had during the regular season. He also scored the winning run in the decisive sixth game. During the three games in Montreal, the fans showed their affection for Robinson and their displeasure at the treatment he received in Louisville. The fans booed all the Colonels as soon as they hit the field in game four, and they continued the booing throughout the game. Conversely, the fans issued raucous cheers for Robinson and the rest of the Royals players throughout the game. The fans' actions helped to cement the bond between the Royals and the city, and it showed that white fans would embrace a black player.

Montreal's fans continued to show their affection for Robinson once the game ended. Robinson wanted to leave quickly to catch a flight to Detroit in order to meet his barnstorming team. The fans, however, wanted to see Robinson before he left and to celebrate the team's triumph. Along with Hopper and other white players, Robinson emerged from the clubhouse and met the throngs of well-wishers. They raised Hopper, the white players, and Robinson on their shoulders and carried them around the field before depositing them back outside the clubhouse. Back in the clubhouse, Robinson still struggled to pack his belongings because people kept wanting to talk to him and congratulate him on his successful season. Hopper, the southern plantation owner, was among the well-wishers. He shook Robinson's hand, praised him as a fine ballplayer and gentleman, and said he had enjoyed having him on the team. Robinson stayed even after all his teammates had left because he still had to face a throng of fans outside the clubhouse. He finally emerged and ran out with fans running after him down Montreal's streets. After fleeing the crowds by car, Robinson finally reconnected with Rachel and headed to the airport.

Once the couple arrived in Detroit, they parted ways. Robinson departed for his barnstorming team, while Rachel returned to her mother's house in Los Angeles. Robinson did manage to leave his team in time to reach Rachel when she delivered their first child, a boy, on November 18. They named their firstborn son Jackie Roosevelt Robinson Jr. With his family life secure, Robinson could focus on the task ahead in his baseball career. He technically remained a member of the Royals, but Rickey promised that he would have an opportunity to make the Dodgers' roster at the end of the 1947 spring training season. Durocher, who would manage the Dodgers in the 1947 season, also seemed open to having Robinson on his roster. He lauded Robinson as one of the best players in the Dodgers' farm system and backed up Rickey's pledge to give the ballplayer a fair chance in the upcoming spring training season.

ON THE ROAD TO THE MAJOR LEAGUES

In the months between the end of the season and the start of spring training, Robinson looked for ways to make money. He did not make any money on his barnstorming tour because of shady practices by the tour's organizers. As a result, Robinson signed a contract with the Los Angeles Red Devils, a professional basketball team that belonged to the National Basketball League (NBL). Professional basketball represented yet another sport embarking upon the practice of integration, and Robinson represented one of three black players on the Red Devils. Robinson had not played competitive basketball since his days at UCLA, yet he quickly adapted and helped the Red Devils win eight of their first nine games. In December, however, Robinson abruptly left the team, possibly because he suffered an injury and did not want to risk his chances of making the Dodgers' roster. His departure from the Red Devils meant that he devoted his entire attention on the upcoming spring training and on the possibility that he could receive his much-earned promotion from the Royals.

To prepare for Robinson's possible promotion to the Dodgers, Rickey worked quietly and efficiently to dispel any remaining opposition to his plans. In a secret poll of Major League owners, fifteen of the sixteen owners had voted in opposition to adding black players to their teams. The Dodgers represented the lone dissenter in the poll. Against that backdrop, Rickey worked hard to ensure that trouble did not erupt at the Dodgers' spring training. Earlier, he had decided to move the site of spring training from Daytona Beach to Havana, Cuba. Even though the Dodgers did not need to follow any segregation ordinances, Rickey decided to house the Dodgers' black players separately from the white players. The Dodgers had four black players in camp—Robinson, Campanella, Newcombe, and Partlow. Rickey had extended tryouts to three other players—including Buster Clarkson, Larry Doby, and Monte Irvin—but he had decided against adding them to the Dodgers' system. Rickey wanted to keep the black players separate from the white players in order to prevent any race-related incidents. He clearly intended to promote Robinson, but he wanted to follow a carefully outlined plan before officially announcing that decision.

As he had done in the previous year, Robinson had a rocky start to his spring training season. When Robinson arrived there, he was overweight, and he worked hard to shed the unwanted pounds. He also suffered from dysentery, and he had a growth on one of his toes removed; he also experienced a recurrence of an earlier back injury. The Royals and the Dodgers trained together in preparation for twelve games in three different countries on the spring training schedule. The two teams would meet first in Panama for three games before returning to Cuba for the next seven games. Then, near the start of the regular season, both teams would travel to Ebbets Field for the final two games. Prior to leaving for Panama, Robinson experienced yet another change when the Royals asked him to switch from second base to first base. Robinson had played well at second base in the 1946 season, and no one else slated to join the Royals seemed likely to challenge him for the starting role. The directive to play at first base represented yet another sign of Rickey's true intentions for Robinson's second spring training with the Dodgers. The Dodgers had established starters at shortstop, Pee Wee Reese, and second base, Eddie Stanky. An opening, though, existed at first base, so that remained the only option for Robinson on the Dodgers' projected roster.

Robinson took the change in stride, and he dazzled the crowds who came to watch him and his three black teammates in Panama. The Royals played against some local teams before they faced the Dodgers, and Robinson easily rounded into form against those opponents. Robinson continued his thrilling play once the Royals started their contests with the Dodgers. He hit consistently, made good defensive plays at first base, and flustered the Major Leaguers while on the base paths. Campanella also drew attention, and he seemed likely to earn a promotion from Nashua to the Royals by the time the regular season started. Newcombe also turned some heads and seemed headed for Montreal along with Campanella. Partlow did not draw as much attention, but he too seemed destined to join the Royals at the end of spring training.

While Rickey focused on paving the way for Robinson to join the Dodgers, a potential revolt arose that threatened to derail his well-laid plans. Prior to the games against the Royals in Panama, members of the Dodgers circulated a petition designed to block Rickey from adding Robinson to the roster. The petition began with four southern-born players on the Dodgers. Those players included two pitchers, Kirby Higbe and Hugh Casey, and the back-up catcher Bobby Bragan. Dixie Walker represented the most significant instigator; he ranked as one of the most popular players on the Dodgers and as an important hitter in the lineup. The four ringleaders, along with Pennsylvania native Carl Furillo, tried to enlist the rest of the roster to join their petition. Stanky and Reese refused as did other players; perhaps out of guilt, Higbe revealed the petition to the team's secretary, Harold Parrott, who promptly informed Rickey.

Both Rickey and Durocher moved quickly to squash the petition and to dissuade any of the players from taking action against Robinson. In the middle of the night, Durocher called for a team meeting and yelled at the gathered players. He essentially told them that their views on whether Robinson should join the team did not matter; if he wanted Robinson on the team, then Robinson would join the team. The players had to accept that reality. Rickey also spoke to the ringleaders individually and tried to shame them for their actions. Bragan and Walker requested that Rickey trade them away from the Dodgers, and Rickey considered their requests before deciding to keep both players. Rickey essentially sent the same message that Durocher sent—the players lacked the standing to determine who did, and did not, join the roster.

Very little of the drama involving the petition played out on the field. Robinson, Campanella, Newcombe, and Partlow concentrated on playing baseball and received enthusiastic support from fans. The only sign of tension arose in the second-to-last game of the series between the Dodgers and the Royals played in Cuba. During the game, a collision happened at first base when the Dodgers' starting catcher, Bruce Edwards, ran into Robinson and knocked him unconscious. The collision happened after Edwards turned for second on a base hit and got caught in a rundown. Robinson jumped in the air for the throw; at that point, Edwards collided with the first baseman as he tried to beat the throw. A trainer came out to tend to Robinson, and the Royals also gathered around him to make sure that he did not sustain a serious injury. Robinson left the game and missed the last game of the series in Cuba. In the *Courier*, Smith tried to downplay the incident as an accident that happened in the middle of an odd situation between first and second base. Robinson too downplayed the incident and pledged to play in the games scheduled for Ebbets Field.

As the regular season quickly approached, Smith took pains to gauge the likelihood that Robinson would open the season with the Dodgers. He noted that Robinson had played well enough to earn a promotion, but that represented only part of the story. For Robinson to earn a promotion and truly become part of the Dodgers' roster, he needed the support of the white players. Smith went through the key players on the Dodgers' roster and listed the odds of whether or not they supported Robinson. He surmised that most of the players would play with Robinson regardless of their personal views, and he correctly predicted that Durocher would support Robinson once he joined the team. Smith, though, struck a negative tone in his column by lamenting that if Robinson did not earn a promotion in 1947, he likely would wait many years before he would receive such an opportunity. A delay in Robinson's promotion would also likely dissuade other owners and general managers from signing black players. Smith concluded his column by asserting that Robinson ranked as a big leaguer and would help the Dodgers rake in profits in the 1947 season.

While that drama played out, Robinson made his first appearance in Ebbets Field when the Royals and the Dodgers concluded their spring training seasons in Brooklyn. Rickey had made the final preparations to promote Robinson when he received a stunning phone call from the commissioner. Chandler's phone call stemmed from an investigation he had conducted into the behavior of the Yankees' Larry MacPhail and Durocher. The two men had a bad history; MacPhail had served as the Dodgers' general manager prior to Rickey's arrival, and the two often clashed. Earlier, Durocher had raised questions about the fact that MacPhail had sat with gamblers during a Yankees' exhibition game in Cuba. Durocher also penned columns, ghostwritten by Parrott, for the *Brooklyn Daily Eagle* that rankled MacPhail. As part of the investigation, Chandler looked into Durocher's personal life and his own associations with known gamblers. Chandler levied fines on the Yankees and on Parrott, but he suspended Durocher for the 1947 season due to conduct detrimental to baseball.

The suspension shocked and angered Rickey since it left him without a field manager at the dawn of the regular season. Additionally, in losing Durocher, Rickey had lost a valuable ally in his plan to promote Robinson. Rickey knew that Durocher would support Robinson against any bias from his teammates as well as opposing teams. The allegations against Durocher also reflected poorly on the Dodgers' image, so Rickey decided to act quickly. Rather than allow the incident to delay his plans, Rickey forged ahead. He again summoned Robinson to his office for a secretive meeting; he wanted to inform Robinson first to prepare him for the inevitable onslaught of the press coverage.

On April 10, the Royals and the Dodgers concluded their series. During the sixth inning, Robinson faced Ralph Branca and bunted into a double play. At that moment, Arthur Mann, an assistant to Rickey, walked into the press box and handed each reporter a sheet of paper that contained two simple typewritten sentences and Rickey's signature. The sentences read: "The Brooklyn Dodgers today purchased the contract of Jackie Roosevelt Robinson from the Montreal Royals. He will report immediately."

6

The Major Leagues and Jackie Robinson's First Two Months

Five days after Arthur Mann casually gave sportswriters Branch Rickey's two-sentence press release, Jackie Robinson appeared in the opening-day lineup for the Brooklyn Dodgers. Robinson's appearance marked the first time in the twentieth century that any Major League team carried a black player on its roster and put a black player in the lineup. Over the first two months of the 1947 season, Robinson appeared to struggle with the burdens placed on him as the first and only African American on any Major League club. He faced hostility from opposing teams, most notably the Philadelphia Phillies, and remained isolated from his white teammates when they traveled outside of New York City. Robinson also generated a significant amount of press coverage and brought large numbers of African American spectators to Ebbets Field as well as other National League ballparks. In June, Robinson's first season appeared to reach a turning point, and he solidified his place in the Dodgers' regular lineup. None of the other fifteen Major League franchises, however, had followed Rickey's lead in signing black players. Though Robinson had proved he belonged in the Major Leagues, the overall pace of Major League baseball's reintegration remained stalled as the 1947 season reached its midpoint.

SOUTHERN CULTURE AND THE DODGERS

When Robinson entered the Dodgers' clubhouse for the first time as a member of the team, he entered a clubhouse dominated by southern-born players. Bobby Bragan, Dixie Walker, and Kirby Higbe, three of the anti-Robinson ringleaders, remained on the team despite their actions during spring training. Bragan had a middling career as a backup catcher, and he had missed the 1945 and 1946 seasons due to his commitments to the United States Army. Instead of jeopardizing his return to the Dodgers after a two-year absence, he pledged to Rickey that he would play to the best of his abilities even if Robinson made the team. Walker and Higbe presented more of a problem since they had played key roles in the Dodgers' success in the 1946 season. The Dodgers had come close to winning the National League pennant. Walker made the All-Star team while earning a .319 batting average, the second best in his career behind the .357 average he had for the Dodgers in 1944. He also compiled other impressive offensive stats—a .391 on-base percentage, a .437 slugging percentage, and a .839 on-base-plus-slugging percentage. Not surprisingly, he led the league with nineteen intentional walks and came in second place in the Most Valuable Player (MVP) race. More importantly, Walker ranked as one of the most popular players on the Dodgers; the team's fans had given him the affectionate nickname of "The People's Cherce," playfully mimicking the Brooklyn pronunciation of "choice" at the time. Higbe also earned All-Star honors while compiling a record of 17–8 with an earned-run average of 3.03. He also received some votes in the MVP race and seemed destined to again lead the Dodgers' pitching staff in the 1947 season.

For all three men, their southern roots framed their opposition to Robinson joining the Dodgers. Bragan, a native of Alabama, had spent his formative years in a deeply segregated society and simply regarded such segregation as the natural order of society. His father operated a construction business, and the black employees always used the back door when they came to the Bragan household. Like Walker and Higbe, Bragan worried about how his family and friends in Alabama would react to him playing alongside a black man. Higbe's grandfather had fought for the Confederacy in the Civil War; during an interview with a New York City radio station, he claimed that he developed a strong throwing arm by throwing rocks at black people. Walker owned a hardware store in Alabama, Dixie Walker Hardware, and spoke affectionately about the society and culture of the Deep South. Any form of integration threatened to undermine that society and culture and, therefore, to tear the three men away from the roots they cherished.

While Rickey did not try to trade either Bragan or Higbe, he did try to trade Walker prior to the start of the 1947 season. Rickey's move came after Walker wrote him a letter asking for a trade-away from the Dodgers, believing that such a trade would represent the best way out of the awkward situation. Rickey worked out a deal with the Pittsburgh Pirates, but then he reconsidered whether such a trade worked for the best interests of the Dodgers. Without Walker's bat in the lineup, Rickey reasoned that the Dodgers would struggle to capture the pennant and to have yet another opportunity to win the franchise's first World Series title. Rickey wanted a winning baseball team in order to prove that his plan to add black players would help, not hurt, the fortunes of all Major League clubs. He went back to the Pirates and pushed them to include Ralph Kiner, then a promising young player, in the deal for Walker. The Pirates balked, and Rickey called off the proposed trade. Walker, along with Bragan and Higbe, remained on the roster when the Dodgers purchased Robinson's contract and put him in the starting lineup.

APRIL 15, 1947, AND ITS AFTERMATH

Robinson's first appearance in Ebbets Field in a Dodgers jersey came the day following his last appearance as a Montreal Royal. The Royals had departed, and the Dodgers and Yankees started a three-game exhibition series to conclude the spring training schedule. Prior to the game, a still-stunned Robinson entered the Dodgers' clubhouse for the first time and received his jersey that bore the number 42. He did not yet have a locker, so he hung his clothes on a nail on the wall. Once he was on the field, Robinson took in the surreal scene. In one day, he had gone from playing first base for the Royals to playing first base for the Dodgers. He comported himself well during the three-game series, notching only two hits but earning five RBIs and playing without errors at first base. In a sign of the future for the Dodgers, black fans came out in large numbers to watch Robinson and the Dodgers. The three games in Ebbets Field drew a record number of fans for a three-game exhibition between the Dodgers and the Yankees.

With the spring training season concluded, many people throughout the country eagerly anticipated the Dodgers' home opener scheduled for Tuesday, April 15. In black newspapers, sportswriters echoed something that Wendell Smith wrote about and warned readers to engage in good conduct when attending Robinson's games. The sportswriters cautioned readers against putting too much pressure on Robinson, otherwise they might hurt him and therefore hurt the larger cause of integrating baseball and other aspects of American society. A few months earlier, Rickey held a dinner with Herbert T. Miller, executive secretary of a branch of the YMCA in Brooklyn, and other black leaders in New York City. At the dinner, Rickey said that African Americans represented the biggest threat to Robinson's success as a member of the Dodgers. Rickey feared that exuberant African Americans would damage his plans by using Robinson as a symbol of triumph, as a political symbol, or even as a symbol of the superiority of their race. He also impressed upon his audience of African Americans the need for proper, moderated behavior in National League ballparks. Rickey's words had the desired effect, and black newspapers sought to tamp down their readers' enthusiasm for seeing Robinson in a Dodgers' uniform.

Robinson prepared for Opening Day by welcoming Rachel and Jackie Jr. to New York City and settling into their hotel room at the McAlpin Hotel in downtown Manhattan. The tiny hotel room could barely accommodate the young family, but the couple deemed it suitable for the start of the season. Robinson's place on the opening-day roster did not guarantee his place on the roster for the rest of the season. His contract paid him the minimum permitted for rookies, so the family faced limited options for more permanent living arrangements. A small electric stove served as the only means in the room for cooking and heating food. Robinson and Rachel would eat separately at nearby restaurants while one of them stayed behind to watch Jackie Jr. Rachel used the shower rod to dry Jackie Jr.'s diapers; baby bottles, silverware, and dishes also added to the room's clutter. Despite the closeness of the space, the young couple enjoyed their reunion after being several months apart, and Rachel again served as a key means of support for her husband. Before he left for Ebbets Field on Opening Day, Robinson jokingly said to Rachel, "Just in case you have any trouble picking me out, I'll be wearing number forty-two" (Eig 2007, 897).

Robinson took the subway from Manhattan to Brooklyn and entered the Dodgers' clubhouse well in time for the first pitch. Only two teammates, pitcher Ralph Branca and outfielder Gene Hermanski, greeted him and welcomed him to the team. The rest of his teammates barely acknowledged his presence in the clubhouse. Acting field manager Clyde Sukeforth, the scout who had brought Robinson to meet with Rickey, penciled Robinson into the starting lineup at first base. Outside the clubhouse, a crowd of twenty-seven thousand people filed into Ebbets Field. The ballpark could hold thirty-two thousand fans, and a larger crowd saw the Dodgers' home opener in the 1946 season. Although midweek afternoon games happened frequently in baseball in the 1940s, many white Brooklyn fans likely stayed away from Ebbets Field because they did not want to mingle with the larger number of black fans they knew wanted to see Robinson make his debut. Since none of them had ever witnessed a Dodgers game featuring a black player, the team's fans perhaps did not know what to expect at Ebbets Field as their team made history.

The twenty-seven thousand fans included Rachel and Jackie Jr., who had an adventure before getting to their seats. Rachel had to contend with an illness Jackie Jr. had since arriving from Los Angeles, and she struggled to find a taxi that would take her from Manhattan to Brooklyn. Once she finally arrived at Ebbets Field, Rachel found a hot dog vendor who would heat Jackie Jr.'s bottles in the same water he used to cook hot dogs. Rachel settled into a section full of African American fans and realized that she had not dressed Jackie Jr. in appropriate clothes for the springtime weather. She had brought clothes appropriate for springtime in Los Angeles, not for the cooler spring weather of New York City. Thankfully, a woman seated next to Rachel wore a fur coat to the game, and she wrapped Jackie Jr. inside the coat. That created one less distraction for Rachel, and she could concentrate her energy on watching her husband make his anticipated debut.

On the field, players from the Dodgers and the Boston Braves completed their pregame rituals in the midst of the opening-day festivities. The entire Dodgers' infield—Robinson, second baseman Eddie Stanky, shortstop Pee Wee Reese, and third baseman John "Spider" Jorgensen—posed for a famous photograph on the steps of their dugout. In the photograph, the players appeared relaxed and ready to take the field as a unified team. Stanky stood next to Robinson and casually had his left hand on Robinson's right shoulder. Though he felt isolated and anxious, Robinson managed a smile for the photographer. The photograph did not tell the full story of Opening Day, of the coolness between Robinson and most of his teammates. When the Dodgers lined up for the national anthem, only Branca stood next to Robinson.

Once the game started, the isolation between Robinson and his teammates disappeared. In the top of the first inning, the first out of the game involved Robinson. The Braves' lead-off hitter, Dick Culler, hit a ground ball to Jorgensen, who promptly threw the ball to Robinson at first base for the first out. The rather ordinary play marked an extraordinary moment in American and baseball history, and fans in the stands reacted accordingly. In the bottom of the first inning, Robinson went to bat for the first time. He faced Johnny Sain, one of the best pitchers in the National League. Many in the crowd rose to their feet and offered their support to Robinson. Robinson responded by grounding out to the third baseman, marking yet another extraordinary moment in a rather ordinary play on the field. Sain did not throw at Robinson or try to knock him out of the game; he followed the rules and induced a groundout for the second out of the inning. The first inning passed without any questionable incidents; Robinson blended into the game not as a black ballplayer but as the first baseman of the Brooklyn Dodgers.

After his first inning groundout, Robinson flew out to the left fielder and hit into a double play in his next two at bats. In the seventh inning, the Dodgers faced a 3–2 deficit. Stanky led off the bottom of the inning with a walk, and then Robinson bunted the ball up the first base line. The Giants' first baseman, Earl Torgeson, cleanly fielded the ball and threw it to the second baseman who had run over to cover first base. Torgeson, however, hurried his throw and hit Robinson on his right shoulder. The ball deflected into foul territory, giving Stanky the opportunity to reach third base and Robinson second base on the error. Centerfielder Pete Reiser followed Robinson to the plate, and he hit a double that brought both Stanky and Robinson across home plate. Leftfielder Hermanski drove in the game's final run on a double. Though he failed to get any hits, Robinson scored the winning run, and his speed had helped to cause the error that put both him and Stanky in scoring position in the bottom of the seventh inning.

After the game, Robinson returned to the clubhouse and eventually found his way out while facing a throng of fans who wanted his autograph. None of the white sportswriters from New York City's newspapers followed him back to the McAlpin hotel. The *Courier* and other black newspapers provided extensive coverage of Robinson's debut, but the more mainstream newspapers provided routine coverage of the Dodgers' first game. Within the New York City tabloids, coverage of the Dodgers ran alongside coverage of the Giants' and the Yankees' respective contests. Ward Morehouse, a writer who covered pop culture for the *New York Sun*, snagged the day's only postgame interview with Robinson by going to his small hotel room at the McAlpin. Rachel left the room to get her dinner, and Robinson responded to the writer's questions while caring for his young son. In the interview, Robinson complimented the Braves' starting pitcher Sain. He also acknowledged that he needed to perform in order to keep his spot with the Dodgers and that he alone could not suddenly change the sentiments of ballplayers who came from the South. Robinson, in other words, did not dwell on the game he had just played, nor did he try to sugarcoat the task he faced with the Dodgers. He recognized the reality of what he faced, and he expressed the calm determination that he could meet and overcome any obstacles in his way.

Two days later, Robinson and the Dodgers returned to Ebbets Field for the second and final game of the opening series against the Braves. The game attracted a little over ten thousand fans, a much smaller crowd than the crowd for the home opener. Robinson's presence on the team had not yet translated into increased attendance figures for the Dodgers, but his presence did not stop the team from winning games. Though Higbe had a shaky outing, the Dodgers won the game by the score of 12–6 to improve to sweep the Braves and improve to a 2–0 record for the 1947 season. More significantly, Robinson collected his first hit with the Dodgers; he reached base two additional times on walks. He also did not commit any errors at first base. With those wins, the Dodgers wrapped up their first series of the 1947 season tied for first place in the National League. The two games had passed without any incidents on the field. Outwardly, Robinson appeared to represent another player on the team, not as someone who elicited strong feelings from his teammates. In reality, a sense of isolation remained between Robinson and his teammates. He spent most of the opening-day contest sitting next to Sukeforth, not his teammates, in the Dodgers' dugout. The obstacles that Robinson alluded to his interview with Morehouse remained for the foreseeable future.

On Friday, April 18, Robinson and the Dodgers faced two new tests. They played their first road game, in the Polo Grounds against the Giants, and they welcomed their new manager, Burt Shotton. Sukeforth had guided the Dodgers to their first two victories; he stepped aside as Shotton arrived to manage the Dodgers for the remainder of the season. Shotton cut a quieter figure than the person originally slated to manage the Dodgers, the brash and outspoken Leo "the Lip" Durocher. The sixty-two-year-old Shotton had started his career in the Major Leagues in 1909 with the St. Louis Browns. He retired in 1923 after playing in only one game in that season. During his career, Shotton played in the outfield for the Browns, the Washington Senators, and the St. Louis Cardinals. Following his retirement, Shotton returned to the Major Leagues to manage the Philadelphia Phillies from the 1928 through 1933 seasons. He then went to Cincinnati and managed the Reds for the 1934 season. He spent the next eleven seasons managing Minor League clubs in the Cardinals' farm system and, later, serving on the coaching staff of the Cleveland Indians.

Shotton seemed like an odd choice to manage the Dodgers during the 1947 season. Following the 1945 season, Shotton seemingly retired from his managing and coaching career and joined the Dodgers as a scout. His relationship with Rickey began during his playing days with the St. Louis Browns when the Dodgers' mogul served as the Browns' field manager. That relationship continued when Shotton joined the Cardinals. Rickey again served as Shotton's field manager, and Shotton managed the team on Sundays when the devout Rickey refused to break the Christian Sabbath. When he joined the Dodgers in April 1947, he refused to wear a uniform. Shotton would occasionally wear a Dodgers' hat, but he would wear a suit and tie while managing the Dodgers. Per Major League rules, Shotton's street clothes prevented him from leaving the dugout during games. If a dispute happened during a game involving any Dodgers players and umpires or the opposing team, Shotton could not enter the field and defend his players or argue with the umpires.

Even though the Dodgers remained in New York City to face the Giants, the first road game of the season presented a test to see how fans in an opposing ballpark reacted to Robinson. The location of the Polo Grounds, the Giants' longtime home ballpark, also sparked concerns from Ford Frick, still the National League's president, about the kind of fans who would attend Robinson's first road game. The Polo Grounds sat near the boundary between Upper Manhattan and Harlem, a predominantly black region of the city. Harlem had long served as a center of African American cultural life, as evidenced by the Harlem Renaissance during the 1920s. The area had also seen a rise in civil rights activism in recent year and had sent the first African American, Adam Clayton Powell Jr., to Congress in the 1944 elections. Powell won on a platform that demanded civil rights, an end to all restrictions that prevented African Americans from voting, and a federal ban on lynching. Those concerns also seeped into articles from the Harlem-based *Amsterdam News*. Like other black newspapers, the *Amsterdam News* issued warnings to its readers about their behavior at the Polo Grounds. The newspaper also raised concerns about what would happen when Robinson faced taunts and harassment on the field.

POLO GROUNDS

Similarly to Ebbets Field, the Polo Grounds represented part of New York City's urban landscape and stood as a symbol of Major League Baseball's connections to urban neighborhoods. There were four editions of the Polo Grounds, which were located in upper Manhattan. The first Polo Grounds opened 1876 and stood until 1889. During its brief existence, the first Polo Grounds served as the home grounds for polo matches as well as for the New York Metropolitans, a professional baseball team that belonged to the American Association. The Metropolitans played from 1880 until 1887; the franchise has no connection to the New York Mets that began playing in the National League in 1962.

The Polo Grounds that served as the home of the New York Giants during Jackie Robinson's career represented the fourth edition of the stadium that bore that name. That version of the Polo Grounds opened in 1911 and boasted one of the most unusual field configurations in Major League Baseball. In order to accommodate other sports, the Polo Grounds' field had an oval shape that created very short left and right fields alongside a very deep centerfield. Many ballparks in the early twentieth century had deep centerfields, but they also had reasonably deep right and left fields. At the Polo Grounds, the distance between home plate and the deepest part of centerfield measured at 483 feet. Left-center field and right-center field, the "alleys" in the outfield, measured at 450 feet and 449 feet, respectively. Left and right fields, however, had significantly shorter dimensions. The distance between home plate and the deepest part of left field measured at 279 feet, whereas the distance between home plate and the deepest part of right field measured at only 258 feet.

The Polo Grounds, Ebbets Field, and other ballparks from the early twentieth century were built to fit into established neighborhoods. They were also built before the home run became a feature of Major League play, hence the odd and vast outfield dimensions. Many fans either walked or took public transportation to the ballparks and sat near home plate, not in the outfields. Ballplayers such as Robinson adapted to the odd configurations at the Polo Grounds. The park itself stood as a symbol of an earlier era in Major League Baseball, an era that came to a close during Robinson's career.

In that tense atmosphere, the Dodgers and the Giants renewed their crosstown rivalry and played two controversy-free games at the Polo Grounds. The Giants won both games by the scores of 10–4 and 4–3, putting the Dodgers two games behind the leaders in the still-early race for the National League pennant. For the first game played on Friday afternoon, a remarkably large crowd of over 37,000 fans filled the Polo Grounds. On Saturday afternoon, an even larger crowd of over 52,000 fans greeted the Dodgers and the Giants. The official attendance figure of 52,355 set a record for a Saturday afternoon baseball game at the Polo Grounds. As expected, a large contingent of black fans came to the games to watch Robinson. Even if many of those fans rooted for the Giants, they also wanted to see Robinson and cheered for him throughout both games.

Though the Dodgers lost both games, Robinson enjoyed some personal success and ended the series with a lofty batting average of .429. In the third inning of the Friday afternoon game, Robinson hit his first Major League home run off the Giants' starter Dave Kolso. Kolso had induced a fly-out to left field when Robinson came to the plate in the top of the first inning, but he did not have the same success against the rookie in the top of the third inning. Robinson connected on Kolso's pitch and deposited into left field to give the Dodgers a temporary lead of 2–1. After he rounded the bases, he shook the hand of left fielder Tommy Tatum, who followed him in the batting order. The ordinary moment again had extraordinary significance. For the first time since the late nineteenth century, a black ballplayer had hit a home run in a Major League contest. His teammate waiting at home plate for his turn greeted him with a handshake, the same as he would have greeted a white teammate after that teammate hit a home run. On the field again, the isolation between Robinson and his white teammates dissipated, and Robinson simply appeared as the Dodgers' first baseman.

Later in that same game, Robinson showed flashes of the style of play that would help make him famous and would help transform the sport. Robinson led off the top of the eighth inning with a hit to right field, a seemingly routine single. Robinson, however, ran fast and turned at first base seemingly in an attempt to stretch the routine single into a double. After turning toward second, however, Robinson stopped. The move successfully confused the Giants' right fielder. Instead of throwing a simple toss to the first baseman, the right fielder hurried his throw, and the ball sailed away from the first baseman. Robinson easily reached second base and then scored on a double from the center fielder Carl Furillo. During the following game, Robinson continued his hitting prowess by getting three hits, two singles and a double. He reached base an additional time on a walk and again played error-free defense at first base.

SETTLING IN FOR THE LONG TERM

In his review of Robinson's first four games, Smith happily related the rookie's progress on the field and his growing popularity among baseball fans. A story that began on the *Courier*'s front page outlined the overwhelming number of letters that Robinson had received from well-wishers across the country. Robinson also received many invitations to events that did not involve baseball, something that angered Rickey. During a press conference, Rickey complained about all the attention and begged people to leave Robinson alone so that he could concentrate on playing baseball. In a separate article in the same edition, Smith asserted that Robinson's early success both at the plate and at first base had assured him of a regular spot in the starting lineup. He also credited Robinson for bringing in large crowds to the Polo Grounds and noted, pleasantly, that the larger crowds remained on their best behavior. They did not engage in overly enthusiastic cheering for Robinson, nor drew unwanted attention to themselves in the ballpark. After only four games, Smith proudly declared that Robinson's addition to the Dodgers had succeeded and that the future seemed favorable for the rookie first baseman.

His early-season success apparently convinced Robinson that he could move out of the McAlpin hotel and settle into more permanent housing. The Dodgers pitched in to help Robinson find a new living space, and news about Robinson's decision seeped into the newspapers. Mabel C. Brown, who lived in the Bedford-Stuyvesant area of the city, called the Robinson's hotel room at the McAlpin and offered them an unused bedroom in her apartment. Unwisely, the couple accepted Brown's offer without first visiting the apartment and without meeting their new landlord. Though Brown did not have a husband or children, the small two-bedroom apartment had only one bathroom. Brown also had a boyfriend who frequently stayed at the apartment, creating more crowded conditions and more competition for both the kitchen and the lone bathroom. Although the room provided the young couple with more space than they had at the McAlpin, they still had to contend with cramped living conditions quite unlike what they had experienced in southern California. Robinson, Rachel, and Jackie Jr. moved into their new living quarters shortly before Robinson faced the biggest test of his nascent career with the Dodgers.

THE BIGGEST CHALLENGE YET

Due to a snowstorm that canceled two games against the Braves in Boston, the Dodgers next took the field on Tuesday, April 22, against the Philadelphia Phillies. Since their debut in 1883, the Phillies had won only one National League pennant. That lone title came in 1915; they promptly lost the World Series to the Boston Red Sox 4–1. Over the next four decades, the franchise often finished in the lower tier of the National League standings. After finishing in fourth place in 1932, the Phillies finished in either seventh or eighth place every season until they finished in fifth place in the 1946 season. The Phillies, however, had not ended a season with a winning record since 1917, and the franchise would not compile another winning record until 1949. While the Dodgers had some hope of contending for the pennant in 1947, the Phillies lacked all such hope. They could not challenge the Dodgers on the field or in the standings, but they could offer a different kind of challenge, particularly to Robinson.

PHILLIES

Founded in 1883, the Philadelphia Phillies stand as one of the oldest and least successful franchises in the National League. Aside from a few brief periods in their history, the team ranked either near the middle or the bottom of the league's standings. The late 1940s represented one of the many times in the Phillies' history when the team meandered through the regular season and watched as two other teams competed for the World Series. The Phillies shared a home ballpark with the American League Philadelphia Athletics, a team with a more successful history. Both teams, however, failed to generate much excitement in the 1940s. The Phillies' lone World Series title in the twentieth century lay thirty years in the future; more disappointment awaited the team in the 1947 season.

In the 1947 season, the Phillies seemed to house a heavy concentration of the southern culture that prevailed in Major League clubhouses. At that time, the Carpenter family owned the Phillies. Robert Ruliph Morgan Carpenter Sr. purchased the franchise in 1943 and turned the club's operations over to his son, Robert Ruliph Morgan Carpenter Jr. The younger Carpenter hired Herb

Pennock to serve as the team's general manager. Together, they seemingly turned a blind eye to the racial sensibilities that field manager Ben Chapman brought into the clubhouse and dugout. Pennock himself joined in the culture by pleading with Branch Rickey to keep Jackie Robinson off the Dodgers when the team played in Philadelphia.

Though the team fired Chapman after the 1947 season, the franchise did not take any steps toward signing a black player until the 1950s. On April 22, 1957, ten years and one week after Robinson made his debut with the Dodgers, the Phillies had a black player in their starting lineup. At that point, every other team in the National League had fielded at least one black player in their starting lineups. Chapman served as a symbol of the Phillies' animosity toward black players, an animosity that persisted many years after his departure from the franchise.

Unseasonable cold weather greeted the Dodgers, the Phillies, and the crowds of less than ten thousand spectators. In the dugout, Phillies field manager Ben Chapman let out a torrent of verbal abuse at Robinson, which shocked and angered those who could hear his words resonate across the field. Chapman had played in the Major Leagues for several teams and had managed the Phillies over the past several seasons. He was born in Kentucky and had spent his formative years in Alabama. He had a history of stirring controversy as both a player and a manager. He frequently yelled insults at opposing players in an attempt to throw those players off their games. He also had a habit of yelling back at fans who taunted him from their seats. His actions occasionally landed him in trouble; in 1934, Chapman made anti-Semitic remarks toward some fans, leading to a petition from some Yankees fans to urge the franchise to get rid of him. Chapman later apologized for his remarks and denied that he possessed any animus toward Jewish ballplayers or fans.

In addition to stirring verbal confrontations, Chapman also showed flashes of a bad temper during his career as both a player and a manager. While playing for the Yankees in 1933, Chapman spiked Buddy Myer, the Washington Senators' second baseman, in a game in Washington, D.C. The incident escalated and led to Chapman attacking Senators' pitcher Earl Whitehill in the Senators' dugout. Fights on the field spilled over into the stands; all three players faced suspensions. Five years later, when Chapman played for the Boston Red Sox, he triggered the first on-field fight in nearly two decades at Fenway Park. Chapman also engaged in fights with umpires. In 1937, he threw a glove at an umpire, which resulted in his ejection from the game and yet another suspension. In 1943, while managing a Minor League team called the Richmond Colts, local police escorted

Chapman from the field after he engaged in a fight with an umpire. That fight resulted in his year-long suspension.

As he demonstrated during his career, Chapman regarded getting under an opponent's skin a part of the way he played and managed baseball. He saw his actions to be well within the boundaries of acceptable behavior on the baseball field. While he later denied possessing any racial bias, Chapman's insults clearly targeted Robinson's skin color and other stereotypes pertaining to African Americans. He frequently directed the N-word at Robinson and referred to the first baseman's thick lips, a facial feature stereotypically associated with African Americans. Chapman also yelled about Robinson's thick skull, another stereotype associated with African Americans that bigots used to prove their superiority. In addition to taunting Robinson, Chapman also taunted Robinson's white teammates and openly questioned whether they truly wanted the first baseman on their team. He warned them that they would contract sores and other diseases if they associated with Robinson and that they could spread those afflictions to their wives.

Near the end of his life, Robinson recalled that the constant stream of insults and abuse he faced from the Phillies made him question his commitment to the "don't fight back" plan he had with Rickey. The insults and abuse attacked Robinson's dignity. He considered marching over to the Phillies' dugout, attacking either Chapman or one of the players who joined in the abuse, and then walking away from the game. Robinson, though, remembered the greater cause he represented and the risks involved in him deciding to fight back against the insults and abuses. He recognized that his failure to adhere to the "don't fight back" plan would likely end any immediate hope for more black players to enter the Major Leagues. Instead of physically attacking the Phillies in their dugout, Robinson concentrated on channeling his anger and on using it to defeat the team in a different manner.

Robinson got his revenge in the bottom of the eighth inning. At that point in the game, the Dodgers and Phillies remained deadlocked in a scoreless tie. Robinson led off with a single to centerfield and then took a sizable lead off first base. He stole second base on a throw that missed the shortstop and bounced away from the fielder. That bounce gave Robinson the opportunity to reach third base. Three batters later, the left fielder Hermanski hit a single, and Robinson scored the game's only run. He allowed his performance to speak for itself and send a message to his harassers.

The Dodgers' victory in the first game of the three-game series did not deter Chapman and the Phillies from trying to agitate Robinson and the rest of the Dodgers. Chapman led the abuse and insults in the second game of the series; he missed the third game due to an illness, but the abuse and insults continued to come from the Phillies' dugout. Chapman's tactics did not help his team on the field. The Dodgers won the remaining two games of the series by the scores of 5–2 and 2–0. Robinson finished the series with a .346 batting average for the season, so Chapman's tactics also failed to distract the first baseman from helping his team win games. While Robinson never fought back against Chapman and the Phillies, his white teammates faced no such restrictions on their behavior. At one point, Stanky called Chapman and the Phillies "yellow-bellied cowards" and dared them to yell at someone who could answer them. Other Dodgers players, including Walker, also expressed displeasure at Chapman and the Phillies and spoke to the press about the incidents. Instead of hurting Robinson, Chapman and the Phillies had only hurt themselves and made Robinson seem sympathetic.

Following the series with Brooklyn, Chapman and the Phillies tried to spin what had happened in order to deflect scrutiny about Chapman's racial animus. Coverage after the series focused on Chapman's behavior and dredged up stories about other instances where he seemed to cross the line between acceptable and unacceptable behavior on a baseball field. By contrast, sportswriters lauded Robinson for his restraint and for rising above the abuse he heard while playing against the Phillies. Chapman tried to explain away his behavior in Brooklyn as part of a long baseball tradition—players and managers tried to get under the skin of their opponents. He noted that white players, like the Italian-American Joe DiMaggio, heard slurs with regard to their ethnicities. To Chapman, the verbal abuse he hurled at Robinson did not stem from any biased feelings he harbored about African Americans. On the contrary, the verbal abuse represented part of the game of baseball, something that Robinson had to expect if he wanted acceptance as a player in the Major Leagues. Most sportswriters, including black sportswriters, and Chandler did not buy Chapman's arguments. To them, Chapman's behavior had no place on a baseball field and exposed the manager's deep bias against African Americans. Chandler warned Chapman against engaging in such abusive behavior while he managed the Phillies.

AN EARLY-SEASON SLUMP

On the heels of that troubling series against the Phillies, Robinson entered a prolonged hitting slump that brought renewed questions about his ability to play for the Dodgers. The Dodgers carried two other players on the roster who could play at first base, but Shotton and Rickey kept Robinson in the starting lineup. They hoped that he could battle through the slump as well as the shoulder injury he had incurred during a collision. During the slump, Robinson's batting average dipped to .273, well below his average at the start of the season and well below his average during the previous two seasons. While the *Courier* referred to Robinson's slump, it also tried to maintain positive coverage of his progress with the Dodgers. In one story, Smith wrote about an interview with Robinson at the McAlpin hotel and the overwhelming number of positive letters he had received from people across the country. Two of those letters came from Mallie Robinson and Zelle Isum, Robinson's mother and mother-in-law. In that same edition of the *Courier*, a story on a different page focused on Robinson as a young husband and new father and joked that Rachel's father initially did not approve of the match. Those articles detail the delicate balance that the *Courier* strove to maintain in its coverage of Robinson. Not only the sportswriters could not ignore Robinson's on-field struggles, they also submitted personal interest stories designed to help their readers invest in Robinson's success. Smith and the *Courier* had played critical roles in getting Robinson to the Dodgers, and they showed no sign of abandoning their effort to continue to promote the viability of adding black players to Major League organizations.

During a series in late April against the Giants in Ebbets Field, Robinson received a boost of support from an unlikely source—heavyweight champion Joe Louis. For over a decade, Louis had ranked as one of the most visible and likable African American celebrities in the United States. Black newspapers followed every step of his successful career; stories about his training sessions drew splashy coverage on sports pages and came with large photographs of the champ in action. Though Louis's career had neared its conclusion in 1947, he still carried a great deal of goodwill. The near-capacity crowd at Ebbets Field warmly greeted Louis as he walked to his seats near the Dodgers' dugout. One he reached his seats, Louis waved at Robinson. Robinson reciprocated by presenting Louis with an autographed baseball. The brief gestures carried some deeper significance. Robinson paid his respects to the champ and acknowledged his support. By waving at Robinson, Louis helped to validate the first baseman's place as a Major League-caliber ballplayer. Louis's wave also symbolized the passing of a torch from one past sports celebrity to a new one who could serve as a national symbol of triumph over racism.

Despite the slump, Rickey remained committed to Robinson and his plan to build a contending team around black players. A sign of Rickey's commitment came on May 3 when he completed a trade involving Higbe, one of the anti-Robinson instigators from the Dodgers' spring training days. Rickey sent Higbe to the Pittsburgh Pirates along with several other players—Gene Mauch, Dixie Howell, Cal McLish, and Hank Behrman. In return, Rickey received $250,000 from the Pirates and an outfielder, Al Gionfriddo. Gionfriddo had played in a game for the Pirates in the 1947 season, and he would play in only thirty-seven games for the Dodgers for the remainder of the season. In eighty-one plate appearances, Gionfriddo amassed a 177 batting average with no home runs and six RBIs. After his thirty-seven games with the Dodgers, Gionfriddo never played in another Major League game. While Rickey received a substantial amount of money from the Pirates, the fact that he took Gionfriddo in a deal for Higbe demonstrated that he simply wanted to jettison the troublesome pitcher from the Dodgers. Rickey wanted harmony in the Dodgers' clubhouse, and he wanted to send a message to the rest of the Dodgers players. To Robinson, Rickey showed that he had faith in the rookie first baseman. To the Dodgers' white players, Rickey showed that he would trade any of them if they did not outwardly accept Robinson as a teammate. Higbe had support among the Dodgers' fanbase, and he had been ranked as the team's top pitcher in the previous season. Neither of those factors saved him from a trade.

A THREATENED BOYCOTT

As the calendar turned from April to May, Robinson needed all the support he could obtain as other teams tested the boundaries of how they could respond to his presence with the Dodgers. On May 1, Robinson broke out of his slump against the visiting Chicago Cubs. Due to bad weather, the Dodgers played their next game on May 6 when they hosted the St. Louis Cardinals at Ebbets Field. The Cardinals had won the World Series in 1946 and seemed poised to defend their title in 1947. For the Dodgers, the series against the Cardinals could serve as the way for them to measure how they competed against the defending champs and how close they stood to their own dreams for postseason glory. Prior to the series, however, several members of the Cardinals seemed to focus more on Robinson and not on a plan to defeat the Dodgers. Harry Walker, Dixie Walker's brother, and a few other Cardinals started to discuss the possibility of staging a boycott to protest Robinson's presence on the Dodgers. The instigators seemed to assume that if enough players joined in their boycott, they could force the Dodgers to bench Robinson and maybe encourage other teams to follow their lead.

Ultimately, the plan to boycott the games against the Dodgers never materialized, yet the threat of such a boycott led to swift action against the Cardinals' players. Sam Breadon, the Cardinals' president, learned about the discussed boycott and met with individual players to put an end to the plan. Breadon, however, wanted additional support, so he turned to the National League's president Frick. The two met in Frick's office in New York City and decided to take a proactive stance against the discussed boycott. Frick gave Breadon a message that he could deliver to the players, a message meant to squash any talk about or plans for a boycott. The players received the message, and all the Cardinals appeared in Ebbets Field for the three-game series against the Dodgers. The series passed without any on-field or off-field incidents; the Cardinals won two of the three games in the series. As a result of the series, the Dodgers lost the lead they had built in the National League standings. They departed from Ebbets Field for the start of a twelve-game road trip that took them to Philadelphia, Cincinnati, Pittsburgh, Chicago, and St. Louis.

The discussed boycott had no effect on the Dodgers-Cardinals series and seemed destined to fade away into oblivion. On May 9, however, the floodgates opened when Stanley Woodward of the *New York Herald Tribune* broke the story about the Cardinals' discussed boycott. In Woodward's retelling of the incident, he exaggerated key details and made the discussed boycott a significant threat facing the entire National League. According to Woodward, discussions about a boycott began in the Dodgers' clubhouse, spread to the Cardinals, and had the potential to spread to the other six teams in the National League. In other words, Woodward alleged that players across all eight National League teams had developed a plan to engage in a strike in order to demonstrate their opposition to Robinson. Woodward also claimed to have the message that Frick passed along to the players through Breadon. Frick allegedly threatened the players with suspension from the National League and warned them that they would stand as outcasts from the sportswriters who cover baseball. He also allegedly claimed that he did not care if the suspensions wrecked the National League because he believed in the righteousness of supporting Robinson over the striking players.

One day later, Woodward backtracked from the claims he had made in his initial article while still trying to claim that he published a true story. In the second article, Woodward admitted that he did not interview Frick. He also had not interviewed any of the players on the eight National League clubs who had allegedly coordinated a strike in protest of Robinson. Woodward, furthermore, even admitted that he did intend to imply he had published the actual message Frick delivered to the players. In the first article, Frick's message had appeared within quotation marks, thereby implying that it represented an on-the-record accurate wording of his message to the conspirators. For those reasons, it seemed highly likely that Woodward had fabricated parts of the story he published on the previous day and had exaggerated the likelihood that the entire National League faced a crisis. Robinson's presence undoubtedly rankled many players in the National League, but no concrete evidence existed that those feelings translated into coordinated action across every National League franchise.

The baseball world focused on Woodward's first article, not his second one, and hailed Frick for his quick actions in support of Robinson. Praise for Frick also spilled over into black newspapers. In one edition of the *Courier*, the top of the sports page included a reproduction of the message that Woodward claimed Frick delivered to the Cardinals players. A headline above the reproduced quote referred to "Frick's Immortal, Uncompromising Statement." Below the statement, Smith published a lengthy article in which he lauded Woodward for exposing the plot against Robinson and effectively leading to the plot's demise. He also lauded Frick and Chandler for acting quickly and for making uncompromising stands in support of Robinson. Smith added some bits of new reporting by highlighting the role that Walter Winchell played in generating support for Robinson and opposition to any potential strikers. Winchell delivered popular radio broadcasts, and he had devoted his last two Sunday broadcasts to denouncing ballplayers who opposed Robinson. Smith also revealed that Robinson had received letters so threatening that the Dodgers had contacted the local police force. In spite of those pressures, Smith noted that Robinson remained focused on playing baseball and on maintaining his composure on the baseball field. He credited Robinson's composure for helping to kill any talk of a league-wide rebellion, for making it possible for Frick and Chandler to support him, and for making his would-be opposition look like troublemakers.

MORE HOSTILITY IN THE NATIONAL LEAGUE

In addition to the dustup involving the Cardinals, Robinson faced real hostility from other teams in the National League. On May 9, the same day when Woodward broke the story about the Cardinals' possible boycott, Robinson and the Dodgers arrived in Philadelphia for a four-game series against the Phillies. The four-game series, which included a scheduled doubleheader on Sunday May 11, marked the first time that the Dodgers played a game outside New York City. Prior to the game, Phillies general manager Herb Pennock called Rickey and begged him to not bring Robinson to Shibe Park. Pennock told Rickey that the Phillies team simply would not take the field if Robinson appeared in the game and alluded to a fear that the city would not accept seeing a black man on the field. In his response, Rickey called Pennock's bluff. Rickey replied that the Dodgers would gladly accept a 9–0 outcome for each of the four games scheduled for Shibe Park. The score of 9–0 represented the recorded outcome for any game that one team forfeited to another team. Rickey's response, combined with a warning from Chandler, squashed any potential that the Phillies would refuse to play against Robinson at Shibe Park. Chandler had warned Chapman and the Phillies against a repeat of the ugliness that marred the earlier series in Ebbets Field. To show that he understood

Chandler's warning, Chapman released a statement in which he insisted he did not object to Robinson playing for the Dodgers. The games remained on schedule, and the Phillies took the field in all four games.

Despite those measures to block a repeat of the first Dodgers-Phillies series, Robinson still faced hostility when he arrived in Philadelphia. The Dodgers typically stayed at the Benjamin Franklin Hotel when they played in Philadelphia, and the entire team had rooms booked at the hotel. The hotel management, however, refused to accommodate Robinson when he arrived with his white teammates. The white Dodgers checked into the Benjamin Franklin Hotel and prepared for the game later that evening. Robinson found accommodations at an all-black hotel, the Attucks, and then joined his teammates at Shibe Park. The episode served as a reminder of the different experiences Robinson faced that set himself apart from his white teammates. While he could blend in as the Dodgers' first baseman on the baseball field, he could not blend in with his white teammates away from the diamond. He remained an African American subject to the rules that treated all African Americans, including athletes, as a separate subset of citizens.

Once he arrived at Shibe Park, Robinson had to face his old nemesis, Chapman. Before the first game, Chapman informed the Dodgers that he wanted to pose for a photograph with Robinson. The photograph would be taken on the field, in front of the large crowd, the reporters and photographers, and members of both teams. In keeping with his pact with Rickey, Robinson agreed to Chapman's request. Rather than shake hands, Robinson and Chapman held the opposite ends of a baseball bat while posing for the infamous photograph. Both men smiled for the photographers, and the image appeared in newspapers in both Philadelphia and New York City. Afterward, Chapman and some of the Phillies still subjected Robinson to verbal abuse similar to, but milder than, the kind of abuse hurled at him during the first series in Ebbets Field. Robinson also later recalled that a few of the Phillies players used their bats as machine guns, pointed them at him, and mimicked shooting at him from their dugout. The Phillies won three of the four games in the series, leaving the Dodgers with a two-game deficit in the National League's standings. More importantly, the actions of Chapman and the Phillies showed that they had not truly learned their lesson and that they intended to use Robinson's race as a way to get under his skin.

Robinson seemed outwardly unfazed by the death threats and other treatments he received in Philadelphia. A column "Jackie Robinson Says" regularly appeared in the *Courier*; Smith likely served as Robinson's ghostwriter for the columns, yet the columns provided insight into the story Robinson wanted to convey about his time with the Dodgers. In one column on the visit to Philadelphia, Robinson provided a pleasant recounting of the photograph he took with Chapman. He referred to Chapman as a nice person who did not actually mean the horrible things that he had said to him during the series at Ebbets Field. In other columns, Robinson recounted the good experiences he had in Pittsburgh against the Pirates and in St. Louis against the Cardinals players who allegedly wanted to avoid playing against him in Brooklyn. Later in his life, when he wrote his autobiography, Robinson would offer different views of his early experiences with the Dodgers. As he played in his first season, however, Robinson used his columns to convey an upbeat image and to insist that other players in the National League accepted him as a ballplayer.

Instead of causing dissension among the Dodgers, the hostility that Robinson faced in his first two months with the team helped to melt his isolation from his white teammates and turn public opinion in his favor. While Robinson still tried to keep to himself on road trips and in the Dodgers' clubhouse, he earned the admiration of his teammates for how he comported himself in the face of hostility. That hostility also opened his teammates' eyes to the additional pressures that Robinson faced, pressures beyond what other rookies experienced in their first seasons. Robinson later recalled that Reese helped him through his tough times with the Dodgers, even at one point standing next to him while hecklers from the stands hurled insults at him. While Robinson continued to receive hate mails, he also received more letters of support, so many, in fact, that the Dodgers had to manage the first baseman's enormous pile of letters. The positive letters came from all areas of the country, including the South. At one point, Rickey joked that the hostility Robinson received actually represented the best thing that happened to the Dodgers. The abuse helped to make Robinson seem sympathetic and bring the team together, something that Rickey predicted would represent the biggest challenge to his plans to add more black players to the Dodgers' roster.

Rickey also showed his support for Robinson in another way—by making it clear that the rookie had a permanent place on the Dodgers' roster. On May 10, Rickey traded Howie Schultz, the backup first baseman, to the Phillies for $50,000. At the time of that deal, Robinson had broken out of slump, but his batting average remained stubbornly below .300. Rumors of Robinson's demotion to the Royals hung in the air, but those rumors dissipated once Rickey concluded the Schultz trade. Once Schultz departed for the Phillies, Robinson represented the only person on the Dodgers' roster who could play at first base. The trade not only solidified Robinson's permanent spot on the Dodgers' roster but also provided hope for players such as Roy Campanella and Don Newcombe who played in the franchise's farm system. Rickey had firmly backed Robinson even in the midst of a slump, and he seemed committed to bringing more black players to the Dodgers in order to build a pennant-winning team.

The extended road trip that began with hostility and humiliation in Philadelphia represented a turning point for Robinson in several ways. He attracted large crowds at Crosley Field in Cincinnati, Forbes Field in Pittsburgh, and Wrigley Field in Chicago. Those crowds disproved one of the persistent arguments against integrated teams in the Major Leagues—that integrated teams would cause attendance declines in Major League ballparks. In the game in Pittsburgh, Robinson had an incidental collision with the Pirates' first baseman, Hank Greenburg, who later apologized and offered him some advice for dealing with adversity. Greenburg had faced similar hostility due to his Jewish faith, and he could sympathize with the rookie. Robinson's teammates, including Stanky, came to his defense when Pirates' pitcher Fritz Ostermueller hit him with a pitch. By the time the road trip ended, Robinson had raised his batting average to .299 and had seemed to become more comfortable both at the plate and in the field. As May turned into June, both Robinson and the Dodgers had appeared to turn a pivotal corner and seemed poised to challenge the best teams in the National League.

Overall, Robinson's first two months with the Dodgers revealed both the promise and the pitfalls of adding black players in a still heavily segregated society. At times, he blended in with his white teammates and appeared to have the respect of players in the National League. At other times, he stood apart from his teammates because he faced taunts and verbal abuse that specifically targeted the color of his skin. He also stood apart because he could not respond to such taunts and abuse and because he received hate mails that led to police intervention. Though Robinson secured his spot on the Dodgers' roster, the overall success of the effort to bring black players into the Major Leagues remained in doubt. Two months after Robinson debuted with the Dodgers, he remained the only black player in the Major Leagues. Even though the Dodgers drew large crowds on the road and at Ebbets Field, none of the other Major League officials seemed poised to follow Rickey's lead and integrate their rosters. Whether more black players would come in Robinson's wake remained a key question as the 1947 season reached its halfway point. A surprising answer to that question ultimately came not from the National League but from the American League and from one of the more eccentric people ever associated with the game of baseball.

7

The Rookie of the Year

During the first two months of the 1947 baseball season, Jackie Robinson secured his spot on the Brooklyn Dodgers' roster and proved that he could uphold the deal he had made with Branch Rickey to not fight back against racist agitators. For the remainder of the season, Robinson continued to prove that he belonged on the Dodgers and dispelled many of the myths that had sustained the color line in Major League Baseball. More importantly, Robinson and his teammates proved that an integrated team could reach the postseason when the Dodgers clinched the National League pennant in September 1947. The Dodgers' successful 1947 season represented one sign of the success of the long-term effort to reintegrate the Major Leagues and of Rickey's plan to build a winning team using black players. Another sign of success came in Cleveland when the Indians' minority owner, Bill Veeck, integrated the American League by adding Larry Doby to his team. On the heels of Doby's addition to the Indians, the St. Louis Browns added two black players, Hank Thompson and Willard Brown. By the time the 1947 season ended, Robinson no longer represented the only black player in the Major Leagues or on the Dodgers' roster. His presence, along with the presence of other black players, seemed to portend the eventual end of all-white teams in the Major Leagues. Additionally, the presence of black players in the Major Leagues came against a backdrop of efforts to end segregation in other parts of American society. Robinson, Doby, and other black players, therefore, stood as harbingers of a future

American society in which legalized segregation no longer existed and in which separate leagues for black players represented relics of American history.

THE REGULAR SEASON CONTINUES

By June 1, 1947, Robinson and the Dodgers had played against the other seven National League teams in at least one series. While they had yet to host the Cubs, the Pirates, and the Reds in Ebbets Field, they had played in every National League ballpark. A familiar pattern had emerged—Robinson brought huge crowds to the ballparks and received cheers from the black spectators who came to see him play even if they did not root for the Dodgers. Away from the ballparks, Robinson and his traveling companion, Wendell Smith, whom Rickey had put on the Dodgers' payroll, looked for alternate accommodations. Neither of them could stay in the same hotel as the Dodgers' white players. With his job at first base secure and with encouragement from his manager Burt Shotton, Robinson played a more aggressive style of baseball and often confounded opposing players as he stole bases, including home. Robinson's aggressive play also helped him raise his batting average and helped him earn the admiration of his team-mates. The Dodgers finished May with a season record of 20–17 and facing a two-game deficit in the National League standings. While Robinson had turned a corner in his season, the Dodgers still faced an uphill battle in their quest to make the postseason and win the franchise's elusive first World Series title.

On June 1, the Dodgers returned to Ebbets Field for an extended home stand against the Cardinals, Pirates, Cubs, and Reds. In those games, the large crowds that greeted the Dodgers on the road started to appear at Ebbets Field. The game against the Dodgers and the Cardinals on that day drew over thirty-four thousand fans, the largest crowd to date at Ebbets Field in 1947. Five other games on the home stand attracted over thirty-thousand fans; other games drew over twenty-thousand fans, a significant improvement over the Dodgers' attendance figures during the 1946 season. Following that extended home stand, the Dodgers once again went on the road and faced the same teams they had faced earlier in the month at Ebbets Field. They ended the month with a shorter road trip against the Braves, Giants, and Phillies before returning again to Ebbets Field and a home stand that went on from July 2 to July 21. The Dodgers ended June with a record of 38–28, good enough for a tie atop the National League standings. By the end of July, the Dodgers had an impressive 63–36 record, good enough for a massive ten-game lead in the National League.

As the Dodgers compiled that impressive record, Smith and the *Pittsburgh Courier* continued to serve as an important conduit between Robinson and black baseball fans. The regular "Jackie Robinson Says" columns carefully avoided any unpleasantness that Robinson endured and took pains to depict a positive image of the first baseman's rookie campaign. In one column published in early June, Robinson noted the good treatment he received in Boston while playing against the Braves. Some Boston fans tormented Robinson in the same way fans in other cities tormented him, but that fact did not appear in the column. Additionally, the column, likely ghostwritten by Smith, referred to a recent column from Boston sportswriter Austen Lake. Lake had written a column critical of Robinson's play at first base; he later issued a clarification that he liked Robinson and did not harbor any racial prejudice against the rookie. He insisted that he simply did not see Robinson as a successful first baseman. Robinson responded by insisting that Lake had every right to criticize him without needing to issue a clarification. In fact, Robinson stated that he wanted sportswriters to criticize him if he made mistakes or errors while playing at first base. Robinson, in other words, called upon sportswriters to cover him like a baseball player and to hold him to the same standards they applied to white players.

The same upbeat message continued in other columns published during June and July 1947. Another column in June covered a very banal topic—hustling in the Major Leagues. In the column, Robinson emphasized the importance of hustling as key to successful individual careers in the Major Leagues and as key to team success. Another column covered his second visit to St. Louis to play against the Cardinals, the team that sparked rumors of a league-wide anti-Robinson strike earlier in the season. Robinson never mentioned those rumors, nor did he mention any poor treatment from the Cardinals' players or fans. On the contrary, Robinson praised the Cardinals' pitcher George "Red" Munger, who had defeated the Dodgers 3–0 on the first game of the road trip. He also looked ahead to the games in Chicago and Cincinnati and lauded one of the Reds' pitchers, Ewell Blackwell. Robinson detailed how the pitcher fooled the hitters and predicted that Blackwell would win over twenty games in the 1947 season. His words proved prophetic; Blackwell defeated the Dodgers 4–0 and won twenty-two games in the 1947 season, the most wins by any pitcher in the Major Leagues.

While the regular "Jackie Robinson Says" columns did not provide much insight into his feelings, they stand as a valuable reminder of the pact he made with Rickey back in August 1945. The columns also stand as a valuable reminder of the reality that Robinson faced during his first season with the Dodgers. Robinson led the National League in getting hit by pitches, yet he never charged the mound or did anything else on the baseball diamond that revealed his displeasure at leading the league in such stat. With Smith as his guide, Robinson carried the same attitude into the columns that appeared in the *Courier*. Both Smith and Robinson understood the larger purpose that lay behind the first baseman's rookie campaign with the Dodgers. Smith had devoted the entirety of his newspaper career to advocating for black players to join the Major Leagues, and the success of that advocacy depended upon Robinson. Had Robinson used the columns to vent the frustration he later vented in his autobiography, the movement of black players into the Major Leagues likely would have stalled for an indefinite period. His columns likely would have caused a distraction for the Dodgers and would have created even more distance between Robinson and his white teammates. The columns also would have given critics the opportunity they needed to argue that black players could not handle the mental challenges of playing in the Major Leagues. Furthermore, at the time those columns appeared, none of the fifteen other Major League franchises seemed interested in signing black players. Robinson, through Smith, needed to present the calm and banal image he presented in those columns because such an image represented the only likely means of success for black players in the Major Leagues.

Smith complemented the banal and generally upbeat tone of the "Jackie Robinson Says" columns in his own regular columns that ran under the title of "The Sports Beat." Since Smith traveled with Robinson, he provided his readers with details about the long road trips and about the first baseman's success against his National League opponents. In a column written during a trip to Boston, Smith reminded his readers about the failed tryouts held with the Red Sox two years earlier as a way to mark Robinson's triumph in such a short period of time. He claimed that Robinson's presence in Boston as a member of the Dodgers should embarrass both the Braves and the Red Sox since both of those franchises had an opportunity to add him to their rosters. Smith seemed to take pleasure in relating how both the teams neglected to understand how World War II marked the death knell for segregation in the Major Leagues and how their denial stood in stark contrast to the city's place as a starting point of the American Revolution.

In another column, Smith regaled his readers with a story of how enthusiastic fans mobbed the Dodgers, including Robinson, at Grand Central Station before the team left on its train ride to St. Louis. He joked that the veteran players navigated the scene, but Robinson and other rookies struggled to make their way to the waiting train. Smith also noted that he ran into Ford Frick on the train and had an extended conversation with him about Robinson. According to Smith, Frick welcomed a conversation with the sportswriter. When asked about the then-recent conflagration with the Cardinals, Frick said that his office had received letters from across the country and only one letter criticized Frick's actions. Frick stood firm and insisted that he could not let the players dictate who could play in the Major Leagues and that he could not remove a player solely because of the color of his skin. He also praised Robinson and the rapid progress he had made while learning to play a new position, the third new position he had learned in three seasons. Near his end of the interview with Frick, Smith broached the delicate topic of the lack of black players on other National League clubs. Frick did not have any predictions as to when another black player would join a franchise, but he pledged to treat that addition as simply another routine transaction. He would not force a club to sign black players, nor would he stand in the way of any owner or general manager who followed Rickey's example.

Smith seemed pleased with Frick's responses, but the lack of black players on other clubs remained a glaring problem for the sportswriter and others who wanted integrated teams. Though Smith had often celebrated the death of the color line in baseball, the color line remained largely intact almost two years after Rickey's and Robinson's first meeting. Robinson still stood as the only black player in the Major Leagues. The Dodgers' farm system boasted several promising black prospects, most notably Roy Campanella and Don Newcombe, but neither player seemed ready to join the Dodgers in the 1947 season. None of the other fifteen farm systems included any black players, and none of the other owners or general managers had publicly committed themselves to signing black players. The Negro Leagues remained the main forum for black ballplayers who wanted to play at the professional level. Progress toward a fully integrated Major Leagues had not yet spread beyond the Dodgers' organization, and the questions of if and when such progress would spread remained unknown.

ROY CAMPANELLA

Roy Campanella, one of Jackie Robinson's earliest black teammates on the Brooklyn Dodgers, has a life story that also embodies the racial divide in American history. Born to an African American mother and an Italian-American father in Philadelphia in 1921, Campanella and his siblings faced the same realities that many biracial Americans faced in the twentieth century. They could not fully assimilate into the world of white America, even though they attended integrated schools in the Philadelphia school system. Campanella dropped out of school at the age of sixteen so that he could pursue a professional baseball career. He had watched many games at Shibe Park near his home in North Philadelphia, and he allegedly had a tryout scheduled with the Philadelphia Phillies. According to that story, the franchise later canceled that tryout once someone discovered Campanella's mixed race background. He then pursued a career in the Negro Leagues and quickly impressed the older players with his baseball skills. Veteran catcher Raleigh "Biz" Mackey became Campanella's mentor and molded him into arguably the top catcher in the Negro Leagues.

In October 1945, before the announcement of Robinson's signing, Campanella almost missed his opportunity to join the Brooklyn Dodgers' organization. Like Robinson, Campanella had a lengthy meeting with Branch Rickey, but he declined Rickey's offer to come to Brooklyn because he thought Rickey wanted him for the Brown Dodgers. A short time later, Robinson and Campanella crossed paths, and Robinson revealed to him Rickey's plan to add black players to the Brooklyn Dodgers. Campanella hurriedly sent a telegram to Rickey, indicating his interest in joining the Dodgers' organization, and he spent the 1946 season in the Minor Leagues with Don Newcombe and the Nashua Dodgers.

Campanella spent his entire Major League career following in Robinson's footsteps with the Brooklyn Dodgers. His debut came on April 20, 1948, just over one year after Robinson's debut. In 1951, Campanella became the second African American, after Robinson, to win the Most Valuable Player award; he became the first African American to win the award multiple times. He also followed Robinson as the second African American player to be inducted into the Hall of Fame. Campanella played his final game on September 29, 1957. He was set to join the Dodgers for the 1958 season, but a car accident on January 28, 1958, ended his playing career. Campanella sustained a broken neck in the accident, and he spent the rest of his life in a wheelchair. In June 1972, the Dodgers retired his number 39 at the same time as they retired Robinson's number 42, further cementing the link between the two former teammates.

LARRY DOBY JOINS ROBINSON IN THE MAJOR LEAGUES

Fortunately, Smith and others who wanted a fully integrated Major Leagues did not need to wait much longer for another sign of progress. That sign did not come from the National League; it came from the American League, specifically from William Louis "Bill" Veeck Jr. Born in 1914, Veeck's life centered on baseball. In 1918, his father accepted William Wrigley's offer to work as the Chicago Cubs' president. Veeck worked as a popcorn vendor at Wrigley Field, and he remained attached to the franchise after his father's death in 1933. Throughout his career in baseball, Veeck developed a well-earned reputation for creative and occasionally outlandish ideas. In 1937, for example, he suggested planting ivy on the outfield walls of Wrigley Field. The Cubs' management followed through on his suggestion, and the ivy-covered walls remain a distinguishing feature of Wrigley Field in the twenty-first century. Veeck left the Cubs in 1941 when he bought a stake in the Milwaukee Brewers, then a Minor

League team that played in the American Association. As a part-owner of the Brewers, Veeck again flexed his creativity with stunts such as weddings at home plate, giveaways involving live animals, and scheduling morning games for fans who worked at nights. Veeck's eccentricity extended to an injury he sustained while fighting in World War II. As a result of his injuries, Veeck lost part of his right leg and wore wooden prosthetics for the rest of his life. He occasionally used the different wooden prosthetics as ashtrays.

A few years after buying a stake in the Brewers, Veeck played a leading role in a story that may or may not have accelerated the date of Major League Baseball's reintegration. In 1962, Veeck published his autobiography, *Veeck—As in Wreck*, and related for the first time his thwarted scheme to purchase the Philadelphia Phillies and transform the team with black players. Veeck's alleged scheme took place after the conclusion of the 1942 season, a season in which the Phillies finished with a dreadful record of 42–109. He claimed that he had secured the necessary financing to purchase the franchise from Gerry Nugent, who had his own financial problems and who could not properly support the Phillies. Veeck also claimed that he planned to work with Abe Saperstein, a sports promoter, and A. S. "Doc" Young, the *Chicago Defender*'s sports editor, to secure the best talent in the Negro Leagues. According to Veeck, his plans fell apart when he revealed his true intentions to Commissioner Kenesaw Mountain Landis. To Veeck, Landis and the other owners arranged for someone else to purchase the Phillies in order to block his plans.

Different historians have disputed the veracity of Veeck's story since the contemporary evidence seems inconclusive. Landis and the other owners did push Nugent to sell the Phillies, and Nugent complied by selling the team to William D. Cox shortly before the start of the 1943 season. Many stories published between the end of the 1942 season and the start of the 1943 season detailed those efforts, and a few stories reported on a meeting between Nugent and Veeck. None of the stories, however, provided any hints about Veeck's deeper intentions for purchasing the Phillies, nor did they conclusively state that Veeck sought to purchase the franchise. Black newspapers, furthermore, never published any stories linking Veeck to the Phillies and to a plan to fulfill their efforts to reintegrate the Major Leagues. Historians who doubt the veracity of Veeck's story point to the absence of such stories as proof that Veeck likely concocted his story for his autobiography. Those historians also note that Veeck misidentified the *Defender*'s sports editor; Fay Young, not Doc Young, worked as the paper's sports editor in the 1940s. Other historians, however, found evidence of Veeck's claims prior to the publication of his autobiography and believe that those earlier claims lend credence to his story.

Regardless of the veracity of his claims involving the Phillies, Veeck did play a leading role in reintegrating the Major Leagues. He had long admired players in the Negro Leagues and, like Rickey, sought to build a winning franchise around black players. After selling his stake in the Brewers, Veeck returned to the Major Leagues by purchasing a minority ownership in the Cleveland Indians during the 1946 season. Veeck again flexed his creative muscles when he joined the Indians. He moved the team to a larger ballpark, Municipal Stadium, that the franchise had used only occasionally for its home games. Veeck also introduced promotions, giveaways, and other stunts that irked his fellow Major League owners. To Veeck, such stunts helped to market the Indians, a team that had not won the American League pennant since 1920. In early July 1947, Veeck made his boldest gambit to date in his career—he signed Larry Doby, the first African American to ever play for a team in the American League.

Born in South Carolina in 1923, Doby had a background similar to Robinson's background. Doby's parents divorced during his childhood, and his father subsequently died in a drowning accident. At the age of fourteen, Doby moved from his native South Carolina to Paterson, New Jersey, to live near his mother. While he attended Paterson's East Side High School, Doby excelled in four sports—football, baseball, basketball, and track. Like Robinson, Doby played on integrated teams in both high school and college. He briefly attended Long Island University after accepting an athletic scholarship to play for the school's basketball team. Doby, however, also signed a contract with the Newark Eagles prior to the start of the 1942 season and played for the Eagles during that season. Doby signed the contract using an alias in order to protect his amateur status and his ability to play intercollegiate sports. Following the 1942 season, Doby spent two years serving in and playing baseball for the United States Navy. Doby encountered the same racial segregation that Robinson encountered in his own World War II experiences, and he never forgot those experiences. Since Doby spent a great deal of time playing for the navy's baseball and basketball teams, he developed friendships with other athletes serving in the navy. He met Marion Motley, one of the first two black players the Cleveland Browns would sign in 1946. He also met Mickey Vernon, a star player for the Washington Senators who later encouraged the Senators' owner Clark Griffith to sign Doby. After the war, Vernon gifted Doby with a set of bats, a gesture that Doby deeply appreciated.

News of Robinson's signing with the Dodgers in October 1945 led Doby to reconsider his postwar plans. Doby had considered working as a teacher or a coach once he received his discharge from the navy. Robinson's signing, however, led Doby to believe that he could pursue a career in professional baseball, specifically in the Major Leagues. Doby received his honorable discharge from the navy in January 1946, and he rejoined the

Newark Eagles. He also returned to his longtime girlfriend, Helyn, whom he married during the 1946 season. Doby made a wise decision to return to the Negro Leagues and to resume his career with the Eagles. The Eagles dominated their league during the 1946 season and captured the World Series title over the Kansas City Monarchs, a team that still boasted some of the top black talent. Doby represented a key player in the Eagles' 1946 success, and he resumed his strong play in the 1947 season. By the season's mid-point, Doby had a .458 batting average. He also had hit fourteen home runs and had thirty-five RBIs. With those numbers, Doby caught Veeck's attention, and the eccentric owner put the finishing touches on his plans to bring Doby to Cleveland.

Veeck did not follow the same careful plan that Rickey followed when he brought Robinson to the Dodgers. He intended to bring Doby directly to the Indians, not to one of the franchise's farm teams. When he joined the club in 1946, Veeck hired Louis Jones, an African American, to work in public relations for the Indians and to help prepare Cleveland's black population for a black player. Veeck recognized Doby's talents; Doby also abstained from alcohol, something he had in common with Robinson and something that made him a good candidate to follow the Dodgers' first baseman. Doby first heard about the Indians' interest in him in mid-June, and Veeck contacted the Manleys on July 1 to work out a deal for their second baseman. Unlike Rickey, Veeck respected the contract Doby had signed with the Eagles and intended to compensate the Manleys. He paid them $10,000 for Doby and promised them an additional $5,000 if Doby remained with the Indians. Effa Manley agreed to those terms; Doby played his final game with the Eagles on July 4 and hit a home run in his final at bat in the Negro Leagues. One day later, Doby arrived in Chicago to join the Indians in their series against the White Sox. Veeck met him at the airport, and a taxi took the two men to Comiskey Park. After a quick press conference, Doby went into the Indians clubhouse, donned his jersey, and walked onto the field as a member of the Cleveland Indians.

Not surprisingly, Veeck made bold and boastful claims when he addressed the press about Doby's signing. Veeck proclaimed Doby's signing signaled the start of a wide-open race to acquire the best talent from the Negro Leagues. He credited Robinson's success with the Dodgers for his decision to grab Doby in the middle of the season lest he allow another Major League franchise to acquire the talented second baseman. Additionally, Veeck saw talented players throughout the Negro Leagues and predicted the existence of a fully integrated Major Leagues within a decade. As he reasoned, Robinson's success and Doby's signing destroyed any relics of the old era in the Major Leagues, an era defined by a color line. While other executives stopped short of Veeck's bold claims, they did praise the signing. Rickey lauded Veeck for making a sound baseball decision and for signing a player who could help the fifth-place Indians in the second half of the season. None of the other owners in the American League tried to block Veeck from adding Doby, and the Senators' Griffith trotted out the old spin that a color barrier had never existed in the league.

Black newspapers joined in the praise directed at Veeck, and Robinson joined them in applauding Doby's arrival in the Major Leagues. Robinson warmly welcomed Doby to the Major Leagues, predicting that the newest member of the Indians would excel in his new challenge. He made a pledge of solidarity with Doby and promised that the two of them would work hard in order to ease the path to the Major Leagues for other black players. In its coverage of Doby's signing, the *Courier* revealed that Veeck had pledged to sign a black player in a meeting with the paper prior to the 1947 season. The newspapers' representatives at that meeting included managing editor William G. Nunn and Al Dunmore, the author of the article. At that meeting, representatives from the newspaper gave Veeck three names to consider—Doby; Monte Irvin, one of Doby's teammates with the Eagles; and Frank Austin of the Philadelphia Stars. Veeck promised to send his scouts to follow those three players, and he also revealed his plans for bringing a black player to the Indians. He criticized the way that Rickey handled Robinson, believing that the Dodgers' general manager put too much pressure on Robinson and engaged in too much fanfare. Instead of bringing a black player through the minors, Veeck insisted that he wanted to immediately add the player to the Indians' roster. Dunmore also revealed that Veeck wanted to add Irvin, but he could not work out a deal for both players at the same time. Dunmore lauded Veeck for his sincerity and predicted that the Indians' owner would soon sign another black player to join Doby on the Indians' roster.

In that same edition of the *Courier*, Smith revealed that Veeck had just barely beaten Rickey to signing Doby. According to Smith, Rickey had worked out a plan to sign Doby and send him to the Montreal Royals, the same plan he had enacted with Robinson. Though Doby did not realize it, the Dodgers had scouted him throughout the 1946 season. Doby also did not know about the Indians' interest in him until Jones, the team's public relations executive, approached him and said that he would join the team within one week. At first, Doby did not believe Jones and thought that someone had decided to play a joke on him. In the rest of his column, Smith related Veeck's plans to add Doby into the Indians' roster and that he tried to spin the Dodgers' failure to sign him in a positive light. The Dodgers had missed out on a good player, but having another team sign Doby actually helped the larger cause of bringing black players into the Major Leagues. Smith argued that Rickey gained an ally in Veeck and gained visible proof that he would not stand alone in using black players to help build winning teams. Veeck's actions, moreover, could help take some of the heat off Rickey and the Dodgers as they pursued the pennant.

Unfortunately for Doby, the warm feelings and support found in the sports pages did not filter into the Indians' clubhouse. Though Doby had played at second base for the Eagles, he could not play that position for the Indians. The Indians had an established second baseman, Joe Gordon, who had won the MVP award in 1942 as a member of the Yankees and made the 1947 All-Star team. It seemed likely that Doby would play at first base, an unfamiliar position for him, if he joined the Indians' regular starting lineup. The Indians, however, already had two established first baseman on the roster—Eddie Robinson and Les Fleming. In his haste to add Doby to the Indians' roster, Veeck had not consulted with the Indians player-manager, shortstop Lou Boudreau, about Doby's playing position. The suddenness of Doby's arrival, combined with the threat he posed to the playing time of two established members of the roster, created some iciness in the Indians' clubhouse. Boudreau met with his players and warned them against any agitation against Doby. He accompanied Doby as the ballplayer introduced himself to his new teammates, but he received a cold reception from Eddie Robinson and Fleming. Doby did not interact with any of his teammates as they warmed up on the field, and he sat by himself on the Indians' bench. Boudreau used Doby as a pinch-hitter in the seventh inning, and Doby struck out in his only at bat. When Doby returned to the dugout, two Chicago police officers, dressed in plain clothes, sat next to him to provide him with protection against any possible violence.

For the remainder of the season, the Indians rose from fifth to second place in the American League, but Doby struggled to secure an established place on the roster. He made only thirty-two plate appearances and finished the season with a .156 batting average, a far cry from the averages he had posted with the Eagles. Doby hit only one double; he did not hit any triples or home runs, and he accumulated only two RBIs. Like Robinson, Doby faced insults and harassment when he did make appearances in games, but he never reacted to the treatment. Despite Doby's performance on the field, Veeck remained committed to the ballplayer and to his plan to bring more black players to the Indians. Doby returned to the Indians' in the 1948 season, this time as an outfielder. With his new position, Doby joined the Indians' regular lineup and regained the form he had displayed with the Eagles. Along with Robinson, Doby helped to dispel the old myths that had blocked black players from the Major Leagues and helped to make the inclusion of black players seem normal.

On July 18, Robinson and Doby received some additional company in the Major Leagues when the St. Louis Browns signed Willard Brown and Henry Thompson. Both Brown and Thompson played for the Kansas City Monarchs, and the Monarchs co-owner Tom Baird made sure that he received compensation for his players. He did not want a repeat of what had happened when Rickey signed Robinson two years earlier. The Browns management paid the Monarchs $5,000 for both players, and that amount satisfied the understandably resentful Baird. Brown and Thompson, however, did not have the same impact that Robinson and Doby had with the Indians. The Browns represented an afterthought among St. Louis's baseball fans, and the presence of two black players did not draw more fans to the ballpark. Brown and Thompson did make history on July 20 when they became the first two black players to take the field at the same time in a Major League contest in the twentieth century. On August 13, Brown again made history when he hit his first home run, the first home run that a black player had ever hit in the history of the American League. By the end of August, however, the Browns released both players and returned them to the Monarchs. While Thompson would return to the Major Leagues in 1949 with the New York Giants, Brown never again played in a Major League game. Unlike the Dodgers and the Indians, the Browns did not seem serious about adding black players. They appeared to sign both Brown and Thompson as a publicity stunt, but abandoned that stunt when it failed to move the franchise out of the Cardinals' shadow.

ROBINSON CONTINUES TO IMPRESS

While those events unfolded in Cleveland and St. Louis, Robinson remained focused on his rookie campaign with the Dodgers and on helping the team win its elusive World Series title. Through July and August, as the Dodgers rose in the National League's standings, Robinson maintained a batting average near .300. He also continued to steal bases, including home, and ended the season by leading the National League in stolen bases with twenty-nine steals. His presence on the base paths helped the other batters in the Dodgers' lineup and provided a spark to the team's offense. Robinson also helped his team by playing good defense at first base; Pee Wee Reese and Eddie Stanky also played good defense and helped to prevent opposing teams from getting on base. With the departure of Kirby Higbe, Ralph Branca anchored the Dodgers' pitching staff and finished the season with twenty-one wins, the highest single-season win total of his career. In the outfield, Dixie Walker, the former anti-Robinson instigator, remained a key part of the Dodgers' lineup. Walker made the All-Star team on his way to a .306 batting average and thirty-one doubles. Since he batted behind Robinson in the lineup, Walker benefited from his teammate's ability to get on base, and he finished the season with ninety-four RBIs.

In addition to contributing to the Dodgers' on-field success, Robinson seemed to grow less isolated from his white teammates. Smith continued to travel with Robinson and reported that the rookie seemed more like a normal ballplayer, and not sideshow, as the season progressed. He reported on one incident that happened when the Dodgers arrived in Illinois for an exhibition game against one of the team's farm clubs. In the afternoon before the night game, many of the Dodgers decided to kill time by playing a round of golf. Smith and Robinson initially formed their own twosome on the course, but Reese later invited them to join his foursome. They finished the round playing with Reese, pitcher Rex Barney, team secretary Harold Parrott, and *New York Times* sportswriter Roscoe McGowan. Smith reported that Reese and Barney treated Robinson in the same manner as they treated their white teammates by joking with him as they completed their rounds. He also reported that Stanky helped Robinson with his defense at first base and provided him some advice on how to play against certain hitters. Another reporter, the *Boston Daily*'s Clif Keane, wrote about a conversation he had overheard involving Robinson and Walker. In the conversation, Walker advised Robinson to stop concentrating on pulling his hits to right field and try to hit the ball to the opposing field. If Robinson worked on hitting the ball the opposite way, he could confound opposing defenses and make it harder for opposing teams to position their fielders. Later in the season, Robinson fell into the Dodgers' dugout while catching a foul ball. He would have crashed onto the dugout floor, but Branca caught him before such a catastrophe could happen.

Even though Robinson seemed to settle in with his teammates, he still kept his distance, and he faced some hostility from opposing teams. During the second half of the season, the worst instance of hostility against Robinson happened in August in a game against the Cardinals at Ebbets Field. For both teams, the series carried postseason implications. The Dodgers had cooled off after their blistering July and had lost their comfortable lead in the National League standings. The Cardinals stood in second place and threatened to dash the Dodgers' hopes for the second consecutive season. The Dodgers won the first two games of the series, a doubleheader played on Monday, August 18, before nearly thirty-four thousand fans. In game three of the series, the Cardinals won by the score of 11–3. To close out the series on Wednesday, August 20, Shotton turned to his ace Branca to win the series and extend the Dodgers' lead over the Cardinals. Branca responded with a solid effort and held a 2–0 lead into the ninth inning. Shotton replaced Branca after the pitcher walked two men; his replacement, Hugh Casey, promptly surrendered the lead, and the game went into extra innings. In the eleventh inning, the Cardinals' Enos Slaughter came to the plate with Stan Musial on first base. Slaughter hit a ball down the first base line, which Robinson easily fielded; instead of throwing to second to try to nab Musial, Robinson stepped on first base to record the out. When Robinson stepped on first base, however, Slaughter spiked him by stepping on the back of his leg near his ankle. The incident could have seriously injured Robinson, possibly severing his Achilles tendon and sidelining him for the remainder of the season. Robinson did suffer a minor injury, and he remained at first base for the rest of the game.

The Cardinals prevailed in the twelfth inning, but the incident between Slaughter and Robinson overshadowed the game's outcome. To many who watched or covered the game, Slaughter deliberately stepped on Robinson's leg as he crossed first base. Slaughter had a reputation for playing hard, but not for playing dirty or for displaying racial animus toward Robinson. That did not stop Parrott from walking into the Cardinals' clubhouse after the game and confronting the players over Slaughter's conduct. Nothing happened after the incident. Robinson did not speak about the play, and no one issued any formal complaints to Frick or to Chandler. The Cardinals left Brooklyn to continue with the rest of their season, and the Dodgers opened a series against the Reds at Ebbets Field the day after the game. The incident, however, served as a reminder of the precarious situation facing Robinson every time he stepped onto the field. Pitchers threw at his head, and runners on the base paths would try to hurt him and prematurely end his rookie season. Robinson could not respond directly to any such incidents; he could respond only by playing well and helping the Dodgers expand their lead in the standings.

In late August, Rickey provided some help for both Robinson and the Dodgers' pitching staff by signing Dan Bankhead, the first African American pitcher in the Major Leagues. When he signed Bankhead, Rickey departed from the plan he had followed with Robinson, Campanella, and Newcombe. He provided Bankhead's Negro League team, the Memphis Red Sox, with financial compensation. He also sent Bankhead directly to Brooklyn, not to Montreal or one of the other farm clubs in the Dodgers' system. Rickey wanted Bankhead to bolster the Dodgers' pitching staff as the team made its final push for the pennant. With Bankhead on the roster, Rickey felt confident that he had someone who could come in from the bullpen and provide Shotton with another option for a reliever. Bankhead's presence also gave Rickey another roommate on road trips and someone who could understand the unique pressures black ballplayers faced in the Major Leagues.

Unfortunately, Bankhead failed to provide the stability that Rickey and Shotton sought from their relief pitchers. With the Memphis Red Sox, Bankhead had an impressive 11–5 record with 124 strikeouts. Those stats, however, did not transfer to his brief time with the Dodgers. On August 26, Bankhead made his first appearance with the Dodgers in his first official game with the club. He appeared in relief for starting pitcher Hal Gregg, who surrendered six earned runs and five hits in only one inning of work against the Pirates. Bankhead pitched for three and one-third innings, surrendering ten hits and eight earned runs. The twenty-four thousand fans who sat in Ebbets Field's seats saw the Dodgers lose to the lowly Pirates by the score of 16–3. Those fans, however, did witness history when Bankhead came to bat in the second inning against the Pirates' starter Fritz Ostermueller. Bankhead hit a two-run home run for his first-ever hit in the Major Leagues and joined a small club of ballplayers who hit a home run for their first Major League hits. For the rest of the season, Bankhead would appear as a reliever in only four games, pitching in a total of ten innings and compiling a record of 0–0. He finished the season with an unimpressive ERA of 7.50 and did not return to the Dodgers' roster in the 1948 season. Bankhead would not make another appearance in the Major Leagues until the 1950 season when he returned to the Dodgers and appeared in forty-one games. He finished the 1950 season with a record of 9–4 and an ERA of 5.50. In 1951, he appeared in fourteen games for the Dodgers before the team released him, and the release effectively ended his Major League career.

ONTO THE WORLD SERIES

Bankhead's struggles did not deter the Dodgers from their path to the postseason and a date with the crosstown rivals, New York Yankees. On Sunday, September 28, the Dodgers closed out their 1947 season with a record of 94–60, good enough for a five-game lead over the Cardinals and the rest of the National League. The Dodgers captured the National League pennant for only the fourth time in the team's history; the team had previously won the pennant in 1916, 1920, and 1941. In those years, the Dodgers lost the World Series to the Boston Red Sox, the Cleveland Indians, and the Yankees. The Yankees loomed again as the Dodgers' last obstacle to a World Series title. Both the Dodgers and the Yankees led their respective leagues in attendance. With their 97–57 record, the Yankees finished twelve games ahead of their nearest rivals, the Detroit Tigers, in the American League standings. The Yankees had won ten World Series titles, the most in the Major Leagues, and boasted an impressive lineup that included players such as Joe DiMaggio and Phil Rizzuto. They also had a promising young catcher, Lawrence Peter "Yogi" Berra, who had appeared in eighty-three games and would appear in six of the seven games in the World Series. Most importantly, the Yankees carried an aura that the Dodgers lacked. The Dodgers had earned the nickname of "the Bums." The Yankees had already constructed the multigenerational dynasty that continues to define the franchise in the early twenty-first century. Yankee Stadium stood as hallowed grounds in the Bronx; creaky old Ebbets Field stood crammed into a city block in Brooklyn. Despite their similar records, the two franchises seemed like a mismatch, and the Dodgers seemed headed into more postseason disappointment.

Prior to the start of the series, the Dodgers' players and fans exuded confidence and excitement. Robinson and the rest of the Dodgers appeared in a parade through Brooklyn's Flatbush Avenue and Fulton Street. The players sat in convertibles and waved to the cheering crowds. Robinson had another reason to celebrate; he had won the Rookie of the Year Award in the first year that the Baseball Writers Association of America (BBWAA) gave the award. Previously, only the Chicago chapter of BBWAA endowed a player with the award. Ironically, Robinson and Walker, who had asked for a trade in spring training, addressed the gathered crowd. For Robinson and Rachel, the World Series acted like a long-anticipated and needed family reunion. Both Mallie Robinson and Zelle Isum took their first airplane rides and joined their children, as well as their grandson, in New York City. Robinson also enjoyed the company of his older brother Mack, and the couple could socialize with the other Dodgers' players and their wives while family members took care of Jackie Jr.

On September 30, before a crowd of over seventy-three thousand fans at Yankee Stadium, Robinson made history again when he became the first African American to appear in a World Series game. The 1947 World Series included another historical first—it marked the first time that the World Series games appeared on television. Those broadcasts brought the series to more fans who could not travel to either the Bronx or Brooklyn and watch the games in person. Due to the historical nature of the series, the first game attracted an array of celebrities and other important figures. An ailing Babe Ruth, who would die of cancer within a year, attended the first game at the stadium where he had once brought fans to their feet. The suspended Leo Durocher, along with his actress wife Larraine Day, joined Chandler, Frick, and other distinguished baseball celebrities in the seats. New York City Mayor William O'Dwyer, who tossed the ceremonial first pitch, stayed to watch the game. U.S. secretary of state George C. Marshall, New York Governor Thomas Dewey, Senator Irving Ives, and future Secretary of State John Foster Dulles added to the special atmosphere in Yankee Stadium. The first game also attracted African Americans from across the country who came to root for Robinson and to witness the best argument to date that black players belonged in the Major Leagues.

Though the Dodgers lost game one by the score of 5–3, Robinson electrified the crowd and made a lasting impression on those who watched the game. As he had done during the regular season, Robinson batted second in the starting lineup, so he made his first appearance in the World Series in the top of the first inning. The lead-off hitter, Stanky, flew out to left field. Robinson calmly walked up to the plate and worked a walk-off of the starting pitcher, Spec Shea. He then stole second thanks to his speed and slightly late throw from Berra. Pete Reiser followed Robinson to the plate and hit a ball that Shea fielded. Robinson misread the hit; Shea and Rizzuto, the Yankees' shortstop, caught Robinson in a rundown between second and third base. Robinson, however, extended the rundown long enough to allow Reiser to reach second base; though Rizzuto eventually tagged out Robinson, Reiser scored on a misplayed fly ball that Walker hit to the left fielder. Robinson's actions had helped the Dodgers secure an early lead in game one. During his next at bat, Robinson again reached base and energized the crowd with his aggressive style. Unfortunately, Branca surrendered the lead in the fifth inning, the only inning in which the Yankees scored any runs, and the Dodgers never recovered.

The second game of the World Series brought more disappointment for the Dodgers, who lost by the embarrassing score of 10–3. Starting pitcher Vic Lombardi lasted only four innings; he surrendered five earned runs while receiving only two runs of support from his offense. Stanky and Reiser committed errors. The game, though, featured some history as Robinson collected his first hit, a single, in the third inning. He notched another hit, a double, in the eighth inning, but his offense failed to spark the rest of the lineup. As the series moved from the Bronx to Brooklyn, the Dodgers faced the reality that most teams with a 2–0 lead in the World Series went on to win the series. The Dodgers needed a change in venue, among other things, to turn the series around and to give their fans the title they had long desired.

Ebbets Field hosted near-capacity crowds in game three, game four, and game five of the World Series, and the large home crowd helped the Dodgers even the series. The Dodgers won game three by a score of 9–8 thanks to multiple-hit games from Robinson, Walker, and Spider Jorgensen. The same pitching issues that had pushed Rickey to sign Bankhead, who had made the only appearance as a pinch-hitter in the World Series, continued to plague the Dodgers. Starter Joe Hatten lasted for only four and one-third innings, and Branca had to come in from the bullpen to provide some relief. In game four, the Yankees jumped to an early 1–0 lead, leading Shotton to remove the starter Harry Taylor from the game before he had recorded an out. The Yankees added another run in the fourth inning, but the Dodgers' pitcher held them scoreless for the remainder of the game. In the bottom of the ninth inning, the Dodgers scored two runs thanks to a game-winning hit from little-used pinch hitter Cookie Lavagetto. The improbable victory gave Brooklyn's long-suffering fans hope that 1947 finally represented the Dodgers' year. In game five, however, the Dodgers' offense disappeared, and the Yankees regained the lead in the series with a 2–1 victory. To help spark the Dodgers' offense, Shotton moved Robinson from second to fourth in the lineup, but the rookie went hitless in game five. Robinson also faced racial taunts from the Yankees, taunts that rivaled the invective Chapman and the Phillies hurled at him earlier in the season. As he did in the past, Robinson never responded to the taunts and tried to keep his focus on prolonging the World Series.

The final two games at Yankee Stadium provided both a tease for Dodgers' fans and more heartbreak. Robinson batted third in the Dodgers' lineup in game six, and he helped to lead an offensive explosion. The Dodgers leapt to an early 4–0 lead by scoring two runs in both the first and third innings; they added four more runs in the sixth inning and counted on their bullpen to hold the lead for the rest of the game. The Yankees tied the game in the bottom of the third inning and added another run in the fourth inning. In the bottom of the ninth inning, the Yankees scored one run, but the Dodgers held on for an 8–6 victory. Game seven pitted Shea, starting his third game of the series, against Hal Gregg, who had pitched well in game four. Neither pitcher dominated the opposition; Shea left the game in the second inning, while Shotton pulled Gregg in the third inning. The Yankees won by the score of 5–2, leaving the Dodgers tantalizingly and disappointingly short of their first World Series. After the game, the despondent Dodgers retreated to the visitor's clubhouse and said their goodbyes. In contrast to the atmosphere at the start of the season, the white Dodgers approached Robinson and congratulated him on his rookie season. Robinson had earned the respect and admiration of his teammates, and the moment provided some hope for the first baseman as he looked ahead to his second season.

THE STATE OF AFFAIRS AT THE END OF THE SEASON

Overall, Robinson had a successful rookie season. He finished the regular season with a well-earned Rookie of the Year Award thanks to his .297 batting average, twenty-nine stolen bases, twenty-eight sacrifice bunts, .810 on-base plus slugging percentage, and strong defense at first base. In the World Series, Robinson played in all seven games of the World Series and had a .259 batting average to go along with his seven hits and three RBIs. Aside from those stats, Robinson brought a different style of play to the Dodgers and to the rest of the Major Leagues. His threat to steal bases constantly challenged opposing teams and often flustered opposing pitchers and catchers. More importantly, Robinson dispelled all the old myths that sustained the color barrier in the Major Leagues. He proved that black players could compete at the Major League level and could withstand the challenges of a full season. By the time of the 1947 season, five African Americans had appeared in the Major Leagues—Robinson, Doby, Brown, Thompson, and Bankhead. Campanella and Newcombe had compiled good seasons in the Dodgers' farm system, and Campanella seemed likely to join Robinson on the Dodgers in the 1948 season. Robinson and other black players still faced hostility, but the era of segregated baseball had ended. The segregation also ended in the press box; Smith moved into a new job covering baseball for the *Chicago American*, a white newspaper, while he still worked for the *Courier*. His move to a white newspaper presaged his membership in the BBWAA in 1948, the first time that the organization welcomed a black sportswriter. The year 1947 marked a season of progress for the Major Leagues; future years would measure the pace of that progress as the Major Leagues underwent other changes that altered the shape of the sport.

Outside of Robinson, the Dodgers, and the Major Leagues, signs of progress appeared that seemed to foretell the end of segregation in other aspects of American society. On December 5, 1946, President Harry Truman issued Executive Order 9808 to create a President's Committee on Civil Rights. Truman sought to use an Executive Order, rather than press Congress to act, because he knew that members of his Democratic Party from the South would block any legislation related to civil rights. The experiences of African Americans during World War II and concerns about the continuation of legalized segregation in the United States compelled Truman to issue his order and create his committee. The committee published its report, *To Secure These Rights*, in December 1947, a few months after the Dodgers lost in the World Series. In the lengthy report, the committee outlined how the promise of freedom and equality stood at the heart of the American experience and outlined the specific rights guaranteed to all Americans. The report further detailed how segregation denied African Americans the basic rights, how the government best secured the rights of all Americans, and how the present time represented the best time for the federal government to promote the rights of African Americans. In its recommendations, the committee urged the federal government to take specific and concrete steps, such as by establishing a permanent Committee on Civil Rights, designed to secure basic rights for African Americans and to end legalized forms of discrimination.

TRUMAN AND CIVIL RIGHTS

When Harry Truman used his presidential power to support civil rights, he took a gamble and risked his ability to win his own term in the 1948 election. Franklin Roosevelt won four terms on the backs of a "New Deal Coalition," a coalition of voters that included a significant number of white prosegregation southerners. In the absence of another viable coalition, Truman would need support from that same coalition in order to win his own term as president of the United States.

Events at the 1948 Democratic National Convention seemed to foreshadow Truman's loss in the November election. At the convention, the delegates endorsed a ticket of Truman and Alben Barkley, a U.S. Senator from Kentucky. The delegates also endorsed a platform that included support for civil rights; such a platform appealed to Truman and to northern Democrats such as Hubert H. Humphrey of Minnesota. Southern Democrats, such as Senator Strom Thurmond of South Carolina, walked out of the convention in protest. They established the short-lived States' Rights Democratic Party; Thurmond and Governor Fielding L. Wright of Mississippi ran on that party's ticket in the 1948 election. Thurmond, Wright, and their supporters, dubbed the Dixiecrats, wanted to assert the power and influence of southerners within the Democratic Party. The Dixiecrats hoped to create a situation where none of the nominees won the needed number of votes in the Electoral College. In such a situation, the election would go to the House of Representatives, and each state delegation would cast one vote. At that point, the Dixiecrats hoped that they could use their votes in the House to make deals and sway the Democratic Party away from civil rights.

Early returns on Election Day looked bad for Truman and favorable for the Republican Party's nominee, Thomas Dewey. Based upon those early returns, the *Chicago Tribune* published a front-page headline "Dewey Defeats Truman." Later returns, however, decisively swung the election in Truman's favor. The Dixiecrats won the electoral vote in only four states, not nearly enough to throw the election to the House. Truman's victory on a civil rights platform foreshadowed a realignment that would shape American politics in the late twentieth century. The victory also gave Truman an endorsement for his support of civil rights and helped to move the country forward on that issue.

In the middle of the twentieth century, baseball remained the American pastime, and changes in the game often reflected changes in the broader American society. Baseball's unmistakable segregation reflected the unmistakable and legalized segregation of American society that began in late nineteenth century. The ending of segregation in baseball, therefore, did not occur in a vacuum. Since segregation had ended in the Major Leagues, it seemed likely that it would disappear from other areas of American society. The process would not move easily or quickly; the majority of Major League organizations remained stubbornly all white, and racial taunts followed Robinson all the way into the World Series. Integration, however, would continue to move across the Major Leagues as it moved within American society over the next decade. By the time the tenth anniversary of Robinson's debut passed, both the Major Leagues and American society had undergone significant changes. Those changes happened gradually, yet they happened and created a world in which segregated sports seemed like a relic from a distant age.

8

The Major Leagues Are a-Changin'

Jackie Robinson spent his entire career in the Major Leagues with the Brooklyn Dodgers. His last appearance for the Dodgers came in game seven of the 1956 World Series, a game that the Dodgers again lost to the New York Yankees. While Robinson's skills had diminished, his legacy upon the world of baseball and the broader American society remained evident. Black players had appeared on the rosters of all but three Major League franchises. The three holdouts—the Detroit Tigers, Philadelphia Phillies, and Boston Red Sox—would finally add black players by the end of the decade. With the prevalence of black players in the Major Leagues, the Negro Leagues faded from relevancy and from existence. All semblance of league play disappeared in the late 1940s, and most all-black teams folded in the 1950s. Outside of baseball, the civil rights movement marched on and scored some significant achievements, most notably the *Brown vs. Board* Supreme Court ruling that struck down segregation in public education. While Robinson did not yet fully immerse himself in the civil rights movement, he did take the first steps into the realm of political activism and demonstrated a willingness to use his fame to address political as well as social issues. Robinson himself embodied the reality that the United States stood on the precipice of change—that change that would seek to address the shortcomings of the Reconstruction Era and would make the promise of America's founding ideals available to all Americans.

ROBINSON LOOKS AHEAD AND GETS DISTRACTED

During the 1947 off-season, Robinson turned his focus away from baseball and toward projects designed to maximize his moneymaking ability. Similarly to other Major Leaguers in the early stages of their careers, Robinson made a modest salary and lacked leverage to demand a significant raise from his team. Rickey also had a well-earned reputation for paying his players small salaries and for turning aside demands for large raises. Instead of hoping for a significant raise from Rickey, Robinson decided to leverage his fame into endorsements and use that money to help establish his family's financial security. He hired an agent, Jules Ziegler of the General Artists Corporation, who helped him secure endorsements for Borden's Milk, Homogenized Bond Bread, and Old Gold Cigarettes. In addition to those endorsements, Robinson scored a deal to appear in *Courage*, a film with an all-black production and acting crew. That film project never materialized, yet it showed that Robinson sought opportunities well outside of the baseball world. Robinson's agent also helped him obtain a deal for Wendell Smith to write his biography and for the ballplayer to appear in vaudeville shows in several cities, including New York. Those deals demonstrated that Robinson recognized the limits of his baseball career. He could earn only limited yearly annual salaries with the Dodgers, and he could play baseball for only a limited number of years. Robinson knew that he needed to think beyond his baseball career and consider how he could make money in ways that did not require him to play baseball.

Robinson's focus on maximizing his moneymaking potential extended into the early months of 1948, distracting him from the upcoming baseball season. In December, a surgery to remove a bone spur from his left ankle temporarily made Robinson dependent upon crutches. The surgery and the recovery kept Robinson away from most physical activity. As he recovered, Robinson decided to expand the vaudeville show from the original four northern cities to southern cities. People in each southern city that Robinson toured feted the ballplayer with good Southern hospitality. The combined lack of physical activity and the indulgences in Southern food led Robinson to experience a sudden weight gain. By the time he left for spring training, Robinson saw his weight balloon to over two hundred pounds. In addition to those distractions, Robinson dealt with the sudden loss of Rev. Karl Downs, one of the people who served as a father figure to him during his adolescent years. Overall, Robinson's off-season both demonstrated his potential outside of the baseball world and tested his ability to balance his responsibilities to the Dodgers with those other interests. At one point, Robinson missed a planned event with Branch Rickey because of the movie project that never happened. He later attended another event in place of the one he missed, yet the incident caused some friction with

Rickey right at the time that he negotiated his 1948 contract. Those incidents established some bad omens for the 1948 season, a season in which the Dodgers yet again hoped to notch their long-elusive first World Series.

Unfortunately for Robinson and the Dodgers, the 1948 season had an inauspicious start. As part of his negotiation for a better contract, second baseman Eddie Stanky refused to report to spring training. Rickey traded him to the Boston Braves, thereby opening the spot for Robinson. Robinson, however, faced the wrath of manager Leo Durocher, who had returned to the club after serving his suspension. Durocher publicly criticized Robinson for his weight gain and challenged him to hit more balls to the opposite field. To Durocher, Robinson pulled too many balls to left field and, therefore, limited his potential as a hitter. Robinson did respond to Durocher's challenges and shed most of the unhealthy weight he had gained in the off-season. He also made a seamless transition to second base and developed a strong chemistry with shortstop Pee Wee Reese. Another positive sign came from the housing available to the Dodgers' players at their spring training site, Ciudad Trujillo in the Dominican Republic. Unlike in the previous year, Robinson and the other black ballplayers stayed in the same hotel as their white teammates. Robinson and the Dodgers, however, faced a scare on their plane trip from the Dominican Republic to the United States. One of the plane's engines failed, and the other came close to failing. Luckily, the pilot managed to avoid a disaster and safely returned the plane to the airport. The team later reached the United States and completed the spring training schedule with a tour through southern states.

The rockiness that Robinson and the Dodgers experienced in spring training translated into a disappointing 1948 season. In the early months of the new season, Robinson struggled to lose the remaining pounds he had gained in the off-season, and he did not play at the same levels he had enjoyed during the previous year. At one point, Durocher benched Robinson, and Rickey put him on waivers, meaning that any of the other fifteen clubs could claim him and add him to their rosters. None of the other clubs put in a claim, and Robinson remained with the Dodgers. In the middle of the season, Rickey made another shocking move by trading Durocher to the New York Giants and reinstituting Burt Shotton as the Dodgers' field manager. At the time of the trade, the Dodgers stood mired in the bottom half of the National League and seemed destined to finish the season with a losing record. Robinson and the rest of the Dodgers, however, responded positively to Shotton's return and finished July standing in third place. The Dodgers flirted with first place in late August and early September, but they ultimately finished the season behind the Boston Braves and St. Louis Cardinals. The third place finish left the Dodgers and their fans with no choice but to look ahead to the 1949 season and to hope that 1949 would finally represent the Dodgers' year.

For Robinson, the 1948 season fell short of his rookie campaign, yet he still attained some notable achievements. The strong chemistry he developed with Reese persisted into the regular season, and the two formed one of the most formidable double-play combinations in the National League. After his stint on waivers, Robinson turned his season around and finished as the team's offensive leader in several categories, including batting average and RBIs. He did not make the All-Star Game, nor did he get much attention in the MVP voting. Robinson did further establish himself as an everyday Major League ballplayer, and he showed some signs that the deal he had made with Rickey back in August 1945 had run its course. During a game in Pittsburgh in late August, Robinson notched his first career ejection following an argument with the umpires over the ejection of his teammate Bruce Edwards. More importantly, Robinson gained an African American teammate who had the talent to remain in the Major Leagues— Roy Campanella. Campanella did not equal Robinson's Rookie of the Year season, but he did show flashes of the talent that would make him one of the best catchers in the Major Leagues. Despite its rocky moments, the 1948 season did provide Robinson with some opportunities to build upon his rookie campaign. Like the rest of his team, Robinson could look forward to the 1949 season with a renewed focus on baseball and on bringing Brooklyn its elusive World Series crown.

MORE DIVERSITY IN THE MAJOR LEAGUES

Outside of Brooklyn, the Cleveland Indians remained the only other Major League team to carry and play at least one black player on its roster in the 1948 season. After his disappointing rookie season, Doby returned to the Indians as an everyday player in the outfield. His place in the starting lineup, as opposed to his role as a bench player and pinch hitter, helped him regain the success he had with the Newark Eagles. Doby finished the season with a .301 batting average and sixty-six RBIs, a significant improvement over his .156 batting average and two RBIs from his rookie season. He had the third-highest batting average on the team, behind only Lou Boudreau and his fellow outfielder Dale Mitchell. Doby's offensive performance helped the Indians win over one hundred games and capture first place in the American League. In the World Series against the Boston Braves, Doby made history when he hit a home run, making him the first African American to hit a home run in the World Series. He finished the World Series with a .318 batting average, the highest on the team. The Indians won the World Series in six games, thereby making Doby the first African American position player to win a World Series title. His teammate, the legendary Satchel Paige, joined Doby in making history as the first African American pitcher to win a World Series title.

Paige's arrival in Cleveland during the 1948 season demonstrated Bill Veeck's commitment to follow in Rickey's footsteps and build a winning integrated team. His debut with the Indians came on July 9, 1948, two days after his forty-second birthday. Paige's debut in the Major Leagues also came twenty-two years after his professional debut with the Chattanooga White Sox, a club that played in the Negro Southern League. The forty-two-year-old rookie started seven games for the Indians in the second half of the 1948 season. Paige finished with a record of 6–1 and a paltry ERA of 2.48. While he faced only two batters in the World Series, his pitching in the regular season helped the Indians stay ahead of the Boston Red Sox and the rest of the American League. Paige's 6–1 record and 2.48 ERA marked the best winning percentage and ERA of his six-year career in the Major Leagues. He arrived too late to make the 1948 All-Star Team in the American League, but his performance did attract some attention in the Rookie of the Year balloting. Together with Doby, Paige further dispelled the myth that black players would breed disharmony on Major League rosters, which helped to prove that integration represented a pathway to success. Both men celebrated winning the World Series, the last one Cleveland won in the twentieth century, with their white teammates and with their black as well as white fans.

In 1949, three new faces joined Robinson, Campanella, Doby, and Paige as African Americans on Major League clubs—Luke Easter, Monford Merrill "Monte" Irvin, and Don Newcombe. All three players spent time in the Negro Leagues, and all three left indelible marks upon Major League Baseball in the 1950s. Easter, who played for the Homestead Grays, joined the Indians' Minor League team in San Diego and emerged as a sensation in the Pacific Coast League. Injuries marred the early part of his career in Cleveland, but he quickly endeared himself to the fans, and he developed a reputation as a home run hitter. Newcombe pitched for the Dodgers and helped to add to the franchise's reputation as a top destination for black ballplayers. While he played for the Dodgers' farm team in Nashua, New Hampshire, he and Campanella formed the first all-African American battery. He joined the Dodgers late in the 1949 season and had an important role in the teams' run at its elusive first World Series title. A stint in the United States Army during the Korean War interrupted Newcombe's career, and he won only nine games in 1954, the year he returned from his army service. In the next two seasons, however, Newcombe again excelled as one of the National League's top starting pitchers. He won a league-high twenty-seven games in Robinson's last season and cemented his place as one of the top pitchers in the Dodgers' history.

Among those three players, Irvin had the rockiest path to the Major Leagues. Born in February 1919, Irvin had a background similar to Doby's, his former teammate on the Newark Eagles. Like Doby, Irvin's family moved from the South to New Jersey, and Irvin excelled at multiple sports in high school. When he first joined the Eagles in 1937, the eighteen-year-old Irvin played under an alias in order to protect his amateur status. Irvin remained with the Eagles until the 1942 season when a salary dispute with Effa Manley led him to play for a team in the Mexican League. After serving with the army in Europe during World War II, Irvin returned to the Eagles and formed a dominant double-play combination with Doby during the team's championship 1946 season. Irvin's success caught the attention of Branch Rickey, who wanted to sign him without paying Manley the $5,000 she demanded. Since Rickey held Irvin's rights, no other team could sign him, and Irvin continued to play for the Eagles. In 1949, Rickey finally relinquished Irvin's rights, and Irvin promptly signed a contract with the New York Giants. Irvin joined the New York Giants on July 8; on the same day, the Giants also added Hank Thompson, one of the players whom St. Louis Browns had briefly employed in the 1947 season. The two men represented the first two African Americans to play for the Giants. Coincidentally, Leo Durocher, the man who was supposed to serve as Robinson's first manager with the Dodgers, worked as the Giants' manager and helped to ease both Irvin's and Thompson's arrival. With Irvin and Thompson on the Giants, seven African Americans played in the Major Leagues in the 1949 season. Although the pace of reintegration moved slowly between 1947 and 1949, it moved forward and provided hope that it would continue into the next decade. The progress also opened the door to other players whom the league did not welcome prior to 1947, players who would join African Americans in transforming the sport.

Near the end of the 1949 season, the same season in which Easter, Irvin, and Newcombe joined their respective Major League teams, a Cuban-born player, Saturnino Orestes Armas "Minnie" Minoso, also joined the Major Leagues. Due to the color of Minoso's skin, he would have faced the same ban that African Americans ballplayers faced until Robinson's signing in October 1945. Born in 1922, Minoso played baseball in his native Cuba and in the United States for the New York Cubans. While playing for the Cubans, Minoso caught Bill Veeck's attention, and Veeck added him to the Indians' farm system. Minoso played in only a handful of games for the Indians before the franchise traded him to the Chicago White Sox. He represented the first black player to join the White Sox's roster. Starting in 1951, Minoso's talents matured, and he ranked as one of the top hitters in the American League for most of the decade. He came in second place in the 1951 Rookie of the Year vote, and he made regular appearances in the annual Major League All-Star Game. More importantly, Minoso's presence helped to open the door to more Latino players who, along with a larger group of African Americans, helped to quicken the pace of baseball's reintegration in the 1950s.

Starting in 1950, the pace of African Americans and Latinos joining Major League teams increased and expanded beyond Cleveland and New York City. Sam Jethroe joined the Boston Braves in April 1950; one year later, Luis Marquez joined the Braves while Ray Noble, Artie Wilson, and Willie Mays joined the Giants. Mays, Irvin, and Thompson made history in October 1951 when they formed the first all–African American outfield in Major League history. The 1953 and 1954 seasons witnessed six Major League teams adding their first black players. Those teams included the Pittsburgh Pirates, St. Louis Cardinals, Washington Senators, the Philadelphia Athletics, and the Cincinnati Reds. The Cubs added Ernie Banks in 1953, who would go on to become a Hall of Famers and one of the most popular players at every play for the franchise. After resisting calls for integration for many years, the New York Yankees finally added their first black player, Elston Howard, in 1955. By the time Robinson retired at the end of the 1956 season, the Major Leagues boasted approximately seventy African American and Latino players across thirteen of the sixteen franchises. The presence of so many nonwhite players did not signal the end of racism in professional baseball, but it did signal that Robinson had ushered in a new era in Major League Baseball. That era had opened the doors to players who would challenge long-held records and lead to bigger shifts in American society.

The African American and Latino players who joined the Major Leagues in the 1950s had careers of varying lengths and experienced varying degrees of success. Mays and Banks had careers that merited induction into the Baseball Hall of Fame; Mays still has the reputation as one of the greatest all-time Major League players. Henry "Hank" Aaron and Roberto Clemente, who joined the Major Leagues in 1954 and 1955, respectively, also compiled Hall of Fame careers. Aaron eventually broke Babe Ruth's all-time home run record, and Clemente dazzled both at the plate and in the outfield. Clemente's untimely death in 1972 has added to his legacy both in Pittsburgh and across the Major Leagues. While Mays, Banks, and Aaron spent some time in the Negro Leagues prior to joining the Major Leagues, Clemente moved into the Pirates system without a stop in the Negro Leagues. Other players who started their careers in the 1950s—including Frank Robinson and Curt Flood—similarly skipped the Negro Leagues. That development further weakened the already beleaguered all-black baseball teams and helped ensure that such teams would not survive in the era of a reintegrated Major Leagues.

THE END COMES FOR THE NEGRO LEAGUES

In hindsight, Robinson's signing with the Dodgers in October 1945 marked the beginning of the end of the Negro Leagues. Rickey's refusal to pay

FRANK ROBINSON AND CURT FLOOD

Both Frank Robinson and Curt Flood owed their careers to Jackie Robinson, and they symbolized the remarkable changes in Major League Baseball that came in Jackie Robinson's wake. Neither Frank Robinson nor Flood played in the Negro Leagues on their way to the Major Leagues. Frank Robinson made his debut with the Cincinnati Reds in 1956 and played for that team through the end of the 1965 season. Afterward, Frank Robinson played for the Baltimore Orioles, Los Angeles Dodgers, and California Angels before ending his career with the Cleveland Indians in 1976. Most notably, during the 1975 and 1976 seasons, the Indians employed him as a player-manager, making him the first African American field manager in the Major Leagues. He continued to manage the Indians into the 1977 season; he later managed the San Francisco Giants and Baltimore Orioles before taking a job as the Major Leagues' Director of Discipline. He returned to managing in 2002 when he joined the Montreal Expos and followed them to Washington, D.C., when they became the Nationals in 2004. He managed them through the end of the 2006 season and finishing with a record of over 1,000 wins as a manager.

Curt Flood changed history in a different way. Like Frank Robinson, Flood joined the Cincinnati Reds in the 1956 season; he played for the Reds for two seasons before a trade sent him to the St. Louis Cardinals. Until the end of the 1969 season, Flood remained with the Cardinals and enjoyed an impressive career that included three appearances in the All-Star Game and two World Series titles. After the 1969 season, however, Flood made his lasting impact upon the game. The Cardinals included him in a trade to the Philadelphia Phillies, a franchise still tainted by its treatment of Robinson in the 1947 season and its reluctance to sign African American players. Flood could not refuse the trade due to the reserve clause in all Major League contracts, but he refused to report to the Phillies and asked Commissioner Bowie Kuhn to declare him a free agent. Kuhn refused Flood's request, and Flood subsequently sued Kuhn in a case that reached the United States Supreme Court. In 1972, the Supreme Court ruled in favor of Major League Baseball, and the reserve clause remained a feature of Major League contracts.

Even though Flood lost his lawsuit, his actions led to significant changes in the relationship between players and franchise owners. His actions strengthened the Major League Baseball Players' Association, a union founded in 1966 under the tutelage of Marvin Miller. Miller used Flood's example to press other players, Andy Messersmith and Dave McNally, to declare themselves free agents. Miller's efforts worked, and the dawn of free agency ended the reserve clause and gave players the power Flood sought in his dispute with the Cardinals.

compensation to the Kansas City Monarchs, combined with his dismissal of the Negro Leagues as a legitimate organization and Robinson's own antipathy toward the Negro Leagues, gave the Negro Leagues a reputation that they could never shed. The Negro Leagues' irreversible decline coincided with Robinson's debut with the Dodgers in April 1947. While Negro Leagues franchises enjoyed a successful 1946 season, the 1947 season brought many empty seats in ballparks and a marked decline in interest. At the end of the 1948 season, the Negro National League dissolved as its best franchises, the Homestead Grays and Newark Eagles, effectively went out of business. The Grays tried to operate as a barnstorming team for one season before folding for good, while the Eagles franchise moved to Houston before finally dissolving. With the demise of the Negro National League, the remaining teams went into a revamped Negro American League, but any semblance of league-based competition disappeared. More teams went out of business in the 1950s as the number of black and Latino players in the Major Leagues steadily increased. The Negro American League ceased operations in 1958; the Indianapolis Clowns remained the last all-black team in professional baseball, but the team did not play competitive baseball. Instead, the franchise operated like a sideshow before finally folding in the 1960s.

Few if any people mourned the loss of the Negro Leagues, but their passing closed a chapter in American sports history. In spite of their problems, the Negro Leagues provided many opportunities for African American ballplayers and entrepreneurs at a time when African Americans had limited opportunities in American society. While the Major Leagues opened their doors to African American players and scouts, they did not hire African American coaches, field managers, or executives. The inclusion of nonwhite coaches, managers, and executives would not commence for several decades after Robinson's debut. Ironically, the demise of the Negro Leagues stood as a reminder of a paradox at the heart of some of the progress toward integration. Integration led to the closure of some of the institutions, such as the Negro Leagues, that offered opportunities for African American talent and gave African American entrepreneurs outlets to build their capital. Such options did not readily exist in predominantly white institutions, such as the Major Leagues, that opened their doors to African Americans as part of the integration process.

THE MOST VALUABLE PLAYER

As those changes happened in Major League Baseball and in the Negro Leagues, Robinson continued his career with the Dodgers. After a disappointing 1948 season, Robinson stayed away from the many banquets and nonbaseball opportunities that greeted him after his rookie season. He joined Campanella on a barnstorming tour and worked as a coach and counselor for a YMCA branch in Harlem. Robinson did take advantage of one nonbaseball opportunity; he signed a contract to broadcast a fifteen-minute show six days per week on WMCA, an independent radio station based in New York City. That contract showed that Robinson devoted part of his attention to his life beyond baseball, and he recognized that he occupied a role beyond that of a baseball player. Ironically, Robinson's contract coincided with a shift in his relationship with the white sportswriters who covered him throughout the baseball season. During spring training, Robinson and a Minor League pitcher, Chris Van Cuyk, got into a heated argument after Van Cuyk almost hit Robinson in retaliation for a comment the second baseman had made earlier in an intrasquad scrimmage. Though Robinson and Van Cuyk apologized to each other for their actions, sportswriters used the story to depict Robinson as a troublemaker. The story came on the heels of a story from Herb Goren in which he accurately quoted Robinson as welcoming roughness from opposing teams because he wanted to play rough against them. A meeting with Commissioner Happy Chandler absolved Robinson of any insinuation that he issued a threat against the entire league. Robinson, though, resented the fact that sportswriters had misinterpreted his words and used an unrelated incident to paint him as an agitator.

Robinson's soured relationship with the press extended to black sportswriters, specifically to Wendell Smith. After the 1948 season, Robinson wrote an article for *Ebony* in which he shared his negative views on his time with the Kansas City Monarchs. His words rankled Effa Manley and others associated with the Negro Leagues. His words, moreover, came from him, not from Smith. The sportswriter had long served as ghostwriter for Robinson; he penned the regular columns in the *Pittsburgh Courier* that allegedly came from the second baseman. After the incidents in spring training, Smith penned a column in which he chastised Robinson for his ingratitude. As Smith reasoned, black sportswriters like himself had pressed for the reintegration of the Major Leagues. They had, in other words, made it possible for Robinson to join the Dodgers and to enjoy the lifestyle he had enjoyed as a Major League ballplayer. Smith, therefore, reasoned that Robinson owed a debt of gratitude, not resentment, to the sportswriters who covered the Dodgers and who served as his conduit to his fans.

The incidents during Spring Training spoke to a deeper truth about Robinson as he embarked upon the 1949 season—he no longer needed to adhere to the plan Rickey had outlined four years earlier. Rickey believed that the reintegration of baseball would fail if Robinson fought back against the inevitable harassment he would face with the Dodgers. Robinson went along with the plan and did not fight back against the harassment he had faced in his first two seasons. As he approached his third season with the Dodgers, however, Robinson seemed intent on adopting a more aggressive and assertive style of play. Rickey did not publicly object; he spoke in defense of Robinson and tried to minimize the confrontation involving Van Cuyk. The same aggressiveness and assertiveness that Robinson used to prepare for his upcoming opponents also fueled his own preparation for the 1949 season. He worked on improving his slide and his ability to hit the ball to the opposite field. He finished spring training with a .521 batting average and a determination to excel at his sport.

After his usual early-season batting slump, Robinson emerged as one of the league's top hitters in the 1949 season. His batting average rose to .361 in the middle of the season, and he came in second place to the Boston Red Sox's Ted Williams in the All-Star Game voting totals. Along with Robinson, the Dodgers sent four other players to the game—Reese, Campanella, Branca, and Newcombe. Robinson continued to display his prowess in the second half of the season and easily won the National League's MVP award. He finished the regular season with an impressive batting average of .342, the highest average in the National League. In addition to his .342 batting average, Robinson compiled 124 RBIs, 38 doubles, and a .960 on base plus slugging percentage. He compiled those impressive statistics as the Dodgers battled the Cardinals for the National League pennant. The Dodgers prevailed by one game and once again faced their nemesis, the New York Yankees, in the World Series. Two years earlier, the Dodgers and the Yankees had battled in a thrilling seven-game game series. In 1949, however, the Yankees easily prevailed in five games, leaving the Dodgers bereft of their first World Series title.

THE HOUSE UN-AMERICAN ACTIVITIES COMMITTEE

In the midst of his MVP season, Robinson briefly entered an arena that would dominate his postbaseball life—political activism. At the invitation of Georgia Congressman John S. Wood, Robinson testified before the House Un-American Activities Committee (HUAC), a committee of the House of Representatives. Created in 1938, HUAC held hearings to investigate people and organizations accused of affiliating with or sympathizing with Communist organizations. After World War II, the onset of the Cold War between the United States and the Soviet Union recharged HUAC and reawakened fears of Communist-inspired subversion within the country. Paul Robeson, an African American actor and singer, had attracted the attention of HUAC because of a comment he had made about the loyalty of African Americans in the event of a war against the Soviet Union. A native of New Jersey, Robeson had excelled at football at Rutgers University before launching his singing and acting careers. Though Robeson served as the team's captain, he would remain on the bench during games against southern schools because those schools did not want to compete against a black player. After graduating from Rutgers, Robeson graduated from Columbia University's law school, but a lack of prospects led him to pursue a career as an actor and a signer. In the mid-1930s, Robeson visited the Soviet

HOUSE UN-AMERICAN ACTIVITIES COMMITTEE

Indirectly, Jackie Robinson's appearance before the House Un-American Activities Committee (HUAC) marked the first time he crossed paths with Richard Nixon. Nixon came to the House of Representatives in 1947 as one of a new generation of politicians shaped by the Great Depression and World War II. Similarly to many of his colleagues, Nixon arrived in Congress with a fierce anti-Communist worldview and a determination to root out Communism in the United States. He joined HUAC in 1947 and became a national star in 1948 due to his role in the case against Alger Hiss. Hiss had served in Franklin Roosevelt's administration in several roles and had accompanied the president to the important Yalta Conference in February 1945. Whitaker Chambers, a former member of the American Communist Party, accused Hiss of espionage and produced evidence supporting his claims. Hiss appeared before HUAC in an attempt to clear his name; Nixon put him under intense questioning, and Hiss did not have a good response to the evidence Chambers produced. The publicity surrounding the Hiss case made Nixon a star and helped him move first into the Senate and then into the vice presidency. A subsequent trial found Hiss guilty of perjury, and Hiss spent three years in federal prison.

As Robinson's testimony showed, HUAC had many different targets during its existence. Its members sought to uncover alleged and real Communist influence in all aspects of American society—sports, popular culture, and most memorably Hollywood. HUAC's investigations of the influence of Communism in Hollywood resulted in a blacklist of actors, writers, and others involved in the entertainment industry. HUAC's work also bled into the efforts of Senator Joseph McCarthy to hold hearings designed to reach a similar goal—uncover and expose a secret network of Communist spies in the United States.

McCarthy's hearings ended in disgrace for the Senator, and HUAC's work also fell out of favor with many politicians and the general public in the 1950s. HUAC's existence, however, embodied the anxiety that many Americans felt about the powerful Soviet Union and the potential influence of Communist infiltrators. That anxiety also impacted the Civil Rights Movement, a movement that became a focus of Robinson's postretirement life. Some in the federal government saw the movement as an outgrowth of Communist infiltration, and they used that as a pretense to spy on civil rights leaders and organizations.

Union and came away impressed by the country. He held on to those views, and the HUAC members clearly wanted another famous African American man in Robinson to refute Robeson's claims that African Americans would not fight for their country in a war against the Soviet Union.

When he received the invitation to appear before the HUAC, Robinson experienced some mixed emotions, and he sought advice for the best course of action. As he did with other major events in his life, Robinson shared his concerns with Rachel. Both of them sifted through the large amount of correspondence they had received after the press reported on Robinson's invitation from the HUAC. Robinson also received advice from Rickey, who eventually helped him craft a prepared response to the committee. Since Robinson had served in the United States Army during World War II, he did not want to give the impression that Robeson spoke for all African Americans or that all African Americans shared his views. At that time, Robinson and Robeson shared different views, though Robinson sympathized with Robeson's views and understood the roots of his frustrations with the United States. Robinson, however, did not want to give the impression that he believed Robeson had no right to his own views or to express those views. He also did not want to become a pawn in any sort of crusade against Robeson or against those who advocated for civil rights for African Americans.

Once Robinson decided to testify before the HUAC, he worked closely with others on crafting a proper prepared response to the committee. Rickey supported Robinson's decision to testify before the committee and helped him prepare his remarks. Both Rickey and Robinson also worked with Lester B. Granger to compose the remarks for the HUAC. Granger had served as the executive director of the National Urban League, and he had earlier testified before the HUAC on an issue similar to the one Robinson planned to address. Granger assured the HUAC members that Communists had not infiltrated African American communities and, therefore, had not persuaded large numbers of African Americans to regard communism as a superior system. Together, they crafted a statement that succeeded in providing the HUAC members with the information they wanted to hear about African Americans and the Soviet Union. The statement also reflected Robinson's views and his reluctance to serve as a proxy for those who wanted to silence all African Americans who advocated for civil rights.

Robinson appeared before the committee on July 19, and he opened his prepared remarks with some attempts to break the tension in the room. He referred to his career as a professional baseball player and to his unease at getting involved in a political issue. As Robinson reasoned, players in his profession needed to appeal to all Americans, not simply to the Americans who shared their political views. The loyalty of African Americans in a war against the United States, therefore, represented a topic far outside of the realm of the topics that baseball players usually discussed in public. Robinson joked that the topic did not connect at all to the Brooklyn Dodgers' regular season record or to the salary increase he had hoped to get prior to the start of the next season. In a more somber tone, Robinson turned to the topic of the testimony, Communism. He noted that meeting and mitigating the threat of Communist infiltration in the United States should unite people across partisan divides. Robinson also referred to the correspondence he had received after receiving the invitation from the HUAC. While he acknowledged that much of the correspondence came from Communist sympathizers, he said some of it came from people who shared Robinson's anti-Communist feelings. Robinson, furthermore, went to the heart of why he had accepted the committee's invitation—a sense of responsibility. He had been given a platform due to his career as a professional baseball player, and he wanted to use that platform to address an issue important to all Americans.

As Robinson continued with his prepared remarks, he went deeper into his reasons for appearing before the HUAC. He did not claim to possess any sort of expertise on the topic of Communism. Robinson, however, did claim expertise on the topic of life as an African American in the United States. For that reason, Robinson felt comfortable talking to the HUAC and could contextualize Robeson's comments about the loyalty of African Americans. Robinson understood the oppression and discrimination that African Americans faced because he had personally experienced both things during his lifetime. He referred to his own role in reintegrating Major League Baseball, a task that he described as unfinished. Robinson expressed pride in the fact that he went first in reintegrating the sport and that he helped ease the inclusion of other players who joined teams in his wake. Though progress had moved slowly, Robinson confidently predicted that the progress would continue throughout the rest of the league. That confidence helped frame the rest of his prepared remarks and his assertion that African Americans did not need to turn to Communism in their efforts for civil rights.

While Robinson spoke, he took great pains to separate African Americans' advocacy for civil rights from any hint of Communist inspiration or encouragement. He insisted that advocacy for civil rights did not equate to sympathy or even support for Communism. To Robinson, African Americans pressed for racial equality in all aspects of American society, including the armed forces, because they supported democracy, not because they supported Communism. He acknowledged that Communists often spoke against racial discrimination and made racial equality a part of their appeal within the United States. Robinson did not, however, credit Communists for opening the eyes of African Americans to racial discrimination in their country or with any progress toward the ultimate goal of racial equality. He insisted that advocacy for civil rights existed before Communists arrived in the country. Robinson, in other words, wanted to impress upon the HUAC members that African Americans pressed for civil rights and racial equality because of their own experiences with racism. They did not press for civil rights and racial equality because they wanted to foster a Communist revolution within the United States.

After making those comments about civil rights and Communism, Robinson directly addressed Robeson and his comments about the loyalty of African Americans. He quickly dismissed the substance of Robeson's comments while acknowledging Robeson's rights to both hold and state his own opinions. Robinson made it clear that he did not agree with Robeson's views though he respected the latter's accomplishments in the field of sports and entertainment. He also recognized that some African Americans supported Communism and would likely side with the Soviet Union should a war erupt between that country and the United States. Robinson tried to draw the committee's attention to another group, pacifists. He surmised that pacifists of all races would try to prevent a war from erupting, and if a war were to erupt, they would support the United States in such a conflict as they did during World War II. Robinson also tried to diminish the standing of Robeson, or any other singular person, as a speaker or representative of a much larger group of people. To Robinson, Robeson did not speak for all African Americans because one person could not speak for the views of an entire race of people. White Americans, consequently, should not grow overly concerned when Robeson or anyone else spoke favorably about Communism.

In his closing, Robinson reiterated his personal views and his belief in the ability to affect change within the United States without resorting to Communism. Robinson referred to his young family as a sign that he had invested in the country's future and in the country's founding ideals. He assured his listeners that he would not turn his back on his country and turn toward the false promise of Communism. He also assured his listeners that he believed the majority of African Americans shared his views, not the views of Robeson. Robinson then went back to a point he had stressed earlier in his remarks, the lack of an automatic connection between Communism and civil rights. He insisted that African Americans, like himself, would continue to fight against racial discrimination and for civil rights. Such behavior did not mean that they supported Communism or even regarded Communists as allies. Robinson proclaimed that he and other African Americans who wanted civil rights and racial equality did not want or need the assistance of Communists in reaching their goals.

Even though Robinson sought help in drafting his remarks, his remarks to the HUAC reflected the views he held in 1949. Robinson sympathized with Robeson's feelings as he had endured similar experiences that framed Robeson's statements about the loyalty of African Americans. As Robinson stressed, he disagreed with Robeson, but he did not want to imply that the government should silence Robeson or others who shared those views. Additionally, Robinson wanted to remain focused on his baseball career and on not alienating the Dodgers' fanbase. While Robinson held strong political views, he had not reached the period in his life when he wanted to devote much of his time to political advocacy. Instead, he wanted to continue his career with the Dodgers and reach his full potential as a professional baseball player.

MORE DISAPPOINTMENT

After completing his testimony to the HUAC, Robinson wrapped up his MVP season with the Dodgers, and he looked forward to continued success in the 1950 season. The Dodgers and Robinson again had a successful season. While Robinson did not repeat at the National League's MVP, he again compiled a batting average that exceeded .300 and made the All-Star Game. The Dodgers came close to defending their title as the National League Champions, but they ultimately finished in second place to the resurgent "Whiz Kids" Philadelphia Phillies. In the middle of September, the Dodgers faced a nine-game deficit, but they won thirteen of their final seventeen games of the season. In an odd twist, the Dodgers played in three consecutive doubleheaders against the Boston Braves in order to make up for rain-canceled games earlier in the season. Those three doubleheaders immediately preceded the Dodgers' final two games of the regular season, and those games came against the Phillies in Ebbets. The Dodgers won the first game to pull within one game of the Phillies, but star pitcher Robin Roberts held the Dodgers to one run in the final game of the season. In that game, the Dodgers and the Phillies both scored one run in the first nine innings. The Phillies then scored three runs off Don Newcombe in the top of the tenth inning. Both Newcombe and Roberts pitched all ten innings. An elated Phillies team celebrated their first National League pennant since 1915, while a dejected Dodgers team faced yet another season without a World Series title.

For the Dodgers, the 1951 season unfolded in a similar fashion. On August 11, the Dodgers had a thirteen-game lead in the National League, and they seemed poised for yet another run against the Yankees for their elusive World Series title. The Dodgers, however, spent the rest of the season watching that impressive lead evaporate as the team entered a late-season swoon. At the same time, the New York Giants experienced a late-season resurgence. Several factors added to the intensity of the pennant race. The Dodgers and the Giants had a long-standing crosstown rivalry. Leo Durocher, who had left the Dodgers under bad terms, managed the Giants; former Dodger Eddie Stanky, whom Rickey had traded to the Braves in 1948, played second base for the Giants. When the season ended, the Dodgers and the Giants stood tied atop the National League's standings with identical 96–58 records. To determine the winner of the National League pennant, the two teams played in a three-game playoff series starting on October 1, 1951. Those games added to the rivalry between the two franchises and ended with one of the most memorable moments in Major League Baseball's history.

Before moving to the Polo Grounds, the three-game playoff series opened with a 3–1 Dodgers' loss before over thirty-thousand fans at Ebbets Field. In the game, Robinson batted in the cleanup position and had one hit in three at bats; his offense futility matched the futility of the rest of the team. The Dodgers' lone run came on a home run from leftfielder Andy Pafko in the bottom of the second inning. Ralph Branca could not hold the slim lead and surrendered the three runs in the eight innings he pitched in the game. For the second game, the Dodgers rebounded with a 10–0 victory before over thirty-eight thousand fans at the Polo Grounds. Robinson set the tone for the game with a two-run home run in the top of the first inning. He added another RBI later in the game. Palko, first baseman Gil Hodges, and catcher Rube Walker joined Robinson in hitting home runs against the hapless Giants' pitchers. For the third game, the teams remained at the Polo Grounds, and the Dodgers carried a 4–1 lead into the bottom of the ninth inning. In the bottom of the ninth, Newcombe faltered. He allowed two singles before getting his first out; he then surrendered one run to cut the Dodgers' lead to 4–2. An injury to a Giants' player gave Dodgers' field manager Chuck Dressen time to take Newcombe out of the game and replace him with Branca. At the time, the Giants had two runners on base. Branca faced Giants' third baseman Bobby Thomson, and Thomson turned the tired Branca's second pitch into a pennant-winning three-run home run. The moment, known as "The Shot Heard 'Round the World," whipped the Polo Grounds into a frenzy and led the Giants' radio announcer to exclaim "The Giants win the pennant!" several times to his excited listeners. Captured on both film and radio, Thomson's home run still ranks among the all-time greatest moments in the sport's history, and it captured the improbableness of the Giants' comeback. The moment also captured the misery of the Dodgers' franchise. Robinson and his teammates lost yet another opportunity to face the Yankees in the World Series and to finally assert their supremacy over the storied franchise in the Bronx.

As the Dodgers endured those near-misses in the 1950 and 1951 seasons, Robinson enjoyed a mixture of success and frustration. Robinson earned raises at the start of each season. For the 1950 season, Robinson signed a contract for $35,000, the most money ever earned in one season by a Dodger. Prior to the 1951 season, Robinson signed a contract that netted him over $39,000, again establishing a salary record for Dodgers' players. Robinson continued to perform at a high level in those seasons, but he faced scrutiny for his more assertive behavior on the field. He occasionally had run-ins with umpires, which resulted in his ejection from the games. At one point in the 1950 season, Robinson grew so frustrated with his treatment from umpires that he wanted National League President Ford Frick to intervene and limit the umpires' power over ejections. Frick did not intervene, and Robinson continued to gain a reputation as a troublemaker. At the end of the 1950 season, Robinson faced more frustration when Dodgers' owner Walter O'Malley declined to renew Rickey's contract. Prior to that decision, O'Malley had successfully engaged in a scheme to purchase a majority of the team's ownership shares. O'Malley thought that Rickey held too much control over the club's personnel, and he wanted to take the franchise in a new direction. O'Malley's decision deprived Robinson of one of his most important defenders and confidants. Robinson and Rickey maintained their close friendship, but Rickey's departure raised questions about Robinson's future with the Dodgers. As he did prior to the 1951 season, Robinson always signed a new contract and remained with the Dodgers for the rest of his career. Questions about his status, however, would remain with him for the rest of his career and would often overshadow his contributions to the Dodgers' continued successes.

ROBINSON DEVELOPS A BAD REPUTATION

The Dodgers' and Robinson's 1952 season followed a similar pattern. The Dodgers again won the National League pennant and again lost the World Series to the Yankees. Frick moved into the commissioner's office, and Warren Giles succeeded him as the National League's President. Like Frick, Giles refused to intervene on behalf of Robinson in his disputes with umpires. In one instance, umpire Frank Dascoli accused Dodgers players of leveling taunts and slurs at him during a game. Giles wrote a letter in response to Dodgers' field manager Dressen and specifically referred to Robinson as one of the offenders even though Dascoli did not name any specific players. Giles ignored Robinson's subsequent protest, thereby establishing a frosty relationship between the two that would last for the rest of Robinson's career. Later in the season, Robinson had to deny reports that he and Dodgers coach Cookie Lavagetto had tried to assault Cubs' field manager Phil Cavarretta during a rain delay at Ebbets Field. Robinson and Cavarretta had yelled at each other across the diamond from the safety of their own dugouts, but a physical altercation never happened. A few weeks later, both Robinson and the normally mild-manner Campanella became embroiled in an argument with an umpire during a game in Boston against the Braves. In the eleventh inning, Campanella objected when the home plate umpire ruled that a pitch hit shortstop Johnny Logan. The decision angered other Dodgers players, and one of them asked the home plate umpire if he shook Logan's hand once Logan scored the winning run. Robinson joined in on the ribbing of the home plate umpire. Frick fined both Campanella and Robinson, and Robinson refused to pay his $75 fine until he had a hearing with the commissioner. Robinson later relented because he did not want to hurt the team's chances of winning the pennant, but the incident and his indignant response damaged his reputation. Robinson started to hear more boos whenever he traveled away from Ebbets Field, and his poor performance in yet another World Series defeat did not help improve his standing among baseball fans.

While Robinson endured those realities and acquired a reputation as a hot-headed troublemaker, his performance on the field did not falter. He finished the 1952 season with a .308 batting average and a league-leading .440 on-base percentage. In the 1953 season, Robinson again compiled a high batting average, .329, as his Dodgers won 105 games and easily captured the National League pennant. Robinson and the Dodgers faced their nemesis, the Yankees, in yet another World Series. He played all six games and enjoyed his best-ever performance in the fall classic. At the end of the series, Robinson had a .320 batting average, 8 hits, 2 RBIs, and 0 strikeouts. As they had in the past, however, the Dodgers failed to win the series, and they watched as the Yankees once again claimed the title. Robinson returned for the 1954 season with a new field manager, Walter Alston, whom he disliked in comparison to his previous managers Shotton and Dressen. He again finished the season with an impressive batting average, .311, but he appeared in only 124 of 154 games. In both the 1953 and 1954 seasons, Robinson played multiple positions in both the infield and the outfield, and he started to face the reality of his aging body. He found it harder to remain in shape and to contain his temper on the field. In one ugly incident against the relocated Milwaukee Braves, Robinson flung his bat in disgust toward his own dugout. The bat, however, slipped out of his hands and landed in the stands. While Robinson had not intended to throw his bat at opposing fans, many around the National League interpreted his actions as a deliberate attempt to injure spectators. The incident made Robinson the target of increasing boos from opposing fans as well as the target of increased criticism from sportswriters, who also had a frosty relationship with the ballplayer. Other on-field incidents further drove a wedge between Robinson, his teammates, and Alston. While Robinson remained capable of playing in the Major Leagues, he contemplated retirement after the 1954 season. He decided to return for the 1955 season because he needed the money to cover his family's growing expenses.

A CHAMPIONSHIP AND RETIREMENT

For both Robinson and the Dodgers, the 1955 season marked a milestone. Robinson returned to the Dodgers in a swirl of rumors of his imminent departure via a trade with another Major League club. He also returned as one of the oldest players on the roster, and accordingly, he appeared in only 105 of the 154 games on the Dodgers' regular season schedule. In May, Alston benched Robinson at the player' own request, and injuries further limited Robinson's appearances for the rest of the season. Despite Robinson's absence and friction between some of the players and Alston, the Dodgers bounced back from a disappointing 1954 season and captured the 1955 National League pennant. The Dodgers' 98–55 record gave them a very comfortable cushion of 13.5 games over the second-place team at the end of the season. With that cushion, the Dodgers clinched the pennant on September 8, the soonest a team had ever clinched the National League title. The Dodgers again faced the Yankees in the World Series, and the aging Robinson played in the series' first six games. After dropping the first two games at Yankee Stadium, the Dodgers seemed destined for the same fate that had befallen them in every previous World Series against the Yankees. The Dodgers won the next three games and stood in the precipice of their first World Series title. A loss to the Yankees in game six set the stage for the Dodgers' thrilling 2–0 victory in Yankee Stadium in game seven. At long last, the Brooklyn Dodgers won the World Series.

Robinson and the Dodgers headed into the 1956 season as the defending champions, yet for Robinson, the 1956 season carried a note of finality. The World Series title had not repaired Robinson's damaged reputation with fans, and he faced fierce boos during a contest in Jersey City. Ironically, he faced those boos in the same place where he had faced raucous cheers one decade earlier when he started his career with the Montreal Royals. He appeared in 117 of the Dodgers' 154 games, a slight improvement over his appearances from the previous season. Robinson finished the season with a respectable batting average of .275, far lower than his average from the height of his career but an improvement over his .259 average of the previous season. The Dodgers repeated as National League Champions and again faced the Yankees in the World Series. In a reversal of the 1955 series, the Dodgers won the first two games at Ebbets Field, lost the next three games, won game six, and then lost in a 9–0 blowout in game seven.

Game seven took place on October 10, 1956, at Ebbets Field, and it marked the final game of Robinson's career. During the off-season, Robinson finally decided that he could continue to support his family through ventures outside of the baseball diamond. His body simply would no longer allow him to play baseball at an elite level, and the Dodgers seemed determined to trade him to another team. A trade did happen on December 13; the Dodgers, who did not know about Robinson's retirement plans, traded him to the Giants in exchange for Dick Littlefield and $30,000. The trade confirmed Robinson's decision to retire, but he did not immediately inform O'Malley or Giants' owner Horace Stoneham about his decision. He had sold the exclusive story of his retirement to *Look*, a popular magazine, for $50,000. The story leaked before the publication date, and an angry O'Malley and Stoneham had to void the trade. Despite a plea from the Giants' management, Robinson remained firm in his decision; his baseball career had ended.

Freed from the obligations associated with his baseball career, Robinson could concentrate more on issues outside of the baseball world. As the civil rights movement had progressed in the 1950s, the events had played heavily on Robinson's psyche, and he wanted to take a more active role in the movement. Robinson also wanted to take advantage of all opportunities available to him in both the entertainment and corporate worlds. He still needed to make money to support Rachel and their three children—Jackie Jr., Sharon, and David. The entertainment and corporate opportunities would provide him with a steady salary and an ability to build upon the reputation he had established as a ballplayer. In the next decade of his life, Robinson would seek to find a balance between his civil rights advocacy and his responsibilities to his salary-paying jobs. Through his efforts, Robinson gained access to the highest levels of government and political influence in the United States. While Robinson would often face frustration, he did establish a standard that other athletes could follow once their playing careers ended. More importantly, Robinson further established himself as a person whose significance extended beyond the sports world and whose experiences often reflected larger stories and shifts in American society.

9

The Presidency, Civil Rights, and Jackie Robinson

Ten years after making his historic debut with the Brooklyn Dodgers, Jackie Robinson faced another challenge—advocating for civil rights. Robinson's retirement from the Dodgers came in the midst of great changes within American society. Within two years of Robinson's retirement, the Brooklyn Dodgers became the Los Angeles Dodgers; that geographic shift mirrored a geographic shift in the United States in the 1950s. More significantly, signs of progress and frustration for civil rights bracketed Robinson's retirement. The movement and its leaders scored significant victories in desegregating public schools and some other forms of public accommodations, but the pace of progress remained slow. Advocates for civil rights continued to face hostility and even violence from those who held power within a segregated society and who felt that change had happened too rapidly. Those realities greeted Robinson as he made the transition from professional baseball to the civil rights movement. He succeeded in using his fame to develop relationships with high-ranking politicians, including Richard Nixon, and pressing them to support federal efforts to promote civil rights. Much like the larger movement, however, Robinson often faced frustration in his efforts to press politicians to support civil rights and to keep the Republican Party honest to its roots as the "Party of Lincoln." Despite those frustrations, Robinson left a legacy for other athletes to emulate. He demonstrated that professional athletes can use their fame to do more than sell products; they can use their fame to help lead the country on a path toward becoming a more perfect union.

ROBINSON'S LEGACY IN BASEBALL—CHANGING DEMOGRAPHY AND GEOGRAPHY

After a comparatively chaotic period in the late nineteenth century, both the American League and the National League entered a prolonged era of stability for approximately the first half of the twentieth century. Once the American League appeared in 1901, teams and leagues no longer appeared and disappeared on a regular basis. The National League carried eight teams—the Boston Braves, Brooklyn Dodgers, Chicago Cubs, Cincinnati Reds, New York Giants, Philadelphia Phillies, Pittsburgh Pirates, and St. Louis Cardinals. The American League also carried eight teams, some of them located in the same cities that carried National League franchises—the Boston Red Sox, Chicago White Sox, Cleveland Indians, Detroit Tigers, New York Yankees, Philadelphia Athletics, and St. Louis Browns. Though some of the team nicknames shifted over time, the location of the franchises remained stable. During Robinson's career, the geographic stability that had characterized the Major Leagues ended. In 1952, the Braves abandoned Boston for Milwaukee; one year later, the Browns vacated St. Louis for Baltimore and became the Baltimore Orioles. After the 1954 season, another geographic shift happened when the Athletics left Philadelphia for Kansas City.

Those geographic shifts came in response to changing residential patterns that arose in the United States in the aftermath of World War II. Improved standards of living, combined with an increase in the number of African Americans living in cities, prompted many white Americans to move to suburbs. Their departure created problems for many Major League teams since those teams depended upon urban fanbases, not fanbases that needed to commute by car from suburbs. The age of many ballparks also added to the problems facing many Major League franchises. Most ballparks showed their age and needed significant upgrades. Since those ballparks sat in the midst of urban neighborhoods, owners had few options for renovating existing ballparks, and with the loss of fans to the suburbs, they looked for other alternatives. The trend toward more geographic shifts that started during Robinson's career continued after he retired and touched his own team, the Brooklyn Dodgers.

Following his successful scheme to remove Branch Rickey from the franchise's ownership, Walter O'Malley had full control over the Brooklyn Dodgers, and he looked for a new facility to replacing the aging Ebbets Field. The Dodgers' home ballpark opened in 1913, in the same era that witnessed the opening of many ballparks still in use in the 1950s. Those ballparks included Sportsman's Park in St. Louis, which opened in 1902, and Shibe Park in Philadelphia, which opened in 1909. In Chicago, Comiskey Park and Wrigley Field opened in 1910 and 1913, respectively. Both Tiger Stadium in Detroit and Fenway Park in Boston opened in 1912, while the original Yankee Stadium opened in 1923. Like some of those other ballparks, Ebbets Field showed signs of age in the 1950s. Its small size and location in the middle of a Brooklyn neighborhood limited O'Malley's options to make improvements, such as increased parking facilities, to the ballpark. Ironically, the franchise that got its nickname from their fans who "dodged" streetcars on their way to Ebbets Field saw many of its fans join in the post–World War II exodus to the suburbs. O'Malley found a new location for the Dodgers' new ballpark in Brooklyn at the Atlantic Yards, an area located at the intersection of Flatbush and Atlantic Avenues. The next parts of the story involving O'Malley and his venture for a new ballpark remain contentious and left many hard feelings among the Dodgers' fanbase.

The key players in the next parts of the story include O'Malley and Robert Moses, New York City's Director of City Planning. O'Malley later claimed that he acted in good faith to find a suitable site for the Dodgers' new ballpark in Brooklyn. He had plans; O'Malley turned to Moses because he wanted the city to use federal funding to purchase the Atlantic Yards property and build the new ballpark. Moses, however, balked at O'Malley's proposal and showed the Dodgers' owner a different site he deemed as more appropriate for a new ballpark. Moses did not favor using federal funds to build another ballpark in Queens; he tried to sell O'Malley on moving the Dodgers to Queens and to build a ballpark on land that would soon house Shea Stadium. O'Malley, in turn, balked at that proposal because he wanted to keep the Dodgers in Brooklyn and did not see the logic in moving them to another part of the city. Frustrated at Moses' refusal to purchase the Atlantic Yards property, O'Malley sought leverage by turning to a city far away from Brooklyn—Los Angeles. O'Malley's next steps brought him scorn from Brooklyn Dodgers' fans for the rest of his life.

O'Malley turned to Los Angeles due to the persistence of Rosalind Wyman, the youngest person elected to Los Angeles' City Council. Born in 1930, Wyman took office in 1953 and immediately set her sights on proving that Los Angeles could serve as the home of a Major League Baseball franchise. She regarded a Major League franchise as a key way of raising Los Angeles' profile. Wyman faced several obstacles—a lack of interest in expansion and geography. At the time, neither the National nor American League owners seemed interested in expanding beyond eight teams, so Wyman would need to entice an existing franchise to relocate to the West

Coast. Such a relocation, however, remained unattractive since St. Louis stood as the westernmost Major League city. That geographic reality meant that any West Coast franchise would face the unappealing prospect of long road trips throughout the long regular season. Despite those obstacles, Wyman remained determined to get a Major League franchise in Los Angeles, and O'Malley came along as the ideal partner. In 1957, O'Malley traveled to Los Angeles, and Wyman took him on a flight over Chavez Ravine, the site she and others saw as the ideal site for a Major League ballpark. O'Malley agreed and delivered a commitment to move the Dodgers after the 1957 season. Wyman's hard work had finally succeeded, and her dream of a Major League franchise in Los Angeles soon came to fruition.

In order to make the move official, O'Malley needed the support of the National League and to sell his fellow owners on the idea of playing Major League baseball on the West Coast. To sell his relocation plans, O'Malley turned to the Dodgers' longtime rival, the New York Giants. The Giants played their home games in the Polo Grounds, a ballpark originally built in the 1890s that underwent a major renovation in 1911 following a devastating fire. Much like O'Malley, Giants' owner Horace Stoneham wanted a new ballpark to replace the aging Polo Grounds, and he saw few options within New York City. Stoneham considered moving the franchise to Minneapolis, the site of the team's Triple A team, but O'Malley encouraged him to accept the deal offered by San Francisco mayor George Christopher. O'Malley correctly surmised that the other owners would approve his franchise's move to Los Angeles if another team accompanied them to the West Coast. Two franchises solved the owners' concerns about long-distance travel, and the owners approved both the Dodgers' and the Giants' relocations to Los Angeles and San Francisco. News of the teams' relocation did not surface during the 1957 season; both teams played their uneventful final seasons in New York City without informing their respective fanbases about their plans to move once the season ended.

Once again, the Dodgers changed the face of Major League Baseball and heralded a new era for the national pastime. The relocation of both the Dodgers and the Giants from New York City to the West Coast changed the geographic scope of the game and reflected broader population trends across the United States. A few years after the Dodgers and Giants made California their new home, the state gained another franchise with the California Angels. The Angels came into the American League as an expansion franchise; other expansion teams in the 1960s included the New York Mets, the National League franchise that replaced both the Dodgers and the Giants in New York City. California gained two more franchises when the Athletics relocated from their second home in Kansas City to Oakland and when the San Diego Padres debuted as yet another expansion team. Eleven years after the Dodgers and Giants relocated to

California, the number of teams in the Major Leagues had expanded to the point where the two leagues needed to divide into two separate divisions. The creation of divisions within both the American and National Leagues added another round to the playoffs, the American League Championship Series and the National League Championship Series. Major League Baseball represented the national pastime both in theory and in fact; teams populated cities throughout the country and carried rosters full of players who reflected the country's diverse population.

The geographic shifts and expansion that characterized Major League Baseball in the 1950s and the 1960s accompanied the growing diversity of the rosters of each Major League franchise. Those changes further emphasized that April 15, 1947, represented a major turning point in Major League Baseball's history. The date of Robinson's debut with the Brooklyn

---

PLAYOFF SERIES

In 1903, the National League and the American League staged the first World Series. The two leagues did not stage a World Series in 1904, but they restarted the tradition in 1905 and carried it forward every year until the strike-shortened season of 1994. With only eight teams in each league, the two leagues did not stage any playoff games aside from the World Series contests. Occasionally, one of the leagues would need to stage additional games prior to the World Series if two teams finished the regular season with the same record. That happened in 1951 with Jackie Robinson's Brooklyn Dodgers and the New York Giants.

With the expansion of the two leagues in the 1960s, Major League officials recognized the need to expand the playoffs beyond the World Series games. Starting in the 1969 season, both the American League and the National League separated into East and West divisions. To determine the two World Series participants, each league staged a five-game League Championship Series between the winners of the East and West divisions. In the first National League Championship Series, the New York Mets defeated the Atlanta Braves; in the first American League Championship Series, the Baltimore Orioles defeated the Minnesota Twins. The Mets went on to win the World Series.

The introduction of divisions and an extra playoff round added yet another layer of changes to those that baseball fans had already experienced since the end of World War II. The teams themselves that participated in the first League Championship Series symbolized change. Three of those teams—Braves, Orioles, and Twins—were relocated franchises. The Braves had moved from Boston to Milwaukee before settling in Atlanta, the Orioles were the former St. Louis Brown, and the Twins were the former Washington Senators. The fourth team, the New York Mets, were an expansion team that had not existed prior to 1962. Change represented the norm in Major League Baseball, and the change did not end in 1969.

Dodgers truly marked the end of an era in Major League Baseball's history and the start of an era of remarkable change that continued for the remainder of the twentieth century. While the rules of baseball remained in the same, the game looked very different after April 15, 1947, than it did before that date. Robinson always remained aware of his place in bringing about major changes, and he sought to use his retirement to press for broader changes in American society.

ROBINSON AND A CHANGING AMERICAN SOCIETY

The changes that characterized Major League Baseball in the years following Robinson's retirement from the sport reflected larger and deeper changes within American society. Some of those changes, particularly the changes stemming from the civil rights movement, had their roots during the latter part of Robinson's career. In 1954, the unanimous majority decision in *Brown v. Board of Education* nullified the practice of racial segregation in public education. That decision marked the culmination of a long-term effort to challenge the constitutionality of segregation in public education and breathed life into the post–World War II civil rights movement. One year later, two events provided additional sparks to the movement. In July, a group of white men in Mississippi lynched Emmett Till, a fourteen-year-old boy who had allegedly whistled at a white woman. *Life*, a popular magazine, featured Till's badly disfigured body lying in an open casket, and the image both shocked and revolted many across the country. In December, Rosa Parks refused to move to the back of one of Montgomery's, Alabama, buses, and her resistance and subsequent arrest led to a successful boycott of the city's buses. The boycott, which led to another successful Supreme Court ruling, also brought into prominence a young minister from Georgia, Dr. Martin Luther King Jr.

CIVIL RIGHTS MOVEMENT

The post–World War II civil rights movement did not represent one linear movement. On the contrary, it represented a multifaceted movement that simultaneously played out on the national, state, and local levels. Several events from the 1950s emphasized the multifaceted nature of the movement. The first of those events came on May 17, 1954, when the Supreme Court issued its unanimous opinion in the *Brown v. Board of Education* case. Chief Justice Earl Warren wrote the unanimous opinion that struck down the system of racial segregation in public education. The Supreme Court's opinion impacted every public school system in the United States. Implementing the opinion, however, happened at the state and local levels. Occasionally, the federal government had to step in and enforce integration orders. That happened in Little Rock in 1957.

The next of those events came in August 1955—the murder of Emmett Till. Till's murder shocked many across the nation. Till's murder highlighted the obstacles civil rights activists faced as they pressed for progress. A native of Detroit, the fourteen-year-old Till was murdered while he visited relatives in Mississippi. He allegedly whistled at Carolyn Bryant, a twenty-one-year-old white woman; Bryant's husband Roy Bryant and half-brother J. W. Milam later abducted Till, beat him, shot him in the head, and then sunk his body in a river. An all-white jury found Bryant and Milam not guilty, and both men freely confessed to their actions in an interview conducted after the trial. Bryant and Milam felt that their actions were justified. Many Americans, both black and white, felt differently, especially after seeing Till's mutilated body in his casket. For many, Till's unjust murder galvanized them into supporting civil rights because he represented an ugly symbol of the realities of racial segregation.

The last of those events came a few months after Till's murder and featured again the interplay of local, state, and national forces. Rosa Parks did not spontaneously decide to refuse to give up her seat on a bus in Montgomery in December 1955; she belonged to a local chapter of the NAACP and had planned for such an act to challenge the city's public transportation rules. Parks and other local activists sustained the boycott in Montgomery; they received support from both the local and national branches of the NAACP and from Dr. King, who soon became a national civil rights leader.

All those factors—geographic changes, expansion in the Major Leagues, the continued influx of nonwhite baseball players, and the emergence of civil rights leaders—shaped the world awaiting Robinson after his retirement. During his career, Robinson's biggest venture into the political world came with his carefully crafted testimony to the HUAC in 1949. Outside of that moment, he occasionally responded to reporters' questions about specific events, such as the bombing of black churches and other forms of resistance white Southerners demonstrated in response to the Supreme Court's actions. Robinson's willingness to respond to such questions added to the bad reputation he developed, particularly when sportswriters compared him to his more reticent teammate Roy Campanella. Once he retired from baseball, Robinson felt freer to take a more active role in promoting civil rights and using his own stature as the man who broke baseball's color barrier to help advance the cause of integration in other areas of American life. As he turned his focus to civil rights, however, Robinson remained mindful of the need to find a career that enabled him to support his family. Like other families across the country, the Robinsons had moved away from New York City and built a dream home in the suburbs.

Fortunately for Robinson, he found a job that gave him the freedom he sought while also providing him with the salary he needed to support his family in an era full of changes.

Robinson's ambitions crossed with the ambitions of William H. Black, the founder of the Chock full o'Nuts company. Black's company had its roots in the economic downturn that accompanied the end of World War I. In 1922, Black started selling nuts at a stand near Forty-third Street and Broadway in Manhattan. Four years later, Black officially founded the Chock full o'Nuts company with a chain of eighteen nut shops in New York City. Once the Great Depression hit, Black realized that his product represented a luxury for too many of his customers. To avoid financial ruin, Black transformed his company. Instead of selling nuts in his shops, Black sold coffee and sandwiches, including a special sandwich that included a mixture of nuts and cheese. The Chock full o'Nuts shops thrived and became part of New York City's cultural landscape. Black developed a good reputation for his employment practices that gave his employees benefits and bonuses and that maintained fair practices for both black and white employees. In the 1950s, Black expanded his business enterprise by selling Chock full o'Nuts products in grocery stores. He also sought to hire someone who could help him manage his company's personnel and who could serve as a promoter for the Chock full o'Nuts brand. Black found what he wanted in Robinson—an African American who could help manage the company's large number of African American employees. Robinson also possessed the gravitas needed to promote the company in a very competitive New York market.

The deal bringing Robinson into the Chock full o'Nuts company happened before his formal retirement from Major League Baseball. Black and Robinson met for lunch in December 1956, and Black made Robinson a formal offer, which Robinson accepted on December 12. Starting in March 1957, Robinson would join the Chock full o'Nuts company as a vice president who had oversight over the company's personnel. The initial terms of the contract lasted for two years and netted Robinson an annual salary of $30,000 per year in addition to other benefits, such as stock options and use of a company car. After two years, Robinson would then get a five-year renewable contract at the same position. Ironically, Robinson agreed to those terms at the same time as he received news of his trade from the Dodgers to the Giants. Additionally, Robinson secured $50,000 from *Look* magazine for the exclusive rights to his story on his retirement from Major League Baseball. Those developments confirmed for Robinson that he had made the right decision to retire at the end of the 1956 season. Additionally, the two contracts helped Robinson secure a sound financial footing for his family before he officially went through with his retirement plans.

ROBINSON AND THE NAACP

Though Robinson had responsibilities to the Chock full o'Nuts company, his new profession gave him the freedom to pursue his passion for civil rights. As he started his new career as a corporate spokesman and personnel manager, Robinson directed his civil rights passions toward the National Association for the Advancement of Colored People (NAACP). NAACP. In 1956, Robinson had received the Spingarn Medal, the highest award bestowed by the NAACP. Established by Joel Elias Spingarn in 1914, the Spingarn medal annually went to an African American who made a notable achievement in the field of human endeavor. Other Spingarn honorees included Walter White, the NAACP's executive secretary who led the organization's anti-lynching efforts; Marian Anderson, an acclaimed singer; and A. Philip Randolph, the International President of the Brotherhood of Sleeping Car Porters who had tried to organize a march on Washington, D.C., in 1941. Other honorees included Paul Robeson and the famous lawyer Thurgood Marshall, who served as the NAACP's council in the *Brown v. Board of Education* case. In the two years after Robinson received the award, the recipients included people at the heart of the civil rights movement—Dr. King and Daisy Bates and the other members of the Little Rock Nine. By receiving the Spingarn Medal, Robinson entered elite company among his fellow African Americans and received recognition that his athletic feats had brought the hope of racial progress for all African Americans.

Robinson took a greater interest in the NAACP at a critical time for the organization. The NAACP had led long-term legal efforts to outlaw lynching and segregation, and those efforts required financial support that annual membership dues alone could not satisfy. In 1953, the NAACP established the Fight for Freedom Fund, a fundraising drive with the goal of raising $1 million each year for the next ten years. With that money, the organization hoped to fund legal efforts to outlaw segregation in time for the centennial of the Emancipation Proclamation, the executive order that President Abraham Lincoln had authorized in 1863. At the behest of the NAACP's leaders, Robinson served as the Chairman of the Fight for Freedom Fund and launched a tour designed to increase NAACP's membership as well as donations to the fund. His tour commenced in 1957, a few months after the successful Montgomery Bus Boycott and a few months before violence erupted in Arkansas over efforts to integrate Little Rock's Central High School. A new organization from the Montgomery Bus Boycott, Dr. King's Southern Christian Leadership Conference (SCLC), competed with the NAACP for fundraising dollars. Additionally, many southern states sought to actively undermine the organization and to prevent it from any further legal challenges to segregation. Despite his lack of fundraising experience, Robinson gave the NAACP what it needed—a charismatic and well-known spokesman who could lend his celebrity status and credibility to the organization's fight for racial progress. Robinson also brought with him a $10,000 check courtesy of his new employer, the Chock full o'Nuts organization, and the same determination that had guided him throughout his baseball career.

On his first tour for the Fight for Freedom Fund, Robinson showed that he could use his celebrity status to help advance the cause of racial progress. Large crowds greeted him throughout his tour in major cities such as Baltimore, Cleveland, Pittsburgh, Oakland, and Los Angeles. The people in those crowds knew him as Robinson the baseball player, and Robinson did not shy away from referring to his baseball career in his speeches. In his prepared speeches, however, Robinson did not focus on his career; instead, his speeches strove to draw his audiences' attention toward the world of civil rights. He wanted to impress upon his audience the same sense of urgency he felt, the urgency that had led him to join the NAACP at the same time as he pursued a career in the corporate world. Robinson saw the NAACP as playing a leading and integral role in the advancement of full citizenship rights for African Americans, and he wanted to shake his audiences out of any sense of complacency they felt about civil rights. He felt so inspired by his successful first tour that he wanted to launch two ambitious plans—a $100 per-plate dinner in New York City and the creation of a committee of artists, entertainers, and athletes who shared his zeal for the NAACP. The members of that committee would emulate Robinson; they would use the power of their celebrity status to raise much-needed funds for the NAACP and to bring more members into the organization's fold. Robinson's success led to increasing demands for his time from local NAACP branches, and it seemingly gave him little room to fulfill the obligations of his jobs with the Chock full o'Nuts company.

Robinson officially reported for his first day of duty with the Chock full o'Nuts company on March 3, 1957. By that time, he had completed his first tour as the Chairman of the Fight for Freedom Fund and had emerged as one of the key spokesmen for the NAACP. As he did with the NAACP, Robinson approached his job with the Chock full o'Nuts company with a great deal of zeal and determination. He took a tour of the company's twenty-seven restaurants, sought to meet with the employees at those restaurants, and visited other locations important to the company's operations. Robinson, however, ran into some friction unlike the kind of friction he had experienced as a baseball player. He disliked having to fire people; he preferred to advocate for the company's employees in the same manner in which he advocated for civil rights and the NAACP. Additionally, when an attempt at unionization among the company's employees failed, some employees lashed out at Robinson and accused him of dissuading the black employees from forming a union. An investigation by the National Labor Relations Board (NLRB) cleared Robinson of any wrongdoing, but the incident hinted at tensions building within the Chock full o'Nuts company. Robinson occupied a delicate position within the company; his job required him to manage and potentially fire employees who no longer met the company's standards. Such a position meant that Robinson could face scrutiny within the company at the same time as he spoke on civil rights issues that touched many nerves, including those of high-ranking politicians.

ROBINSON AND THE PRESIDENCY

During his baseball career, Robinson had the opportunity to meet many politicians, including the two people who served as the president and vice president of the United States in 1957—Dwight Eisenhower and Richard Nixon. Robinson's meeting with Nixon left a deep impression upon him and led to a lasting relationship. Nixon came from Whittier, California, a community approximately twenty-five miles away from Pasadena; Nixon also followed sports, and he could carry a conversation with Robinson about the latter's athletic feats. Additionally, both men shared similar views on Communism. Robinson views had not shifted since his testimony before HUAC in 1949. That same committee had helped to launch Nixon's political career and had helped to demonstrate his fiercely held anti-Communist beliefs. Robinson also became an admirer of Nixon because of his willingness to speak on civil rights issues. In the 1950s, neither the Republican nor the Democratic Party had a strong history in regards to civil rights. The Democratic Party still had a strong presence in the segregated South, and the Republican Party had moved on from its roots as the party of Abraham Lincoln and emancipation. Nixon represented one of the few politicians who spoke out in favor of civil rights, and that willingness earned him respect from Robinson. As part of his advocacy for the NAACP and civil rights, Robinson included direct appeals to politicians such as Eisenhower and Nixon. Such appeals brought mixed results for Robinson and put him on the frontlines of political controversies involving civil rights in the 1950s and 1960s.

Robinson started sending letters directly to the White House in 1957 in response to debates over the proposed Civil Rights Act of 1957, the first such act coming from the federal government since the 1870s. He wanted to add his voice to those who supported the measures found in the proposed legislation and who wanted to move the bill through the roadblocks in Congress. Both Eisenhower and Nixon supported the proposed legislation, but Congress still included many segregationist lawmakers who belonged to the Democratic Party. Robinson's championing of the bill brought him closer to the Eisenhower administration and earned him personal visits from E. Frederic Morrow. Morrow worked for Eisenhower as an Administrative Officer for Special Projects, making him the first African American to work in such a capacity for the President of the United States. The Civil Rights Act of 1957 passed through both houses of Congress, and Eisenhower signed the legislation into law on September 9 of that year. While imperfect, the Civil Rights Act of 1957 helped to empower the federal government to take action in protecting the rights of African Americans. The legislation, furthermore, helped to cement the bond between Robinson and Eisenhower's vice president, Nixon.

Though Eisenhower had supported the Civil Rights Act of 1957, Robinson saw Nixon as the stronger champion of civil rights within the executive branch. During a tour of Africa, Nixon delivered what Robinson regarded as a powerful defense of civil rights in a speech that also had anti-Communist overtones. Nixon delivered his remarks in response to criticism from Communists about racism in the United States; he made a firm pledge to advocate for civil rights until all Americans had access to equal opportunities. Robinson expressed his gratitude to Nixon, and Nixon responded with his own warm regards for the former ballplayer. At that point in his career, Nixon had likely made the decision to run for the presidency in the 1960 election, and he likely wanted to cultivate Robinson as a key ally and campaign surrogate. Such political calculations, however, do not diminish the connections that Nixon and Robinson forged over civil rights. Nixon noted that some parts of the Civil Rights Act of 1957 had to be "watered down" in order to secure passage through Congress. He assured Robinson that he would press for stronger legislation once he became president, and Robinson chose to believe him. Robinson genuinely saw Nixon as a champion for civil rights and accepted the vice president's public and private words as evidence that he would carry through with his promises.

In 1957, another event related to civil rights sharpened Robinson's belief that Nixon stood as the true champion of civil rights within the Eisenhower administration. As a consequence of the *Brown v. Board of Education* ruling, the Central High School in Little Rock, Arkansas, planned to enroll nine black students. According to the plan, the nine students would officially enroll in the Central High School on September 4. Arkansas governor Oral Faubus, however, blocked that plan when he called upon the Arkansas National Guard to go to Little Rock and to "preserve the peace." Instead of "preserving the peace," the Arkansas National Guard blocked the nine students from entering the high school. The move angered Eisenhower, who sought to persuade Faubus to enforce the Supreme Court's ruling and to integrate the high school. Eisenhower's inaction made him look weak; his decision to avoid a direct confrontation with Faubus gave the impression that he would not enforce federal civil rights regulations above the opposition of southern states. On September 20, federal judge Ronald Davies ruled against Faubus and ordered the National Guard to leave Little Rock. Three days later, the nine students finally entered Central High School, but a large mob of angry whites rioted once they learned that the students had entered the school. To protect the students from mob violence, local police officers escorted the students out of the school and drove them away from the crowds.

The reaction of the white rioters, and the seeming silence from Eisenhower himself, angered Robinson and others affiliated with the NAACP. Robinson wired an angry message to the White House, blasting Eisenhower for his appeal for patience. Daisy Bates, the head of the Arkansas branch of the NAACP, called upon the president to personally guarantee the safety of the nine black students. She insisted that unless Eisenhower made such a gesture, the nine black students would not again attempt to enroll at the Central High School. Though Eisenhower had disagreed with the *Brown v. Board of Education* ruling, he believed in enforcing the law and felt appalled at what had transpired in Little Rock. On September 24, Eisenhower federalized the Arkansas National Guard and ordered them to defend the integration of the Central High School. To accompany the National Guard, Eisenhower also delivered one thousand paratroopers from the 101st Airborne to Little Rock. Under the auspices of the federalized National Guard and the 101st Airborne's paratroopers, the nine black students safely entered the Central High School. Some of the security measures put into effect in September remained in place throughout the entire academic year. Eisenhower's actions drew praise from Robinson, yet the entire experience showed that a distance existed between the president and champions of civil rights such as Robinson. Eisenhower took the steps that he did in September 1957 because he believed in following and upholding the law; Robinson wanted to see something else from the nation's elected leadership. He wanted to see something that Eisenhower could not provide in 1957—a deep and fierce commitment to using federal power to advance civil rights against the intransigence of state and local governments.

Despite his dismay over Eisenhower's delayed actions, Robinson could review his first full year of retirement as a success. He found a well-paying and prestigious job that gave him the flexibility to work with the NAACP and pursue his passion for civil rights. More importantly, Robinson emerged as a credible authority on the issue of civil rights. He made a well-regarded appearance on *Meet the Press*, a prestigious news program that featured politicians and heads of state from around the world. Robinson also saw success with his Fight for Freedom Fund and had approximately fifteen hundred attendees pay $100 apiece for a dinner to celebrate the fund. In addition to the accolades he earned from the NAACP for the successful Fight for Freedom Fund efforts in 1957, Robinson won accolades from New York-based organizations such as the Young Adult Fellowship of the Salem Methodist Episcopal Church in Harlem. The NAACP elevated Robinson to its board of directors and made him a co-chairman of the Life Membership Committee. Robinson even made a dangerous venture into the deep South in an effort to recruit more African Americans to join the NAACP and to help commemorate "Jackie Robinson Day" in Mississippi. Overall, Robinson showed in his first full year of retirement that he could translate his success on the baseball diamond to success in other parts of his life. Robinson, though, also showed flashes of aggressiveness and frustration on the baseball diamond, and those same tendencies also surfaced in his advocacy for civil rights.

In May 1958, Eisenhower again waded into the issue of civil rights and again did not deliver a message that resonated with Robinson. On May 12, both Robinson and Eisenhower attended the Summit Meeting of National Negro Leaders in Washington, D.C. Robinson heard Eisenhower deliver a speech in which he urged African Americans to exercise patience in regards to progress on civil rights. Additionally, Eisenhower raised questions about the approach that organizations such as the NAACP had used to press for civil rights, an approach that focused on legal remedies. To Eisenhower, using legal remedies to change laws would produce limited results. As Eisenhower reasoned, people's feelings on race and civil rights sustained segregation and animated opposition to attempts to change laws supporting segregation. He insisted that merely changing laws would not change people's feelings and, therefore, the legalistic approach to advancing civil rights would not fully solve the problems involving race and civil rights in the United States. The overall tone of Eisenhower's message and his emphasis on patience frustrated Robinson, who decided to respond directly to the president using stationery from the Chock full o'Nuts company.

Robinson's letter, dated May 13, focused on both Eisenhower's plea for patience and his criticism of using a legalistic approach to advancing civil rights. Early in the letter, Robinson's sense of frustration and thinly veiled anger showed when he described his initial reaction to Eisenhower's call for patience. According to Robinson, he felt like standing up and delivering a cry of dismay when he heard the president make his plea. To emphasize his frustration, Robinson reminded Eisenhower about the amount of patience African Americans had exhibited for a very long period of time in American history. Robinson declared that African Americans could not patiently wait until enough Americans let go of their racism and embraced equal rights for all people. African Americans wanted the rights promised to them in the country's founding documents. Robinson argued that the president's strategy of patience emboldened segregationists such as Faubus; it did not bring the country closer to equal rights for all Americans. He concluded his letter by making a request to Eisenhower for a bold statement in favor of civil rights supported by a demonstration of the president's willingness to use federal power to advance civil rights measures. Robinson insisted that such a statement, combined with the use of federal power, would assure African Americans that they would soon possess all the rights guaranteed to them through the Constitution.

In addition to expressing his displeasure with Eisenhower, Robinson also started to challenge the leadership of the NAACP and to nudge the organization in a different direction. Since the NAACP focused its energies and financial resources on legal challenges, the organization did not often sponsor the kind of direct action that other civil rights organizations sponsored. Robinson wanted a bolder form of leadership from the NAACP, specifically from the organization's leader Roy Wilkins. He wanted Wilkins to push more aggressively for fewer delays in implementing the *Brown v. Board* ruling and to be more supportive of African Americans engaged in civil rights demonstrations. Though Robinson remained affiliated with the NAACP, he openly criticized Wilkins and took a leading role in a youth march that the organization did not organize or sponsor. The youth march, first suggested by A. Philip Randolph, took place in Washington, D.C., in October 1958. Robinson, his wife Rachel, and their son Jackie Jr. joined approximately ten thousand people in marching to raise awareness of the attacks black children endured from police officers in southern cities. While the march gave Robinson the outlet to engage in the kind of action he saw as necessary for the advancement of civil rights, it did not resolve the tensions that existed between him and Wilkins. The march, moreover, further highlighted the distance between himself and Eisenhower since the president did not meet with any of the marchers. Eisenhower's refusal to meet with any of the participants led Robinson to reconsider his views of the Republican Party, but it did not lead him to reconsider his affiliation with the NAACP. Robinson remained with the organization and continued to lead the Fight for Freedom Fund, though he dissented from the tactics favored by Wilkins and other NAACP leaders.

Despite those tensions with Eisenhower and the NAACP leadership, Robinson enjoyed a successful first two years in retirement and established a solid foundation for his continued employment as well as his activism. His initial contact with the Chock full o'Nuts company ended in 1958; he received a new five-year contract that went into effect in 1959. Around the same time as he received that contract, Robinson also secured a job with the WRCA radio station based in New York City. Every Sunday evening, he hosted a half-hour program, *The Jackie Robinson Show*, that featured both local and national political leaders. A few months after launching his weekly radio program, Robinson added yet another outlet for his activism, a regular column for the *New York Post*. Similar to his weekly radio program, Robinson's columns for the *Post* focused on local, national, and international politics, not on sports. Though Robinson occasionally played golf, he rarely watched baseball games and had no connection to the relocated Dodgers franchise. Robinson wanted to focus on civil rights as well as on politics, and the upcoming 1960 presidential election provided him with the opportunity to both hone his political voice and use his platform to help elect the next leader of the free world.

ROBINSON AND THE 1960 PRESIDENTIAL ELECTION

Since the Constitution blocked the popular Eisenhower from running for a third term, the 1960s presidential election represented an enticing opportunity for ambitious politicians from both parties. In the Republican Party, Nixon had the clearest path to the nomination due to his eight years of service as Eisenhower's vice president. By the time of the Republican Party's convention in July 1960, Nixon faced no competition for the nomination, and he won all but ten of the votes from the party's delegates. He chose former Senator Henry Cabot Lodge Jr. of Massachusetts as his running mate. Ironically, Lodge had lost his Senate seat to John F. Kennedy in the 1952 election; Lodge spent the next seven years as the United States' ambassador to the United Nations. The Democratic Party witnessed a more contentious process before selecting its nominee, Senator Kennedy of Massachusetts. The youthful Kennedy directly confronted and overcame concerns about his age and his Catholic faith; he represented only the second Catholic nominated for a major party's presidential ticket. For his running mate, Kennedy selected one of his colleagues from the Senate, Lyndon Baines Johnson of Texas. Johnson had also battled for the party's nomination, and Kennedy felt that Johnson's addition to the ticket would help him win support in the Southern states. The forty-three-year-old Kennedy and the forty-seven-year-old Nixon represented a new generation of politicians that had served in World War II and entered politics in the immediate postwar era. During the general election campaign, the two men discussed many issues, including an issue deeply important to Robinson—civil rights.

Since Robinson did not officially belong to either the Republican or Democratic Party, he sought to exert his influence with both parties as they selected their nominees. He used his column in the *New York Post* to share his political views and to promote the candidates he felt would advance civil rights. Though he did not belong to the Republican Party, he remained drawn to Nixon and to many of the principles that both the vice president and the party advocated—including support for capitalism and opposition to Communism. Robinson devoted one of his columns to touting Nixon's record and to announcing that he could see himself supporting Nixon in the general election. Among the Democrats, Robinson favored Senator Hubert H. Humphrey of Minnesota. To Robinson, Humphrey had the most impressive record on civil rights among the Democrats vying for the party's nomination. Robinson showed his support for Humphrey by campaigning for him during Wisconsin's primary and by helping him to establish one of his campaign offices in Washington, D.C. Humphrey, however, lost both the Wisconsin primary and the party's nomination to Kennedy, someone whom Robinson disdained. Robinson saw Kennedy as someone who would accommodate the segregationists within the Democratic Party, not as someone who would use the power of the presidency to press for civil rights.

Civil rights ranked as an important issue in the 1960 presidential election because of events that had happened in the 1950s and because the movement had entered a new phase in the early part of the year. On February 1, 1960, in Greensboro, North Carolina, four black students from North Carolina Agricultural and Technical State University staged a sit-in at the Woolworth's lunch counter. The four students staged the sit-in to protest Woolworth's policy of refusing to serve black patrons at the lunch counter; the students had purchased items without any problems, but employees refused to serve them coffee. After remaining at the lunch counter until the store closed, the students resumed the sit-in the following day, and more students joined their protest. Over the ensuing weeks and months, more students steadily joined in the sit-in at the Woolworth's, and the sit-in movement spread to other businesses and other southern cities. All the sit-ins adhered to the nonviolent, civil disobedience philosophy championed by King, and it attracted much attention in the press. The sit-ins also helped give birth to the Student Nonviolent Coordinating Committee (SNCC), an organization that would play a large role in civil rights protests over the next decade. For those reasons, it seemed likely that the next president would face the same issues that Eisenhower had faced during his second term. The next president would need to decide how much, if any, federal power he would exert over the objections of state and local officials to promote civil rights.

Once the parties had selected their nominees, Robinson met with both Nixon and Kennedy in an attempt to gauge their willingness to promote civil rights once they took the oath of office. Robinson's meeting with Nixon deepened his resolve to support the Republican Party's nominee, while his meeting with Kennedy deepened the chasm between the two men. In his retelling of the meeting, Robinson claimed that Kennedy tried to offer him money in return for his support. Robinson angrily rejected the offer, and he continued to express skepticism about Kennedy's sincerity on civil rights. Kennedy tried again to solicit Robinson's support; he sent Robinson a letter outlining his reasons for working with the segregationists in the Democratic Party and emphasizing his personal antipathy toward any form of discrimination. The letter did not alter Robinson's views of Kennedy, but the campaign continued to try to make amends. Robinson turned down an invitation to work with the Democratic Party on shaping the party's platform for the 1960 election, and he refused to credit Kennedy for inserting strong resolutions on civil rights into that platform over the objections of segregationists. Robinson, furthermore, criticized Kennedy's decision to select Johnson as his running mate since he believed that Johnson would join Kennedy in accommodating those segregationists within the party. Those experiences confirmed Robinson's preexisting views of both nominees, and they cemented his resolve to help Nixon become the next president of the United States.

Robinson did not shy away from voicing his views on both Nixon and Kennedy, using both his radio program and his regular newspaper column to share those views with his audiences. His open support for Nixon, and his harsh criticism for Kennedy, occasionally generated some pushback from his readers and listeners, but that pushback did not deter Robinson. One incident further increased the tension between Robinson and Kennedy's campaign. Robinson served as a trustee for the African-American Students Foundation; in 1960, the foundation wanted to bring a group of African college students into the United States so that they could enroll at American schools. The foundation needed funding to help support the students, and Robinson appealed directly to Nixon for that funding. At first, Robinson believed that Nixon had convinced the State Department to sponsor the students, and he shared the good news in his newspaper column. The foundation, however, had already accepted an offer directly from Kennedy that exceeded the amount the State Department had planned to allocate to the students. Kennedy used his family's funds to offer the foundation enough money to support the students for three years, and the foundation accepted the offer without informing Robinson. In a subsequent column, Robinson tried to explain what had happened, and the mishap further deepened the chasm between himself and the Kennedy campaign.

Shortly after that mishap, tensions again flared between Robinson and the Kennedy campaign. While campaigning for his older brother in New York, Robert Kennedy gave an interview to a radio station and used the interview to attack Robinson. That interview prompted an angry response from Robinson. While delivering a speech in the Senate, Senator Kennedy accused the State Department of trying to undermine his plan to support the African-American Students Foundation. That speech prompted yet another angry response from Robinson who clearly felt that both the Kennedy brothers had attacked his credibility in an effort to blunt his criticism of the Senator's record on civil rights. The incident did not reflect well on Robinson, who appeared detached from the foundation and unclear on the sequence of events that led to the foundation getting money from the Kennedy family. The incident, more importantly, ended any pretense that Robinson would try to use his influence within the Democratic Party. He took a leave of absence from his job and his newspaper column so that he could focus on his newest endeavor—helping Nixon win the 1960 presidential election.

Robinson's involvement in the 1960 presidential election demonstrated his stubbornness as well as the limits of his political influence. He traveled across the country to campaign for Nixon, yet neither Nixon nor other campaign staffers appeared to value Robinson's support. On the contrary, both Nixon and his staffers behaved in ways that rankled Robinson and made him question his earlier assessments of the Republican Party's nominee. Nixon's campaign did not travel to Harlem, and it encountered a major stumble in October when police in De Kalb County, Georgia, arrested King for his participation in a sit-in. The judge sentenced King to four months of hard labor, a sentence that could have resulted in his death. Robinson appealed directly to Nixon to intervene, but Nixon refused. Robinson reacted with a great deal of dismay and nearly left the campaign over Nixon's refusal to intervene on behalf of King. Making matters worse for Robinson, Kennedy did intervene by calling both Georgia governor Ernest Vandiver and King's wife, Coretta. The gestures from both nominees signaled a possible shift in the politics of civil rights from the Republican to the Democratic Party. On Election Day, most of the African Americans who participated chose Kennedy, thereby helping him secure a narrow victory. Robinson maintained his support for Nixon through Election Day, but his stature had failed to persuade African Americans in joining him and voting for the Republican nominee.

ROBINSON, NELSON ROCKEFELLER, AND A CONTINUED QUEST FOR CIVIL RIGHTS

Overall, Robinson lost more than he gained by actively campaigning for Nixon in the 1960 election. Other African American leaders swung their support to Kennedy and questioned Robinson's steadfast support for Nixon, particularly after the episode involving King. Additionally, for the first time, Robinson faced criticism for his work with the Chock full o'Nuts company. During the campaign, the NAACP appealed to the AFL-CIO for money to help with the organization's efforts to register African American voters. The AFL-CIO refused and cited Robinson's alleged role in blocking the efforts of Chock full o'Nuts employees to form a union as the reason for their refusal. Though Robinson denied that he held anti-union animus, he did work with William Black in preventing the unionization of the company's employees. He also faced criticism from friends who supported Kennedy and lost his regular column with *New York Post*. Even worse, some people, including Robert Kennedy, tried to use Rachel as a conduit to pressure Robinson to withdraw his support for Nixon and cease his campaign schedule. All those unpleasant experiences highlighted the dangers of Robinson's involvement in political campaigns. He risked undermining his reputation and in losing the lift he had built for himself since his retirement from the Brooklyn Dodgers.

Despite those risks, Robinson maintained his interest in politics following the 1960 election. Soon after Election Day, Robinson shifted his focus away from the defeated Nixon since his defeat seemed to portend the end of his political career. Additionally, Nixon's behavior during the campaign had disappointed Robinson, and it did not match the perception Robinson had of the former vice president as a warrior for civil rights. Robinson quickly latched on to New York governor Nelson Rockefeller, one of Nixon's campaign surrogates and someone who seemed to have a bright future in both state and local politics. In their private conversations, Rockefeller convinced Robinson of his commitment to civil rights. Unlike Nixon, though, Rockefeller buttressed his verbal commitments with concrete actions. While Nixon had avoided Harlem during his campaign, Rockefeller joined Robinson in a meeting in Harlem and in fielding questions from the African American audience. Additionally, Rockefeller aligned himself with King; he traveled with King on his own private plane and traveled with him to rallies at black churches. Rockefeller seemed to have a promising future within the Republican Party; that promising future provided Robinson with an opening to keep alive his own political interests despite the setbacks endured during the 1960 presidential election.

As Robinson developed a connection with Rockefeller, he saw an improvement in his connections to President Kennedy and other members of the Kennedy administration. Like his predecessor, Kennedy faced conflicts in southern states that stemmed from civil rights activism. The sit-in movement continued into his presidency, and an organization called Congress on Racial Equality (CORE) sponsored a Freedom Ride to promote policies outlawing segregation in public transportation. In 1961, a Freedom Ride that originated in Washington, D.C., faced attacks from white southerners as the riders journeyed to their destination in Mississippi. Attorney General Robert Kennedy, who supported the policies that ended segregation in public transportation, voiced his displeasure at the attacks and pledged to use the power of his office to enforce antidiscrimination laws. Robinson responded warmly to the Attorney General's response; he also lauded the attorney general when he sent U.S. Marshals into Alabama to protect the Freedom Riders. The actions of both President Kennedy and Attorney General Kennedy led Robinson to reconsider his earlier opposition to both men, but it did not persuade him to formally join the administration or the Democratic Party. Robinson liked his official independence from both parties since he felt such independence gave him a platform to push both parties on the issue of civil rights.

In 1962, Robinson again experienced some highs and lows that illuminated the risks he faced by engaging in politics. The *Amsterdam News*, a black weekly newspaper, hired Robinson to write a regular column, and Robinson used that column to voice his views on politics and civil rights. Robinson remained critical of President Kennedy in his columns, yet he also offered words of praise when Kennedy used his power to advance civil rights policies. Robinson himself faced criticism when he waded into a controversy in Harlem involving the establishment of a new steakhouse that would compete with an established steakhouse owned by an African American businessman, Lloyd Von Blaine. Both race and religion factored into the controversy; the new steakhouse's owner, Sol Singer, and the landowner who had leased Singer the land, Frank Schiffman, were white and Jewish. Schiffman also owned the Apollo Theater, so a group known as the Harlem Consumers Committee picketed the theater. The protests carried the stench of anti-Semitism, and Robinson decried them in one of his columns. In response, the protest's leader, Lewis Michaux, turned his fire against Robinson. The group held protests outside the Chock full o'Nuts headquarters and tried to get Robinson fired from his job with the company. Roy Wilkins offered his voice in support of Robinson, while a new organization called the Nation of Islam tried to further fan the anti-Robinson sentiment. Eventually, cooler heads prevailed, and Michaux and Robinson resolved their differences. The incident highlighted growing tensions within the broader civil rights movement; tensions focused on the involvement of white Americans. Robinson despised discrimination in any form, and he remained a leading voice on the importance of civil rights. At the same time, Robinson faced severe criticism for the first time since his retirement and experienced firsthand the consequences of taking strong stands on controversial matters.

None of those incidents could overshadow the greatest honor Robinson received, induction into the Baseball Hall of Fame in July 1962. Though Robinson had distanced himself from his baseball career and the world of Major League Baseball, he felt genuinely touched by his induction. Ironically, one of the other inductees in that same year was Bob Feller, the long-time Cleveland Indians pitcher who predicted that Robinson would fail in the Major Leagues. Robinson, however, did not display any animosity toward Feller, nor did he dwell on the trying times he had endured as the first black player in the twentieth century. His short yet heartfelt speech paid tribute to his fellow inductees; Branch Rickey; his mother, Mallie; and his wife, Rachel. Robinson also thanked the Baseball Writers Association of America for inducting him in his first year of eligibility, a far cry from the tense relationship he had with many sportswriters when he played with the Dodgers. He closed his speech by thanking the fans who had supported him throughout his career and by stating that he hoped to use his platform to continue to help those with less fortunate lives. His speech nicely encapsulated his worldview—gratefulness for those who helped him and a determination to look beyond baseball to help create a more just world.

Robinson's induction into the Baseball Hall of Fame in his first year of eligibility served as a nice coda to the first part of his retirement. His induction showed that the world of Major League Baseball had not forgotten about him and his contribution to the sport. His foray into the political world had not produced the results he had hoped; Nixon lost yet another election in 1962, and the election for the governor of California, and he declared his political career over. Robinson tried to convince Nixon to change his mind, as he continued to harbor mixed feelings about the Kennedy administration. Additionally, the recent controversy in Harlem made Robinson the target of some very ugly rhetoric and demonstrations that aimed to get him fired from his job with the Chock full o'Nuts company. Robinson, however, remained a respected figure and a prominent leader within one of the most prominent civil rights organizations. When he delivered his Hall of Fame speech, Robinson could reflect proudly on his accomplishments and could look ahead with confidence. Sadly, Robinson's remaining years brought more heartache and frustration as his body steadily broke down and his family endured a terrible tragedy.

10

The End of the Road

Through the first six years of his retirement, Jackie Robinson appeared to fulfill his dreams for a fulfilling life beyond the world of Major League baseball. He had a well-paying job that gave him the freedom to support his family and pursue his passions for civil rights activism. Additionally, Robinson ranked as one of the most respected leaders of the NAACP, a prestigious organization, and a living icon in American society. Robinson also asserted his influence with two consecutive presidents, had a close relationship former vice president Richard Nixon, and had an admirer in Attorney General Robert Kennedy. In 1962, the Baseball Writers Association of America honored Robinson with induction into the Baseball Hall of Fame, thereby cementing his place as one of the all-time greatest ballplayers. Robinson seemed to have a full life and to have discovered the ideal way to transition from the sports world to the corporate and business worlds.

Robinson's outward successes masked a troubled family life and growing tensions related to his civil rights activism. In his retirement, Robinson lived in Stamford, Connecticut, a predominantly white community that initially did not welcome his family. All three of the Robinson children—Jackie Jr., Sharon, and David—struggled in that environment. Jackie Jr., the eldest son, lived a tragically short life marked by a tour in the Vietnam War and recovery from drug addiction. Robinson himself struggled to maintain the same balance between his corporate career and his advocacy for civil rights that he had maintained during the early years of his retirement. He eventually lost his job with the Chock full o'Nuts company and became alienated from the factions within the civil rights movement that embraced militancy. His efforts to shape presidential politics also failed even though his old friend Richard Nixon won the 1968 presidential election. By the time of Nixon's victory, Robinson had forsaken their earlier alliance and had grown disenchanted with the direction of the Republican Party. As Robinson faced those disappointments, he faced another stark reality—his once-athletic body steadily declined under the weight of heart disease and diabetes. Though Robinson's body failed him, his mind remained sharp and remained focused on carrying on the work he had started when he signed with the Brooklyn Dodgers in 1945. He used his last public appearance to chide Major League Baseball for its lack of progress in the coaching ranks and to remind the world of his impact upon American society.

THE ROBINSON FAMILY

When Robinson debuted with the Dodgers in 1947, his immediate family consisted of him, Rachel, and their son Jackie Jr. Three years later, on the heels of Robinson's MVP season, Rachel gave birth to their second child, a daughter they named Sharon. Three years after Sharon's birth, Robinson and Rachel welcomed their third child, a son they named David. With their expanded family, both Robinson and Rachel sought a spacious home outside the cramped confines of New York City. Though they had planned to settle in their native southern California, Robinson and Rachel decided to make the New York City region their permanent home. They did, however, want to find a space that reminded them of southern California and that would provide them with a family-focused refuge. The tiny apartments and houses available near Brooklyn did not meet their dreams. They wanted a home in a more suburban environment, an environment not readily welcoming to African American families in the 1950s.

Since their first residence at the McAlpin, the Robinson family had faced some discomfort and outright hostility as they settled in different locations. In 1948, Robinson, Rachel, and Jackie Jr. moved into the top floor of a two-family house in Flatbush, near the site of Ebbets Field. A family friend had purchased the house with the intention of welcoming the Robinsons to live in the second floor at the reasonable rental price of ninety dollars per month. Some white families opposed the Robinson's presence, but the family quickly developed a close friendship with the Satlow family. Sarah Satlow had refused to sign a petition opposing the sale of the Robinson's house to a black family; she and Rachel formed a long-lasting friendship and helped Robinson respond to his fan mail. The

Satlows' children also formed a friendship with Jackie Jr., and the other white neighbors also welcomed Jackie Jr. into their yards and homes. After spending a year in Flatbush, Robinson, Rachel, and Jackie Jr. moved to St. Albans, a section of Queens that had attracted a few other black residents. Instead of renting an apartment or a floor in a larger house, the Robinsons purchased a house in St. Albans and settled there for a few years. Though the neighborhood had other black families, Jackie Jr. still stood out as one of the few black children in the area. A few of the Robinsons' white neighbors had opposed their arrival into St. Albans, but the family had positive experiences with their neighbors and even welcomed additional family members into their home.

After spending a few years in their home in St. Albans, Rachel started to look for the family's forever home in a more suburban setting. During her search, Rachel encountered the prejudice that many black families encountered as they sought to pursue their dreams of an integrated society. Rachel found a home near the New York-Connecticut border, but the seller took the property off the market. She had similar experiences at other locations in Connecticut; owners would refuse to show her houses within her price range, and her real estate agent self-consciously steered her away from properties in her own neighborhood. Rachel finally found some luck and support when a reporter from a local newspaper heard about the prejudice she had experienced in her search. The newspaper had worked on a series uncovering racial prejudice in the state's housing policies, and Rachel's experiences confirmed what the newspaper had uncovered. It targeted the town of Stamford, and the residents responded by inviting Rachel to a meeting at the home of the Simon & Schuster publisher, Richard Simon. Rachel had a pleasant meeting with the town's residents, and she found the ideal spot for her family's future home later that same day.

The land that Rachel found seemed to represent an oasis very unlike the urban areas that had surrounded her family's earlier homes. Two ponds and a lake framed different parts of the land; small rolling hills also adorned the property and gave the land the peaceful look that appealed to both Rachel and Robinson. The Robinsons secured a mortgage, purchased the property, and then worked to build their dream forever home. Stamford's residents welcomed the Robinson family. Robinson and Rachel had hoped to move into their home in the summer of 1954 so that their children could start the school year in their new Connecticut schools. Construction delays, however, pushed back their move-in date. Rachel Simon, Richard Simon's wife, gave Robinson and Rachel a solution when she offered them her family's summer home in Stamford. Grateful, the Robinsons moved into the Simons' home in August 1954 and put their home in St. Albans on the market. Robinson faced some gentle chiding in the black press for moving his family from New York City to suburban Connecticut. The chiding did not deter Robinson, and the family formally took possession of their house on 103 Cascade Road in February 1955. Robinson and Rachel finally had their dream home, but the idyllic setting for their home could not remove them fully from the realities of American life.

Both Robinson and Rachel remained aware of the fact that their children lived in environment surrounded by white families with white children. Their neighbors remained very friendly, but Jackie Jr., Sharon, and David often stood out as the only black children in their classes, on their teams, and at their church. Robinson and Rachel tried maintaining friendships with other African American athletes, such as Floyd Patterson, and with families they knew from their days living in New York City. They also enrolled their three children in Jack and Jill, a club that sought to build friendships among black children. Neither Robinson nor Rachel wanted their children to endure the prejudice and hatred that they had faced, and they acted in the best of intentions when raising their children. Sharon and David adjusted to living in Stamford, and both of them embraced having a living icon for a father and a loving mother with her own independent career in nursing. Jackie Jr., however, carried the same name as his iconic father and struggled in that shadow.

Jackie Jr.'s troubles began during his seemingly normal, suburban adolescence. He played on the local little league team coached by his father, and he attended the same local public school as his younger siblings. Once he entered high school, Jackie Jr.'s demons emerged, and he lost interest both in playing sports and in attending school. Upon the advice of Dr. Kenneth Clark, the same psychologist whose observations helped to propel the *Brown v. Board* ruling, Robinson and Rachel sent Jackie Jr. to the Stockbridge School, a boarding school in Massachusetts. Initially, Jackie Jr. seemed to thrive at the Stockbridge School, but his time at the boarding school ended in 1962. Jackie Jr. refused to comply with the school's dress code; he also fought with classmates and failed in his courses. After returning briefly to a high school in Stamford, Jackie Jr. engaged in his worst behavior to date. The sixteen-year-old cleaned out his bank account without telling his parents and then traveled to California with one of his friends who also did not inform his parents about his plans. Once they reached California, the teenaged duo planned to earn money by picking fruit. The duo, however, ran out of money when they reached Texas and arrived in California too early for the fruit harvest. Frustrated and penniless, Jackie Jr. finally called home, and Robinson arranged for the teenagers to return to Stamford.

The aborted trip to California marked the beginning, not the end, of the tensions that Jackie Jr. brought into his family. In the ensuing years, Jackie Jr. would become enmeshed in the Vietnam War, a prolonged event that defined the outlook of many men and women of his generation. He also would develop a drug addiction, another phenomenon linked to his generation, and he would struggle with that addiction for nearly the rest of his life. As he watched his eldest son enter a downward spiral, Robinson himself would also enter a downward spiral related to his health. His downward spiral began with a seemingly routine operation, which quickly sapped strength away from his once-athletic body.

JACKIE ROBINSON JR.

With his birth in November 1946, Jackie Robinson Jr. belonged to the baby boom generation, the term given to the Americans born in the decade following World War II. In many ways, the Vietnam War defined the worldview of Jackie Jr. and others of his generation. The war stemmed from the conclusion of World War II. Prior to the war, France controlled Vietnam, then called French Indochina, as part of its colonial empire. Vietnam declared its independence from France in 1945, and forces led by Ho Chi Minh fought against the French forces that wanted to reclaim the country. Minh had the backing of the USSR and China, so Cold War considerations were also factored into the United States' involvement in the conflict. The Geneva Accords in 1954 temporarily divided the country at the 17th parallel, and the United States made a commitment to supporting the government in South Vietnam. Minh had control over North Vietnam, and battles occasionally erupted between forces from the two governments.

During the 1960s, President John Kennedy and Lyndon Johnson drastically escalated the United States' involvement in what had become an all-out war in Vietnam. Both men defined the conflict in Cold War terms—the United States needed to uphold the government in South Vietnam and prevent its demise at the hands of Minh's forces. If Minh were to succeed, then the unified Vietnam would add to the world's Communist states and would symbolize a proxy victory for the USSR. Johnson used a mysterious incident in Gulf of Tonkin in August 1964 to gain congressional support for vast powers to prosecute the war and to increase the number of servicemen sent to Vietnam.

Like many others who fought in Vietnam, Jackie Jr. quickly became overwhelmed by the reality of the conflict and by the lack of clear objectives for the United States. Jackie Jr. did not represent the only young man who came home from the war with deep psychological scars and with a drug addiction. On the home front, stories about the battlefields in Vietnam led many young men to avoid the draft and led many baby boomers to join a vocal antiwar movement. That antiwar movement did not end America's involvement in the Vietnam War. America's involvement ended ingloriously in 1975 when American officials and others scrambled to leave on helicopters as Minh's forces swept into South Vietnam.

IRREVERSIBLE PHYSICAL DECLINE

Robinson may rank as one of the greatest athletes who played in the Major Leagues. During his collegiate career at UCLA, his athleticism propelled him to letter in four varsity sports—football, baseball, basketball, and track and field. Robinson wowed crowds with his skills at running back, challenged his Olympic-medal-winning brother's skills at track and field, and dazzled on the basketball court. Once he reached the Major Leagues, Robinson flummoxed opposing pitchers by aggressively attacking the base paths. He stole home plate nineteen times in his career, a remarkable number for a feat that requires a tremendous combination of speed and savvy. Robinson occasionally struggled with his weight in the off-season, and he underwent minor surgery to remove some bone spurs from his ankle. For most of his baseball career, however, Robinson remained in good physical shape. He could play multiple positions on the baseball diamond, and he continued to frustrate pitchers and catchers, like the great Yogi Berra, with his base-stealing prowess late into his career.

Sadly, within a few months of his retirement, Robinson received a sobering diagnosis of diabetes, the same illness that afflicted his older brothers Edgar and Mack. When Robinson received his diagnosis, he also learned that his seemingly athletic body had already begun its inexorable decline. The same doctor who diagnosed Robinson's diabetes also informed him that his body had deteriorated at a rate remarkable for a man in his late thirties who had played professional sports. Robinson's diagnosis forced some changes in his life. He learned how to inject himself with insulin and to modify his diet. His insulin injections quickly became part of his daily routine along with his work for the Chock full o'Nuts company, his service to the NAACP, and his activism in the political world. Despite those attempts to manage his illness, diabetes continued to ravage his body, and his stressful work contributed to his poor health in his retirement years.

The next physical blow to Robinson's body came in 1962, the same year in which he enjoyed his Hall of Fame honors. With his diabetes diagnosis, Robinson tried to engage in some moderate physical activity such as tennis and golf. By the time 1962 ended, however, Robinson had to sacrifice his moderate physical activities due to painful arthritis and torn cartilage. A seemingly routine surgery in January 1963 turned life-threatening when he suffered from postsurgery complications. A staphylococcal infection that started in his knee soon spread throughout his bloodstream; he had to take heavy doses of penicillin and insulin to fight the infection and manage his diabetes. Robinson occasionally lost consciousness and became so delirious that he did not recognize Rachel when she visited him in the hospital. He did recover and return home, but his return coincided with Jackie Jr.'s ill-fated decision to clean out his bank account and move to California. The near-death experience, combined with yet another setback for his eldest son, weighed heavily on Robinson as he tried to look forward to 1963.

Even as Robinson sought to restart his busy schedule and reconnect with his wayward eldest son, he could not ignore the dismaying signs from his body. The gray-haired Robinson needed to use a cane, a startling change for a man who once ran over defenders, excelled at track and field, and stole bases throughout his Major League career. In addition to his diabetes, Robinson also suffered from heart disease, another silent chronic illness that threatened to further weaken his already-declining body. Robinson's illness combined with his recovery from his knee surgery prevented him from making his long trips in support of the NAACP's fundraising efforts. He remained determined to help the organization from his home in Stamford and to continue his civil rights activism as well as his involvement in political campaigns. As the years progressed, Robinson ran into headwinds from new facets of the civil rights movement, facets that favored tactics appalling to him. He also faced a Republican Party that decided to move in a direction far away from the ideal that Robinson preferred and that propelled him to see the Democratic Party as the better alternative.

A TIME OF TROUBLES

In spite of the stresses with Jackie Jr. and his deteriorating health, Robinson maintained his active involvement with the NAACP and the larger civil rights movement. As he recovered from his knee surgery, Robinson resumed his regular newspaper column and helped to raise money in support of the critical protests in Birmingham, Alabama. The city had emerged as a focal point of civil rights protests in 1963 because of its seemingly entrenched segregation laws and the ferocity of Eugene "Bull" Connor, the outgoing Commissioner of Public Safety. In moments captured in photographs and on television, Connor used the city's police officers to attach protesters with dogs and fire hoses. The ugly scenes attracted national and international attention and spurred President Kennedy to announce his support for a new Civil Rights Act. Robinson traveled to Birmingham to provide support for the protesters and to meet with King, the Reverend Ralph Abernathy, and other leaders of the protests. In June, Robinson and Rachel started a new tradition by holding an "Afternoon with Jazz" concert at their home in Stamford. The concert featured top musicians such as Dizzy Gillespie and raised over $15,000 for the SCLC's efforts in Birmingham.

The adulation that Robinson received when he visited Birmingham and the success of the "Afternoon with Jazz" fundraiser obscured some ominous signs for him in 1963. Malcolm X, who dissented from the approach of the major civil rights organizations, criticized Robinson as a pawn of white liberals who feared militancy among African American protesters. Robinson also faced some heat from the NAACP since he used the "Afternoon with Jazz" fundraiser to support the SCLC and since he devoted one of his columns to critiquing NAACP leader Roy Wilkins. To Robinson, the jealousy the NAACP showed toward the SCLC and SNCC harming the unity was needed to successfully advocate for civil rights. He fervently believed that a cross-racial movement focused on integration through peaceful means—the tactics of the NAACP, SCLC, and SNCC—represented the best hope for civil rights progress in the United States. Robinson regarded Malcolm X as a fringe actor within the larger movement and struggled to understand why Malcolm X and the Nation of Islam received a great deal of media attention. Later in 1963, Robinson and the rest of his immediate family attended the famous March on Washington and heard King deliver his famous "I Have a Dream" speech. Robinson appeared to stand as a towering figure, but the ground beneath him had started to shift in a direction that would bring him more grief than adulation.

A sign of trouble ahead for Robinson came in 1964 when he faced the expiration of his first five-year contract with the Chock full o'Nuts company. While the company had tolerated his activities on behalf of civil rights, that toleration appeared to expire at the same time as Robinson's contract officially expired. Additionally, Robinson faced internal pressures since the quality of the company's workforce appeared to decline while talks of unionization arose. Robinson hesitated to confront underperforming workers, and that hesitation undermined his position within the company. In July, the company fired six employees who had attempted to unionize their fellow employees. The move happened without Robinson's knowledge or consent; his job as the head of personnel for the company meant that such decisions should happen only with his approval. When Robinson complained, William Black accused him of questioning the company's judgment, and Robinson realized that his role within the company remained tenuous. The six fired workers filed a complaint and blamed Robinson, though he had nothing to do with the decision to fire them from the company. To make matters worse, the company rehired the six workers, again without Robinson's consent or knowledge, and effectively neutered Robinson's role within the company. In February 1964, around the time that his contract expired, Robinson tendered his resignation. News reports indicated that Robinson left the company under amicable terms and wanted to devote his energies to Nelson Rockefeller's presidential campaign. Robinson's resignation, however, represented a personal and financial blow that likely added to the stress on his frail body. Black had made Robinson the scapegoat for an ugly incident at the company and had undermined Robinson's dream of balancing his civil rights advocacy with a well-paying corporate job.

As Robinson's career with the Chock full o'Nuts company came to an end, he experienced additional troubles due to his strong distaste for Malcolm X. Robinson used one of his columns to support Ralph Bunche, the first African American to win the Nobel Peace Prize. Bunche won the award in 1950 for his effort to help secure the 1949 Armistice Agreements between Israel, Syria, Lebanon, Egypt, and Jordan. He had also played a role in the formation of the United Nations, participated in the March on Washington, and expressed support for the civil rights movement. Bunche, however, had also attracted the scorn of Malcolm X when he openly criticized the Nation of Islam. Malcolm X, in turn, chastised Bunche for caring about the well-being of people around the world at the expense of the well-being of African Americans. Adam Clayton Powell Jr., who represented Harlem in the U.S. House of Representatives, joined Malcolm X in downplaying Bunche's importance to African Americans and to the civil rights struggle. Such criticism infuriated Robinson, and he used his November 19, 1963, column to attack both men. He claimed that both Malcolm X and Powell lacked the character and leadership that Bunche possessed and that they could learn much from studying the career of the Nobel prize winner. Robinson also questioned the relevancy of Malcolm X and Powell among African Americans and implied that neither man had the standing to critique Bunche as they had been out of touch with issues happening in the United States.

The dustup between Robinson, Powell, and Malcolm X came less than a week before an event that sent shockwaves through the country—President Kennedy's assassination in Dallas, Texas. Though Robinson had not supported Kennedy in the 1960 election, he expressed remorse at his sudden death and admiration for the ways the president had evolved while in office. Kennedy's assassination quieted one of Robinson's critics. Malcolm X commented that he regarded the assassination as "chickens coming home to roost" and did not express any remorse over the event. His comments led to his suspension, and eventual exile, from the Nation of Islam, thereby temporarily depriving him of a platform he could use to critique others. In addition to temporarily removing one of Robinson's vocal critics, Kennedy's assassination also shifted the situation for the upcoming presidential election. President Lyndon B. Johnson, Kennedy's vice president, ran for his own term on a platform dedicated to civil rights. That created a potential dilemma for Robinson, who remained committed to Rockefeller and the Republican Party. Rockefeller faced competition from Senator Barry Goldwater of Arizona, whose candidacy promised to take the party in a different direction.

BARRY GOLDWATER

Jackie Robinson held on tightly to his dream for having both the Republican Party and the Democratic Party to compete for African American voters. He correctly believed that having both major political parties compete for African American voters would give those voters political leverage to enact civil rights legislation. It would also prevent one party from taking African Americans for granted and from making empty promises. He spent nearly a decade pressing for that dream, giving up only when it became obvious that most Republican voters had a different dream for their party.

Barry Goldwater's nomination marked the effective end of Robinson's dream and symbolized the emergence of a post–World War II conservative movement. Goldwater appealed to Republican voters in the southern and western states who wanted a change from the kind of governance that characterized Dwight Eisenhower's administration. To such voters, Nelson Rockefeller, Robinson's preferred candidate, did not represent the kind of principled, small-government, conservative leadership that their country and their party needed. Goldwater held out the promise of stronger leadership in international affairs against the USSR and the reduction of the federal government's involvement in people's lives. His opposition to the Civil Rights Act of 1964, which he regarded as an example of federal overreach, strengthened his candidacy to win the party's nomination. Goldwater's views, however, did not match the tenor of the electorate in 1964, and he lost in a landslide to Lyndon Johnson.

Though Goldwater lost the 1964 election, he did succeed in transforming the Republican Party. The Richard Nixon who ran and won in the 1968 election did not resemble the Nixon who ran and lost eight years earlier; he adopted some of the conservative views espoused by Goldwater. More notably, near the end of the 1964 campaign, actor Ronald Reagan filmed a memorable commercial for Goldwater. Sixteen years after filming that commercial, Reagan won a landslide election while promoting views that resembled those of Goldwater. Goldwater, not Rockefeller and Robinson, shaped the direction of the Republican Party in the late twentieth century.

For Robinson, the 1964 election marked a turning point in his political affiliations. He fervently backed Rockefeller because he regarded the governor of New York as symbolic of the political party that could compete with the Democratic Party for African American voters. Robinson wanted that competition to avoid the potential of one party taking African American voters for granted and, therefore, failing to deliver on policies that would improve the lives of African Americans across the country. Goldwater, however, appealed to extremist elements in the Republican Party that valued states' rights above civil rights. Robinson feared that a party under Goldwater's leadership would reject African American voters and would potentially leave such voters dependent upon a Democratic Party that had yet to shed its segregationist history. Making matters worse for Robinson, his old friend Nixon had endorsed Goldwater, and the rest of the party's elders seemed prepared to nominate the Senator as its standard bearer in the 1964 election. Robinson tried to prevent Goldwater's nomination; he openly called the Senator a bigot and pleaded with other Republican leaders, such as Pennsylvania governor William Scranton, to craft a platform favorable to civil rights. None of those efforts worked. At the convention, Robinson vainly tried to assert the power of black delegates, but Goldwater secured the nomination on the first ballot. A dejected Robinson rebuffed an overture from Goldwater and refocused his energies on the only major party that seemed interested in civil rights, the Democratic Party.

When Robinson turned his attention to the Democratic Party, he focused on supporting Senator Hubert H. Humphrey of Minnesota. Robinson knew that President Johnson would easily win the nomination, but he remained wary of the president because of his past associations with southern segregationists. Johnson had signed into law the landmark Civil Rights Act of 1964, the same bill that Kennedy had supported before his death and attendees at the March in Washington urged Congress to pass. In the Senate, Humphrey had played a leading role in getting the bill approved, and Robinson valued his efforts. Robinson regarded Humphrey as more of a true believer in civil rights than Johnson, and the two developed a close bond. Johnson selected Humphrey as his running mate, and Robinson served as a national chair for the Republicans for Johnson Committee. In November 1964, Johnson won in one of the most lopsided victories in American presidential history. He secured 486 electoral votes to Goldwater's 52; Goldwater won his home state of Arizona and, in a sign of the future, five states in the deep South. In Robinson's adopted home state of New York, his old nemesis Robert Kennedy won the Senate race over the incumbent Kenneth Keating. Keating represented the kind of Republican Robinson wanted to lead the party, and his defeat further soured Robinson on the potential of the party in seriously courting African American voters.

Robinson's sour mood after the conclusion of the 1964 election matched his increasingly sour outlook on life. By the end of 1964, violence had seemingly become a commonplace response to civil rights advances. In the summer of 1963, Byron De La Beckwith murdered Medgar Evers, a NAACP field secretary, outside his home in Jackson, Mississippi. One year later, Ku Klux Klan murdered James Chaney, Andrew Goldman, and Michael Schwerner in Philadelphia, Mississippi. Robinson lamented that those murders, along with other violent incidents, helped make the militancy of Malcolm X an ascendant force within the civil rights movement. Robinson remained steadfast in his anti-militancy values, but he recognized that more youth-focused groups such as SNCC embraced militancy and sought to move beyond King's practice of nonviolent civil disobedience. He found himself adrift. Robinson had witnessed his dream for a civil rights–focused Republican Party collapse with Goldwater's nomination, and he lacked a firm place within the civil rights movement. Since his resignation from the Chock full o'Nuts company, Robinson had also failed to find employment. He tried to channel his despair into a new venture, one that he hoped would help him regain his footing and reestablish his standing as a civil rights advocate.

A NEW START AND OLD PROBLEMS

On January 4, 1965, Robinson celebrated the official dedication of his newest project, the Freedom National Bank, located at 275 West 125th Street in Harlem. Ghana's Alex Quaison-Sackey, the first African to serve as the president of the United Nations' General Assembly, performed the ribbon cutting at the ceremony. Robinson served as the chair of the bank's board, and he hoped that the bank would serve as an example of how a black-owned business could provide financial assistance to African Americans. He worked tirelessly to gain investors in the bank and to expand its assets. When King received his check for winning the Nobel Peace Prize, he deposited the funds in the Freedom National Bank. At the end of the bank's first year of operations, it had assets totaling nearly $10 million. Robinson's bank quickly emerged as the most successful black-owned bank in the United States. The quick and amazing success of the bank gave Robinson the footing to engage in other ventures, such as a venture to build affordable housing and one to establish a life insurance company. While neither of the ventures succeeded, they showed that Robinson had internalized the lessons from the earlier part of his retirement. He no longer worked for a corporate boss; he served as a business leader who used his business to serve the African American community in New York City.

While Robinson entered a new phase in his retirement, he remained interested in politics at both the state and national levels. Any qualms that Robinson had about President Johnson dissipated as the president followed up his support for the Civil Rights Act of 1964 with the Voting Rights Act of 1965. Robinson never developed a close bond with the president, nor did he fully commit to supporting the Democratic Party. He vainly kept alive the hope that the Republican Party would actively seek black voters and would, therefore, make African Americans a powerful voting bloc within the American electorate. That hope compelled Robinson to work with two key Republicans in New York—Governor Rockefeller and John V. Lindsay, a candidate for the U.S. House of Representatives. With Robinson's support, Rockefeller won reelection in 1966, and Lindsay won his House race. Robinson proved that he could guarantee black voters for politicians, and that success made him a valuable asset within New York politics. His place on the national political stage remained more mixed since he refused to consistently belong to one party and to help one party's slate of candidates win.

While Robinson maintained his interests in business and politics, events in the mid-1960s also rekindled his connections to the world of Major League Baseball. In 1965, Robinson joined ABC as a commentator for the twenty-seven games broadcast throughout the season. Robinson also published two books and tried to mend fences with Walter O'Malley. That effort ended in failure since the Dodgers' owner remained angry at Robinson for retiring instead of accepting his trade to the Giants. Near the end of the year, Robinson dealt with the sad news that Branch Rickey had died at the age of eighty-four. Robinson still held warm feelings for Rickey, and those feelings surfaced when Robinson spoke about his friend's death. The sadness that Robinson felt at Rickey's passing matched the sadness that he felt in his family life, specifically with his eldest son, Jackie Jr. The eldest Robinson child continued to lead a troubled life, and his troubles weighed heavily on the minds of his parents.

In the aftermath of his misadventure in California, Jackie Jr. made another poor decision that would alter the course of his life—he enlisted in the United States Army. Jackie Jr. did not make that decision in order to emulate his father; the two had a distant relationship at the time of Jackie Jr.'s decision. On the contrary, Jackie Jr. enlisted in the army because he thought it would help him find a sense of purpose and discipline missing in his life. Ironically, he reported to Fort Riley for basic training, the same base where his father had spent his basic training two decades earlier. Both Robinson and Rachel supported their son's decision and hoped that a stint in the army would help Jackie Jr. get his life on track. Jackie Jr., however, enlisted in the army at a time when President Johnson decided to escalate the United States' involvement in the Vietnam War. The Vietnam War served as a proxy battle between the Soviet Union and the United States; Johnson did not want to preside over a loss against the Communist North Vietnam and raise doubts about the United States' ability to win the Cold War against the Soviet Union. He used the Gulf of Tonkin incident in August 1964 to get approval from Congress for his escalation plans, and those plans went into full effect starting in 1965. Johnson's escalation plans, therefore, coincided with Jackie Jr.'s enlistment and with the conclusion of his basic training. Unlike his father, Jackie Jr. would leave the United States and would gain firsthand experiences about the ravages of total warfare.

Jackie Jr. left for Vietnam in June 1965, and he experienced the war's horrors throughout his deployment. He turned nineteen on November 18,

1965; one day later, he nearly died in an ambush by North Vietnamese forces. Jackie Jr. escaped the ambush with a wound in his left shoulder; the two men on either side of him did not survive despite his attempts to rescue them from the gunfire. He received the Purple Heart and spent a week in the hospital, but the psychological wounds he suffered did not heal. Even though he remained troubled by the ambush and the loss of two friends, Jackie Jr. returned to the battlefield for about another year. In that time, Jackie Jr. endured the full reality of life for a young African American man in the army in Vietnam. He experienced the racism that other African American soldiers faced, and he developed a drug addiction due to the rampant drug use within the army. The combination of the war's horrors, the racism, and the drug use left Jackie Jr. scarred and a noticeably changed young man once his deployment ended in late 1966. He could not disguise his scars from his parents, who remained unable to fully grasp what had happened to their eldest son and to help him recover from those scars.

The alienation between Robinson and his eldest son matched the alienation Robinson felt from many of the changes happening within America in the mid-1960s. In 1965, Robinson mourned the assassination of his frequent critic, Malcolm X, and he remained alarmed at the emerging radicalism within the civil rights movement. He disliked the term "Black Power," a term that gained frequency among civil rights leaders, particularly among young leaders such as SNCC's Stokely Carmichael. To Carmichael and other young activists, the term "Black Power" represented the next logical step in the civil rights movement and a needed break from King's focus on nonviolent civil disobedience. To Robinson, the term connoted a fondness for using violence to advance political goals and overlooked other effective ways, such as voting, that advanced political goals without the need to employ violence. SNCC's decision to evict its white members and to invite a new group, the Black Panthers, to a meeting further added to Robinson's concerns about the direction of the civil rights movement. He could not support the embracing of violence and "Black Power," and as a result, he seemed like an outsider to a movement with roots in his breaking of the Major League color barrier.

Even though Robinson played a key role in Rockefeller's successful reelection bid, his days as a powerful influence within the political world and his status as an icon seemed numbered. During Rockefeller's campaign, Robinson watched as members of the Congress of Racial Equality peppered the governor with questions about his family's financial interests in South Africa, a country governed by racial apartheid. Robinson could not quell the protestors; his presence did not dissuade the protestors from launching their invectives at the governor, nor did it convince them that Rockefeller represented the best option in the race. At the same time as Rockefeller won his second term as New York's governor, former actor Ronald Reagan won his race for Governor of California. Reagan did not come from the Rockefeller wing of the Republican Party; he had campaigned for Goldwater during the waning days of the 1964 presidential election. His victory in California worried Robinson since it served as proof that Goldwater, and not Rockefeller, had won the battle to shape the Republican Party. It appeared unlikely that Robinson would have a future within the Republican Party or that the party would welcome him as an ally.

Robinson faced stresses and disappointment in other areas of his life. In his retirement, Robinson had devoted much of his time to golfing, and he had a dream of opening a country club that would welcome black patrons. Even though he represented a living sports icon, Robinson could not join the High Ridge Country Club in Stamford solely because of the color of his skin. With his business partner Bill Hudgins and other African American investors, Robinson tried and failed to secure a parcel of land that he could use to build his nondiscriminatory country club. On the heels of that disappointment, Robinson entered into an internal NAACP battle with Roy Wilkins. Robinson valued Wilkins' leadership, but he thought that the NAACP needed a new direction and new leadership. Wilkins had recently prevailed over an attempt from younger NAACP members to elect a new leader for the organization and new leadership to the NAACP's board. A disgusted Robinson felt like quitting, and Wilkins fired back at Robinson's criticisms with a few of his own for the former ballplayer. In addition to feuding with Wilkins, Robinson reacted negatively to a rumor that King intended to run in the 1968 presidential election on an anti–Vietnam War platform. Despite the experiences of his son, Robinson still supported the war effort and thought that King should focus his energies on civil rights in the United States. Unlike his recent experiences with Wilkins, Robinson's disagreement with King remained respectful and civil. He continued to value King's leadership, particularly as he witnessed more turmoil and the continued decline of his eldest son.

From his perches as a special assistant to Rockefeller and as a regular columnist for the *New York Amsterdam News*, Robinson watched all the unrest unfold as a result of the growing anti–Vietnam War and Black Power movements. Major cities across the country saw damaging riots as protestors clashed with police forces. Those riots escalated in 1968 as the anti–Vietnam War movement gained steam and as people reacted with shock and dismay at King's assassination. In the heated atmosphere, Robinson fended off attacks that he embodied an Uncle Tom, a derogatory term for an African American who appeared excessively deferential and loyal to white people. Robinson also again received death threats, but he remained steadfast in his resolve to support Rockefeller and to express his views in his column. In the midst of that turmoil, Robinson learned that

Stamford police had arrested Jackie Jr. on charges of drug and weapon possession. Jackie Jr. had both marijuana and heroin on him at the time of his arrest in addition to a .22 caliber revolver. After posting Jackie Jr.'s bail, Robinson and Rachel sent him to the Yale-New Haven Hospital, Rachel's place of employment, for treatment. Jackie Jr. did not serve any time in prison; instead, he remained under extended supervision and treatment for his drug addiction.

Jackie Jr.'s arrest in March 1968 represented the latest in a string of problems that stemmed from his stressful upbringing and life-altering tour in Vietnam. When Jackie Jr. returned from Vietnam, his parents learned that he had fathered a child with a former girlfriend. He did not stay long in Connecticut; soon after returning home, Jackie Jr. went to Colorado and continued the drug addiction that began in Vietnam. Jackie Jr. later testified that he had tried different kinds of illegal drugs, including LSD, both during his time in Colorado and once he returned to the New York City area. As a result of his drug addiction, Jackie Jr.'s behavior escalated. He participated in burglaries, and he even became a drug dealer. In the months leading to his arrest in Stamford, Robinson developed a heroin addiction. Oddly, Jackie Jr.'s arrest and the revelation of his drug addictions brought him closer to both Robinson and Rachel. As their son underwent treatment, Robinson and Rachel gained a better understanding of Jackie Jr.'s experiences in Vietnam and how those experiences put him on the path toward drug addiction. He turned to drugs as a way to cope with the death and violence he witnessed and with the inability to fully share those experiences with his parents.

The rest of year 1968 brought even more trials for Robinson. He had a new job working for the Sea Host chain of restaurants, but that job provided him little beyond a steady paycheck. King's assassination deeply pained Robinson, and he bemoaned the riots that erupted in the days following the assassination. A few weeks after the assassination, Robinson walked his eighteen-year-old daughter, Sharon, down the aisle. He did not fully approve of the marriage; Sharon's husband physically abused her, and their marriage ended in divorce one year later. Robinson lost his mother, Mallie, in May; she collapsed in her driveway in Pasadena, and Robinson could not see her before she passed away. In the next month, Robinson joined the rest of the country in mourning the assassination of Robert Kennedy while also trying to explain away his past and more recent criticisms of the former attorney general. Kennedy had served as one of New York's Senators since 1965, and he had mounted a seemingly successful bid for the Democratic Party's nomination. His assassination came moments after he won the California primary and less than five years after his older brother's assassination. In August, Jackie Jr. escaped from his treatment and recovery program, the Daytop Rehabilitation Program. Police found him and a nineteen-year-old companion in a hotel room in Manhattan; they charged her with prostitution and booked Jackie Jr. with a related charge. Instead of heading to prison, Jackie Jr. received a suspended sentence and returned to Daytop to continue his treatment.

Robinson's very bad year extended through the presidential election and into the early months of 1969. Instead of trying to exert influence within the Republican National Convention, Robinson stayed away and accepted that the party would nominate his old friend and ally Nixon. The Nixon that ran for president in 1968 did not resemble the same man that Robinson had hoped would make civil rights a key plank of the Republican Party's platform. The Nixon who ran in 1968 selected Spiro Agnew, the governor of Maryland with a spotty record on civil rights, as his running mate and deliberately targeted voters wary about racial progress. Robinson openly endorsed and campaigned for Humphrey, the Democratic Party's nominee, which put him at odds with Rockefeller. Following the 1968 election, which Nixon won, Robinson left his post as a special assistant to Rockefeller. He also lost his regular column with the *New York Amsterdam News*, meaning that he lacked the means he had previously used to shape politics. Soon after taking the Oath of Office, Nixon rebuffed an attempt by Robinson and other black leaders to hold a meeting with the new president in the White House. All those events combined to highlight Robinson's powerlessness as the 1960s ended. His dream to serve as an important power player within state and national politics had vanished. Neither the governor of New York nor the president of the United States wanted or needed his support, and civil rights leaders regarded him as outdated. Those experiences darkened his outlook for racial progress in the United States and shaped his actions during the final years of his life.

TRAGEDY

With the loss of his role in Rockefeller's administration and of his newspaper column, Robinson had fewer responsibilities that occupied his time. He remained the chairman of the Freedom National Bank, his most successful business venture, but he lost his job with the Sea Host restaurant chain. While he did not enjoy his job with Sea Host, the job did provide him with a steady income that he needed to support his family. Prior to losing his Sea Host job, Robinson embarked on a new plan to provide for his family by trying again to enter the housing industry. In 1970, he joined with three real estate investors to establish the Jackie Robinson Construction Corporation, a venture that aspired to build affordable housing for African Americans. With his new venture, Robinson helped to secure his family's financial future. He had life insurance, and he and Rachel owned two apartments in Manhattan that would provide them with some additional income once they were sold to new buyers. Despite some setbacks, Robinson had realized his dream of providing for his family's financial security. His family still experienced some inner turmoil, but they did not need to worry about money or about their ability to afford their comfortable home in Stamford.

As a new decade dawned, Robinson's relationship with his children matured. In May 1970, Robinson and Rachel wanted to show their gratitude for how Daytop had helped Jackie Jr. with his recovery. They decided to host a picnic at their Stamford house, and Jackie Jr. served as one of the leaders of the day's festivities. Before Jackie Jr. returned to Daytop, he had a tender moment with both of his parents. That moment helped Robinson to move beyond the pain he had felt at his eldest son's downward spiral into drug addiction. That moment also gave Robinson a glimmer of hope that his eldest son could make a full recovery and lead a productive and happy life. His other son David graduated from high school in 1970, and Robinson gave the commencement address at the graduation ceremony. On Christmas Eve of that year, Sharon married Joe Mitchell, a good man she had met while pursuing a nursing degree at Howard University. Jackie Jr. spent that Christmas season with his family before voluntarily returning to Daytop to continue his recovery.

The happy Christmas of 1970 for the Robinson family seemed to foretell a good future. Sharon had a happy marriage, David had started his first year at Stanford University, and Jackie Jr. had seemed to finally turn a corner on his recovery from his drug addiction. In the early months of 1971, Jackie Jr. started the transition from being patient to employee at Daytop. He had graduated from the treatment program in November 1970, and he showed a willingness to talk openly about his experiences. Father and son appeared together at events designed to raise awareness about the warning signs of drug abuse and the stresses abuse placed upon families. Both Robinson and Jackie Jr. spoke at those events and used their personal experiences as a means of helping other families in similar situations. Robinson and Rachel had continued to hold annual "Afternoon of Jazz" events at their home in Stamford, and they planned the 1971 event for the end of June. They wanted to use the money raised from the event to support Daytop, and Jackie Jr. immersed himself in the planning of the concert. David came home from Stanford to help his older brother, and the Robinson family seemed to be enjoying a period of peace after years of heartache.

That peaceful world was shattered during the early morning hours of June 17, 1971. With Rachel away in Holyoke, Massachusetts, for a conference, Robinson spent the night of June 16 with Sharon and David. Jackie Jr. had spent the night working in New York City; he used David's car to drive himself to and from Stamford. While driving back to Stamford on the Merritt Parkway, Jackie Jr. lost control of the car; the car careened wildly into an abutment and other objects on the side of the road. The impact of the crash killed Jackie Jr. instantly, and police officers arrived at the Robinson house in the middle of the night. A shaken Robinson could not go to the morgue and identify his eldest son's body. That task fell to David; Sharon accompanied her father to Holyoke so that they could break the terrible news to Rachel. When she heard the news, Rachel had an emotional breakdown that continued once she returned to Stamford. The family held Jackie Jr.'s funeral on June 21 and the "Afternoon of Jazz" as planned on June 27. The successful concert briefly helped with the family's grief, but sadness soon settled again in the Robinson house.

In the months following Jackie Jr.'s death, the different members of the family grieved in their own ways. David left the country for an extended tour through both Europe and Africa; at the end of his travels, he decided against returning to Stanford University. He did stay close to home, as did Sharon. A chasm, however, opened between Robinson and Rachel as each of them turned their grief inward. While the couple eventually overcame their distance, Robinson's persistent health problems added to the family's sadness and sense of despair. Robinson understood that he had neared the end of his life. His business decisions had secured his family's financial future, yet he feared about losing whatever time he had left with Rachel, David, and Sharon. Robinson still wanted to make an impact, but his body betrayed him and limited what he could do in his final years.

THE END OF THE ROAD

Even though Robinson cared for his diabetes with regular insulin injections, his hectic schedule prevented him from giving his body the rest it needed. The stress that he endured as he lost status in the political world, faced hostility from younger and more militant civil rights activists, and watched his son become addicted to drugs further weakened his body. In the summer of 1968, Robinson went to his doctor to seek a diagnosis for chest pain, and the doctor discovered that Robinson had suffered a mild heart attack. The attack did not cause any permanent damage, but it did underscore the fragility of Robinson's health. Concerns about Robinson's health led Rachel to take a leave of absence from her job in 1969. During a doctor's appointment in that same year, Robinson received a grim prognosis. The diabetes had ravaged his body to the point that the doctor could not detect a pulse in Robinson's legs. Such a development led the doctor to conclude that Robinson would die within three years. The prognosis rocked both Robinson and Rachel. Rachel tried to cope with the news, while Robinson tried to move on as if he had years of a healthy life in his future.

One year after receiving that grim prognosis, Robinson received more bad news. In August 1970, as he worked on planning a Miss Black America pageant and securing a loan for his company's newest building project, Robinson experienced fatigue and discomfort in his legs. He went into a hospital for tests, and the results showed the further damage that diabetes had wreaked upon his body. Robinson suffered from weight loss, high blood pressure, and high blood sugar. Worse, the results showed that Robinson had suffered a mild stroke; he would suffer two more strokes within the same month. While the strokes did not affect his speech, they caused internal damage to his brain. Robinson suffered from a loss of balance and sensation on the left side of his body. He also slowly lost sight in both of his eyes due to ruptured blood vessels and subsequent hemorrhaging. In addition to the growing blindness, Robinson also suffered from persistent shortness of breath and chest pains. In February 1971, a doctor finally diagnosed Robinson as suffering from diseases in both his heart and lungs. Those newest diagnoses added to the medication Robinson took to manage his health, serving as stark reminders of the closeness of his death. Though Robinson's spirit and determination remained strong, his body would never recover and would not give him the time he wanted to continue to impact the world.

Despite his health problems, Robinson maintained a busy schedule and sought ways to remain involved in current events. Around the same time as he received his heart and lung disease diagnoses, Robinson went to Chicago to meet with the Reverend Jesse Jackson, a former ally of King who had emerged as one of the next generation of civil rights leaders. Robinson had served on the board of Operation Breadbasket, one of Jackson's organizations, and attended the formal launching of Jackson's new organization People United to Save Humanity (PUSH). He also dabbled in other enterprises, but he also became alarmed and pessimistic about the violence he saw in the country. In September 1971, the deadly assault at Attica State Prison destroyed whatever feelings Robinson still held for Rockefeller, the man who ordered the assault in order to suppress a prisoner-led uprising. Robinson nearly became a victim of the violence that arose in Harlem in response to the murder of two police officers. In the midst of that violence, he found the time to attend benefits, dinners, and other events that honored him as well as other important people in his life. The constant travel and events helped Robinson gain a sense of purpose and helped him manage his grief over Jackie Jr.'s death.

As the sorrowful year of 1971 closed, the Robinson family briefly sought some solace on a vacation in Jamaica. Robinson used the vacation to taste his first alcoholic drink and enter the ocean for the first time. Though

Robinson had traveled widely and had participated in many sports, he had never learned how to swim. Guided by his two surviving children, Robinson waded into the ocean and enjoyed a genuine, yet short-lived, moment of happiness with his family. His return to the United States meant a return to the stark reality that his death seemed imminent. The bleeding in his brain had nearly robbed him of his sight; experimental laser surgery tried to stop that bleeding and to save the little remaining sight he had in his left eye. His legs had worsened, and Robinson often experienced pain while walking. Those ailments, combined with his pessimistic assessment of American politics, kept him out of the 1972 presidential election cycle. He held out hope that Humphrey would win the Democratic Party's nomination, but he lacked the platform as well as the inclination to get involved in yet another presidential election.

Instead of getting involved in the election cycle, Robinson spent most of 1972 collecting accolades from different groups. In May, Robinson received an honorary degree from Bethune-Cookman College in Florida and from Sacred Heart University in Connecticut. He also received an award named after Jackie Jr. from Relatives Alerts to Rehabilitation through Education, a group that he had spoken to the previous year shortly before his eldest son's death. Robinson even attended an Old Timers Day at Dodgers Stadium in Los Angeles and watched as the Dodgers became the first team to retire his number 42. When Robinson arrived at Dodgers Stadium, his physical condition shocked his former teammates. Instead of looking like a former athlete in his early fifties, Robinson looked and walked like an elderly man. On October 15 of that same year, Robinson again visited a ballpark, this time Riverfront Stadium in Cincinnati. Commissioner Bowie Khun invited Robinson to Game Two of the World Series between the Reds and the Oakland Athletics in order to formally commemorate the twenty-fifth anniversary of his debut with the Dodgers. Robinson tossed the ceremonial first pitch and used the occasion to make a pitch for the hiring of black coaches and field managers. He did not, however, feel any bitterness on that day. On the contrary, Robinson basked in the adulation of the fans and of the players who wanted to show their affection for one of baseball's living icons.

Game Two of the 1972 World Series marked the last public appearance of Robinson's life. On October 24, Rachel arose as normal and started to prepare breakfast for herself and Robinson. Suddenly, Robinson came out of their bedroom and proclaimed his love for Rachel. He then collapsed in Rachel's arms; he died on his way to the hospital. At the age of fifty-three, Robinson had suffered a fatal heart attack. Robinson's funeral took place on October 29; his pallbearers included his former teammates Don Newcombe, Ralph Branca, and Pee Wee Reese. Dignitaries from both the political and sports world attended Robinson's funeral, and Jackson delivered the eulogy. Fittingly, Robinson's burial took place in Brooklyn at the Cypress Hills Cemetery, the same place that served as the final resting place for his son.

Near the end of his life, Robinson contributed to a new biography titled *I Never Had It Made*. In the biography, Robinson provided a different perspective on his life, different than the optimism that had guided him as he broke the color barrier and sought to advance civil rights within the United States. In the book, Robinson took a critical look at his support for Nixon and at the assumptions he had made earlier in his life. He also took the time to address his critics and to defend the three white men whom critics labeled as his sponsors—Rickey, Black, and Rockefeller. At the same time, he took aim at the owners who refused to hire black coaches and field managers, yet he refused to wallow in anger or self-pity. Robinson closed his book with the title of the autobiography—"I never had it made." That phrase nicely summed up Robinson's life and accomplishments. He worked hard for all his accomplishments, and he did so in a world that refused to provide any advantages to African American men.

In spite of the setbacks Robinson experienced in his postretirement dreams, he left behind a strong legacy for himself, his family, and Major League Baseball. His successful construction company provided an income for Rachel for many years, and his two surviving children have had productive as well as happy lives. Three years after Robinson challenged Major League Baseball to hire black coaches and managers, the Cleveland Indians made Frank Robinson the first black field manager in league history. The twenty-fifth anniversary of Robinson's debut with the Dodgers sparked a renewed appreciation for his legacy. Within the next decade, all teams in Major League Baseball retired the number 42, and players wore the number on April 15 to honor his memory and impact upon the sport. Robinson never "had it made," but his actions made it possible for African Americans to enjoy successful careers in Major League Baseball. His actions outside of the baseball world helped to move the country further down the convoluted path of racial progress. Robinson's life serves as an example for other athletes who want to use their platforms to advocate for causes beyond sports. His experience shows that the path between sports and politics as well as other forms of activism contains many obstacles. Robinson's experience also shows that athletes can travel along that path and leave legacies that reverberate for years following their deaths.

Why Jackie Robinson Matters

Jack Roosevelt Robinson's life lasted for only fifty-three consequential and historic years. His life span tracked the evolution of American society from the segregated world of the post–World War II era to the world of civil rights and meandering progress that characterized the early 1970s. People who lived during Robinson's life span witnessed the collapse of the American economy, the emergence of the movie and television industries, the devastation of World War II, the civil rights movement, and the moon landing. People who lived from 1919 to 1972 also witnessed the transformation of the Major Leagues from an exclusively white enterprise to an enterprise that better reflected the racial makeup of American society. That transformation happened because of Robinson, a man who accurately claimed that he "never had it made" during his lifetime. Robinson emerged as the most important and consequential African American athlete of the twentieth century because of his own talents and determination. He had assistance from powerful men such as Branch Rickey, but Robinson himself played in the games, took the abuse, and proved conclusively that African Americans could compete in Major League Baseball. Once his career ended, Robinson proved that famous athletes could use their platforms to advance causes unrelated to sports. Robinson not only paved the way for the widespread acceptance of African Americans in professional sports but also served as a model for how other athletes could build upon their fame and lead fulfilling lives once their short playing careers ended.

Robinson's path to emerging as the most important and consequential African American athlete in the twentieth century began in Cairo, Georgia, a community shaped by the twin legacies of slavery and the unrealized dreams of Reconstruction. His parents supported themselves through sharecropping, the best option available to them in the rural South in the early twentieth century. As Robinson's parents discovered, the sharecropping system rested upon the same assumptions and dynamics that characterized slavery. White southerners owned the land and used the labor of African Americans to tend to the land. White landowners expected their black laborers to defer to their authority and to remain pliant as well as subservient. Jerry and Mallie Robinson discovered what happened when African Americans decided to challenge that system and to assert more autonomy over their lives. In the wake of that decision, Jerry Robinson abandoned his family, and Mallie Robinson faced eviction from her home as well as a permanent move to the other side of the country. Jerry Robinson's actions also foreshadowed his youngest son's assertiveness, a trait that he often needed to suppress in order to ensure that the project to reintegrate the Major Leagues would succeed.

Robinson's path continued in Pasadena, California, the city that welcomed Mallie Robinson and her young family in 1920. Mallie's decision to move out of Georgia and to join family members on the other side of the country played a critical role in her youngest son's emergence as the most important African American athlete in the twentieth century. Pasadena provided Robinson with the opportunity to play multiple sports and to participate in four sports at the varsity level at UCLA. Robinson had the good fortune to emerge as a star running back, adept basketball player, talented track-and-field athlete, and successful baseball player at a time when some top-level universities opened their varsity teams to African Americans. He did not break barriers at UCLA, but he did gain valuable experience in competing with integrated teams and confronting racism from opposing players. Robinson also caught a taste of life as an athletic star; his feats as a running back earned praise in newspapers across the country. Overall, his time at UCLA provided him with valuable experiences he used later in his life as an African American in the Major Leagues.

In addition to preparing Robinson for his career path to the Major Leagues, his time in Pasadena led him to meet Rachel Isum, the most important person in his life. Rachel served as Robinson's constant companion and biggest supporter as he played for the Montreal Royals and the Brooklyn Dodgers. She traveled with him to his first spring training, witnessed the abuse he suffered on the baseball diamond, and helped him build his suburban oasis away from baseball. Once Robinson retired, Rachel joined him in supporting the civil rights movement and shared with him the great joys and deep sorrows that came with raising their

three children. Rachel and Robinson had rough patches in their relation-
ship, but those patches seemed to make their relationship stronger and
resilient enough to persist until Robinson's death. Rachel's presence in
Robinson's life made his groundbreaking career possible. To Branch
Rickey, she symbolized that Robinson had a stable life, the kind of life he
wanted for the first player breaking the color barrier in the Major Leagues.
Rachel, therefore, not just represented as the most important person in
Robinson's life; she also played a pivotal role in the reintegration of Major
League Baseball, a successful venture that altered American society.

Providentially, the venture to reintegrate Major League Baseball gained
momentum as Robinson emerged as a star athlete at UCLA in the years
immediately prior to World War II. African Americans played in leagues
classified as the Major Leagues in the late nineteenth century, but an
unwritten "gentlemen's agreement" removed them from the Major Leagues
in the 1890s. While Major League Baseball evolved into its modern form,
black baseball players pursued careers in separate all-black teams and
leagues. On those teams and leagues, black players displayed that they
could play baseball at a professional level, a point that many black sportswriters emphasized in their columns. Starting in the late 1930s, the *Pittsburgh Courier*'s Wendell Smith launched the most aggressive push to
reintegrate the Major Leagues. He wrote a series of articles, interviewed
Major League officials, and made public pitches for teams to add black
players to their rosters. Even though Smith did not see much success in his
crusade, he demonstrated a determination to get black players into the
Major Leagues. His efforts led him to emerge as the key leader of the movement to reintegrate the Major Leagues and as a point person officials would
consult if they wanted to extend tryouts to black players.

Though he did not know Smith or directly participate in his efforts to
reintegrate the Major Leagues, Robinson indirectly aided Smith's efforts.
College teams represented one of the few outlets that featured both black
and white athletes. Stories about Robinson's feats at UCLA appeared in the
Pittsburgh Courier and other newspapers across the country. His successes
at UCLA marked the first time that sportswriters learned about his name
and noticed his athletic skills. More importantly, Robinson's presence on
predominantly white UCLA teams helped to condition sports fans to seeing black athletes compete with and alongside white athletes. His presence
and the presence of other black athletes on college and Olympic teams did
not eliminate prejudice within sports. Their presence, however, foreshadowed the future of American sports and supported Smith's contention
that black baseball players could play on Major League teams with white
teammates.

World War II created many disruptions in American society, but it
aided Smith's efforts to reintegrate the Major Leagues and positioned

Robinson to pursue a career in professional baseball. The Double Victory Campaign that arose during World War II tied the country's triumph over the racist Axis regimes to the triumph over racism within the United States. As Smith put greater pressure on Major League officials in his columns, activists engaged in protests outside of Major League ballparks to put additional pressure on franchises to integrate their teams. A few politicians, most notably New York City Mayor Fiorello LaGuardia, joined in putting pressure on Major League teams to sign black players and to give those players realistic opportunities to succeed. Robinson seemed removed from those efforts; he had left behind athletics to enlist in the United States Army. Once his time in the army ended, he fortuitously met with someone who had played in the Negro Leagues. Robinson learned that that he could try out for the Kansas City Monarchs, one of the top teams in the Negro Leagues, and could make a living as a professional baseball player. World War II brought a sense of urgency to Smith's crusade to reintegrate the Major Leagues and helped to bring that crusade to its successful conclusion in October 1945. World War II also brought Robinson to the Negro Leagues and put him in position to sign his historic contract in October 1945 and become the long-desired first person to break the unwritten "gentlemen's agreement."

Robinson did not represent the first African American to compete in professional sports in the United States in the twentieth century. Earlier in the century, Jack Johnson became the first heavyweight champion of the world by defeating former champion Jim Jeffries in a much-publicized fight in Reno, Nevada. Several decades later, Joe Louis not just won the heavyweight title over Germany's Max Schmeling—he emerged as a national hero for defeating a man who symbolized Nazi Germany. The early years of the National Football League (NFL) welcomed some black players before closing its teams to nonwhite athletes until the mid-1940s. The effort to reintegrate the Major Leagues, and the Brooklyn Dodgers' signing of Robinson in October 1945, attracted much attention due to baseball's place in American society. Baseball represented the national pastime in a way that professional boxing and the NFL did not in the mid-twentieth century. Baseball had the pull of representing a uniquely American sport as well as a sport that reflected American society. Adding a black player to a Major League team had implications beyond the sport. A black Major League player suggested that African Americans could integrate other aspects of American society, a prospect that thrilled and terrified different groups of Americans in the mid-twentieth century.

In 1946, the same year when Robinson began his career with the Montreal Royals, four black athletes played professional football. Kenny Washington and Woody Strode played for the NFL's Los Angeles Rams, while Bill Willis and Marion Motley played for the Cleveland Browns of the

All-America Football Conference (AAFC). Those four players endured some scrutiny and racism, but nothing they faced was close to what Robinson faced with the Royals and then with the Dodgers. Professional football in the mid-1940s did not yet occupy a prominent place in American society that it occupied later in the twentieth century. Seeing black players on an NFL or AAFC team did not inspire the same type of symbolism as the sight of Robinson on the Dodgers and on Major League diamonds. Robinson did not represent the only African American breaking barriers in professional sports in the mid-1940s, yet in some ways he did represent the lone African American in American professional sports. Robinson played in the national pastime, Major League Baseball, a sport that had a special place in American society. For that reason, Robinson's success had greater implications for the rest of American society; his success could, and did, signal that racial segregation would disappear from other facets of American society. Robinson's presence in the Major Leagues could, and did, inspire greater backlash from other players and fans who wanted to maintain the pre-1947 status quo.

Robinson's place as the first African American in the Major Leagues in the twentieth century and the implications associated with that achievement marked him as the most important African American athlete of that century. To break the color barrier in the Major Leagues required more than talent on the baseball diamond, something that Rickey recognized when he sent out his scouts to look for the ideal player. The Negro Leagues in 1945, the only year in which Robinson played in those leagues, contained multitudes of good athletes and of players who had paid their dues. Players such as Satchel Paige and Josh Gibson had an abundance of talent and had endured the long road trips, low salaries, and poor ballpark conditions that came with playing in the Negro Leagues. Paige and Gibson, however, had also jumped their contracts and had engaged in behavior that Rickey did not want in the first player he signed. Robinson provided Rickey with the complete package—athletic talent, a stable personal life, and avoidance of vices such as alcohol. Additionally, Robinson had the discipline to not fight back against the prejudice he encountered in his career. All those factors made Robinson the ideal player to reintegrate the Major Leagues and to shoulder the responsibility of proving that African Americans could dominate America's national pastime.

During his first season with the Dodgers, Robinson faced early tests that demonstrated how fiercely many people responded to the presence of a black player in the Major Leagues. His teammates launched a short and ill-fated conspiracy against him, and other players in the National League allegedly threatened to boycott games against the Dodgers. The biggest test that Robinson faced came when the Dodgers faced the Philadelphia Phillies, a northern team with southern sensibilities. Phillies field manager

Ben Chapman and some Phillies players viciously taunted Robinson from their dugout in an effort to knock him off his game and to assert that he remained an unwelcomed guest to many within the Major Leagues. Robinson did not respond directly to those insults, nor did he respond to other slights he faced on baseball diamonds across the league. By checking his temper and remaining focused on the larger purpose of his entrance into the Major Leagues, Robinson dispelled myths and made the reintegration of the Major Leagues an unqualified success.

In addition to having the mettle to deal with strong racism and scrutiny, Robinson also proved that he possessed the talent to play baseball at the highest professional level. Baseball did not represent Robinson's best sport at UCLA, but he honed his skills with the Monarchs and Royals and enjoyed a Hall-of-Fame-caliber career with the Dodgers. He ended his career with a .311 batting average, multiple All-Star Game appearances, a Rookie of the Year award, and an MVP award. Like the rest of his teammates, Robinson struggled in his postseason appearances before he finally celebrated success with a World Series title in 1955. The stats that Robinson compiled tell only part of the story about his baseball skills. Robinson brought a different style to the Major Leagues that changed how other athletes played the game. He drew upon his past as a running back and track athlete to race around the base paths, steal bases, and get inside the minds of his opponents. Robinson's skills added another dimension to his uniqueness and to the way he changed the Major Leagues. Other players and teams had to adapt to him and to the emergence of players who emulated his style and who made his style commonplace in the Major Leagues.

Due to Robinson's success, Major League Baseball saw both a different style of play and a much more diverse player population than it had prior to 1947. Larry Doby joined the Cleveland Indians a few months after Robinson debuted with the Dodgers; the St. Louis Browns briefly added Hank Thompson and Willard Brown to their roster later in that same season. Satchel Paige, Roy Campanella, Willie Mays, Henry Aaron, and Don Newcombe ranked among the top black players who joined the Major Leagues during Robinson's career. After Robinson's retirement, black players continued to dominate both leagues. Those black players included Latinos— such as Roberto Clemente, Felipe Alou, Matteo Alou, Jesus Alou, and Luis Tiant—who would not have played in the Major Leagues prior to 1947 due to the color of their skin. An African American player, Curt Flood, launched an unsuccessful lawsuit that challenged the reserve clause in players' contracts. Flood's unsuccessful lawsuit did pave the way for the introduction of free agency and for the ability of players to have more control over their livelihoods. In 1974, Aaron surpassed Babe Ruth as the all-time leader in home runs, a record that stood until Barry Bonds, another black player, hit his 756th home run in 2007.

All black players who entered the Major Leagues after April 15, 1947, owe a tremendous debt to Robinson and his willingness to shoulder all the responsibilities that came with breaking the color barrier. The diversity in the Major Leagues' rosters marks another reason that Robinson ranks as the most consequential and important African American athlete of the twentieth century. His success did represent the success of an entire race. By proving that he could play at the Major League level, Robinson proved that all players with black skins could play at the Major League level and could rank among the greatest ballplayers in American history.

While Robinson's performance on the baseball diamond represented a key part of his legacy, his contributions to issues and involvement in events away from the baseball diamond made his legacy more important as well as enduring. The first time that events drew Robinson away from the baseball diamond came in 1949 when Congress asked him to testify before the House Un-American Activities Committee (HUAC). Robinson's testimony came in response to comments that another famous African American, Paul Robeson, made about the loyalty of African Americans during the Cold War against the Soviet Union. Congress's decision to ask Robinson to respond showed the place he held in American society. To many Americans, Robinson represented an entire race both on and off of the baseball diamond. To many, he spoke for all African Americans when he dissented from Robeson's views and expressed his love for the United States.

Aside from his testimony to HUAC, Robinson's impact on the world beyond the baseball diamond came in the area of civil rights. Robinson himself represented a civil rights icon—he broke the unwritten color barrier in Major League Baseball that denied opportunities to African Americans and others who could not pass as white. From his first game with the Brooklyn Dodgers in April 1947 to his last game in October 1956, Robinson could never simply focus on baseball. His career with the Dodgers served as an example of progress in the broader post–World War II civil rights movement. Local and national politics shaped Robinson's career, and Robinson's career shaped local and national politics. Robinson understood the special nature of his career and, therefore, of his status in American society. He understood that he could not shy away from that status even after he retired from baseball and that he could use his status to shed light on civil right injustices that many white baseball fans could ignore in their daily lives.

Robinson deliberately used his status as a civil rights icon to advocate for causes important to him, and that determination extended to his family. Robinson and Rachel did what many families did in the post–World War II era—they sought to build a home in a suburb and enjoy the comforts of life away from crowded urban areas. They ultimately settled on a custom-made home in Stamford, Connecticut, a home that Rachel struggled to secure because of the racism of many white suburbanites. With a home in the suburbs, Robinson again symbolized progress in civil rights, particularly in the housing policies that had deliberately discriminated against black homeowners. Robinson personally demonstrated that black families could live in suburbia and could enjoy the benefits of suburban life—good schools, little leagues, and the financial security of a home. The comfortable trappings of suburban life in Stamford, Connecticut, stood in stark contrast to the discrimination that African Americans faced throughout the country, and that Robinson wanted to make a focus of his retired life. Robinson tried to straddle both worlds, but he occasionally encountered the tensions that came with trying to live a comfortable suburban life and advocating for civil rights.

To fulfill his dream of living in his own home in suburbia, Robinson took a well-paying job with the Chock full o'Nuts company as soon as he retired from the Dodgers. The job provided him with the financial security he sought and the freedom to pursue both his civil rights and political advocacy. By taking the job, however, Robinson unintentionally put himself in an awkward position. The job with Chock full o'Nuts required Robinson to do more than simply show up in an office and sell the company to customers. It required him to manage the company's workforce and to enforce measures that sought to discourage unionization. His job responsibilities did not always complement his focus on civil rights and political campaigns, two things that could make many people uncomfortable and that could put the company in a bad place with its customer base. Eventually, Robinson's role with the company became untenable, and it highlighted the challenges he faced in his retired life. He wanted to express his views, but he faced consequences that he never faced on the baseball diamond. Robinson had a steady job in the Major Leagues; his advocacy for civil rights and specific politicians cost him his job in the corporate world.

Robinson did not engage in civil rights and political advocacy solely as a hobby or as sideshows to his paid employment. He took civil rights and politics seriously and believed that he could use his status to affect change in both arenas. A ghostwritten column appeared in the *Pittsburgh Courier* throughout his playing career, and Robinson maintained that practice during his retirement. While Robinson did not always write those columns, they served as his unfiltered views on civil rights and politics. Interestingly, those columns rarely mentioned baseball. Though he retired at the young age of thirty-seven, Robinson did not seem to have any qualms or second thoughts about moving on from his professional baseball career. He seemed more than ready to replace his baseball career with work on civil rights and political advocacy. Baseball gave him stature; civil rights and political advocacy gave him a sense of purpose. Since Robinson held such deep passions for civil rights and political advocacy, he made some missteps and neglected to see the nationwide shifts away from his views. His passions in those two areas, however, also cemented his status as the most consequential African American athlete of the twentieth century.

While Robinson remained current on civil rights issues during his playing career, his retirement freed him to devote more time and to speak openly about topics such as integration in public schools. Since Robinson broke the unwritten color barrier in Major League Baseball, he made a natural transition from baseball player to credible civil rights spokesman. He had lived through the experience of integration, so his words carried a special kind of weight. Robinson's success, furthermore, added to his credibility and helped to blunt any criticism that integration in areas of American society outside of baseball could never occur. He himself showed that integration could happen, that African Americans could stand on equal footing with white Americans, and that old myths of racial superiority and racial inferiority lacked any factual basis. Robinson represented a living symbol of the success of integration and of the potential for integration in other parts of American society. He had not intended to represent the last barrier breaker in American society; he wanted others to learn from his experiences and to enjoy more opportunities than he and others from his generation had done earlier in the twentieth century.

In addition to his stature as a barrier breaker, Robinson also made a smooth transition from baseball to civil rights because his views complemented the dominant views of civil rights leaders in the late 1950s. Like Robinson, civil rights leaders sought integration into American society and to assert the rights due to African Americans according to the nation's founding documents. His views and experiences fit the mindset of the NAACP, an organization that honored Robinson and welcomed him as one of its leading fundraisers. Rosa Parks' defiance of a segregation order on a Montgomery bus in December 1955 mimicked Robinson's behavior in the face of racism—she did not fight back. Parks' actions sparked a successful boycott that ended at the same time of Robinson's retirement. That boycott brought Dr. Martin Luther King Jr. national attention, and his philosophy of nonviolent civil disobedience resembled Robinson's behavior early in his career. While Robinson had a temper, he did not advocate for violent means in an effort to achieve more civil rights for African Americans. In the late 1950s, he remained optimistic about the potential for civil rights' progress, and he fit in seamlessly with a movement geared toward nonviolent civil disobedience.

Robinson's entry into civil rights and political advocacy did not always please the politicians who became the target of his attention. Politicians often used athletes and celebrities for campaigning and photograph opportunities. Robinson quickly showed that he had no interest in engaging in such theatrics; he took his advocacy seriously and expected politicians to listen to his views. President Dwight Eisenhower discovered the tenacity and seriousness of Robinson's civil rights and political advocacy in the aftermath of the resistance to the integration of the Central High School in Little Rock, Arkansas. Robinson saw Eisenhower as moving too slowly and unjustly asking African Americans to remain patient for basic rights that all Americans had a right to enjoy regardless of their skin color. Eisenhower clearly did not anticipate that response from Robinson, and he likely assumed that he had acted appropriately as well as swiftly in support of the order to integrate Little Rock's high schools. The incident between Eisenhower and Robinson set a pattern for Robinson's encounters with politicians. Robinson had no qualms about challenging politicians, including the president of the United States, and he demanded that they support legislation expanding civil rights for African Americans.

When Robinson engaged in civil rights advocacy in the late 1950s, he did so with an eye on a very important contest—the 1960 presidential election. The Constitution prohibited Eisenhower from running in 1960, thereby making Vice President Richard Nixon the presumed frontrunner for the Republican Party's nomination. Robinson and Nixon seemed to have a special kinship. Both men came from southern California, and both men had experience with poverty on their way to successful lives. Nixon and Robinson had met during the latter's baseball career, and Nixon appeared to express admiration for Robinson as both a ballplayer and a barrier breaker. Nixon, furthermore, seemed to have a more open mind and a greater willingness to use federal power to advance civil rights. To Robinson, Nixon represented the best option for African American voters in the 1960s. Nixon also presented Robinson with the best opportunity to realize his dreams for African Americans—a Republican Party that competed with the Democratic Party for support from African American voters.

Robinson turned to civil rights and political advocacy at a time of transition for the two major parties. Both the Republican and Democratic Party had their roots in the nineteenth century and had cultures shaped by the Civil War. The Republican Party had a strong antislavery focus, while the white Southerners who wanted to maintain slavery populated the Democratic Party. Abraham Lincoln, the first Republican to serve as president of the United States, used federal power to end slavery; after Lincoln's assassination, Republicans in Congress continued to use federal power to advance civil rights and enforce racial equality. The Democratic Party, on the other hand, contained reactionary white Southerners who wanted to replicate the culture of slavery. Those divergent histories continued to define both parties in the mid-twentieth century—the Democratic Party remained the party of those who favored legalized segregation, while the Republican Party held on to its history as the party of Lincoln. Following

World War II, however, the civil rights movement started to scramble those legacies, and it created complications for Robinson. The Democratic Party had begun to actively court black voters, and a Democratic president Harry Truman had taken the first steps to again use federal power to advance civil rights. At the same time, the Republican Party seemed poised to move in a different direction. Robinson had a vision for the Republican Party that many within the party did not share, and that limited the effectiveness of Robinson's influence.

As Election Day approached in 1960, Robinson had good reason to remain wary of overtures coming from the Democratic Party's nominee, John F. Kennedy. Pro-segregation southerners continued to hold positions of power within the party, and any president from the Democratic Party would need their votes in Congress to get legislation passed into law. Kennedy himself seemed very nonchalant about civil rights and gave King the impression that he would not prioritize using federal power to challenge state and local officials over their segregation laws. Nixon, on the other hand, honed the good impression he had made on Robinson when he seemed more open than Eisenhower to supporting civil rights.

In October, less than one month before Election Day, Kennedy took an action that altered the dynamic of the race and undermined Robinson's argument for Nixon. Local authorities in DeKalb County, Georgia, arrested King following a sit-in, and King faced the prospect of a hard prison sentence that could result in his death. Kennedy intervened and spoke to local authorities in the hopes of getting King freed from jail; Nixon refused to take such action despite pleas from Robinson. King walked away from jail after someone posted his bond; Kennedy's gambit had worked. Robinson had good reason to doubt the intentions of someone from the Democratic Party, but he should have recognized that a shift had started to occur that had the potential to redefine the parties in the 1960s. The incident involving King foreshadowed that shift, and it would interfere with Robinson's efforts to engage politicians of both parties on civil rights.

In the aftermath of Kennedy's victory in the 1960 presidential election, Robinson remained stubbornly committed to his dream of having both the major political parties compete for African American voters. Robinson maintained a working relationship with Nixon and even urged him to remain in politics after his disappointing loss in the 1962 gubernatorial race in California. Robinson's dream, however, crashed on the shores of political reality. Though reluctantly, President Kennedy and his brother, Attorney General Robert Kennedy, did react strongly against violence toward civil rights activists and pushed local officials to eliminate laws mandating racial segregation. Near the end of his life, President Kennedy threw his support behind the bill that became the Civil Rights Act of 1964, a bill that his successor Lyndon Baines Johnson maneuvered through

Congress. The actions of President Kennedy and President Johnson showed that a shift had happened and that the best hope for Robinson and other African American voters came with the Democratic Party, the one-time party of the Confederacy and southern segregationists. Robinson came to accept that reality only after he witnessed what happened in the 1964 election season—the arrival of a conservative wing of the Republican Party that moved the party away from its legacy as the party of Lincoln. He committed himself to backing Nelson Rockefeller, yet the New Yorker could not withstand the tide of passionate support for Arizona Senator Barry Goldwater. Goldwater did not want Robinson's support, and his nomination effectively killed Robinson's dream for two political parties that would compete for African American voters.

Robinson's frustrations and missteps in the political world came at a time when his civil rights advocacy seemed to lose its effectiveness. He remained a civil rights icon, yet in the context of the mid-to-late 1960s, he seemed like an icon from a distant part of American history. Robinson's focus on nonviolence and his appreciation for white allies, such as Branch Rickey, clashed with the growing militancy within the civil rights movement. Instead of following the ideals of King, many within the movement followed the views of Malcolm X and of the members of the Student Nonviolent Coordinating Committee (SNCC) who turned away all white members. Robinson also ran afoul of civil rights activists when he tried to support local politicians and business leaders who in the eyes of those activists perpetuated racial discrimination. At that point in his life, Robinson both could not and would not change his views. He passionately believed in civil rights, but he did not share the passion for militancy that many activists shared in the 1960s. He took a different view of the term "Black Power," believing that it should refer to economic power and political power through the ballot box. For those reasons, Robinson seemed like a man out of step with time. He represented a symbol of the country's past, not an example of its future potential.

Robinson's frustrations and failures during the last decade of his life do not diminish his stature as the most important and consequential African American athlete of the twentieth century. On the contrary, those frustrations and failures emphasize how he stood as a symbol of a rapidly changing American society in the twentieth century. In his earlier years, Robinson symbolized the frustrations of many African Americans who stood as second-class citizens within American society. Once his signed his first contract with the Dodgers organization, Robinson represented a harbinger of the integration that represented American society's future. Robinson's career showed how integration would work in American society and the obstacles the integration process would face from those who wanted the segregated status quo. Once his career ended, Robinson symbolized the different phases of the post–World War II civil rights movement. He seamlessly blended in with the early phase that emphasized building allies, promoting integration, and nonviolent civil disobedience. He stood apart from, and seemed bewildered by, the direction the movement took later in the 1960s. In that way, he symbolized many people who supported the goals of civil rights progress but could not abide by the more militant and separatist means many activists adopted in latter part of the decade.

In many ways, Robinson's life story symbolizes a uniquely American success story and cements his stature as the most important and consequential African American athlete of the twentieth century. His lifetime demonstrated the hopes, the realized dreams, and the frustrations of American Americans across five decades of the twentieth century. Robinson's accomplishments forever altered American society; his success in Major League Baseball proved that legalized racial segregation would not last and that integration represented America's progress toward a more perfect union. The celebrations that occur every April 15 across Major League Baseball stand as a testament to Robinson's stature as the most important and consequential African American athlete of the twentieth century. No other athlete receives the kind of treatment that Major League Baseball accords Robinson every season. No other athlete's number has been retired by every team in the sport. Other athletes had better and longer careers, but no one had a career like Robinson. No one else broke the barriers, dispelled the myths, and took the abuse that Robinson took when he wore a Dodgers jersey for ten seasons. Other athletes would have crumbled under the weight that Robinson carried, and others would have fought back when they faced the harassment that Robinson endured. Robinson possessed the unique combination of talent and fortitude necessary to bring himself and countless others to the Major Leagues. Even though reintegration remained a work in progress at the end of Robinson's life, his efforts did produce some significant successes and did move the country beyond the deeply segregated world of his birth.

Decades after Robinson's debut with the Dodgers, baseball fans can see the lasting legacy of his accomplishments every time they visit a Major League ballpark or watch a Major League Baseball game on television. Every ballpark posts Robinson's retired number 42 in Dodger blue near the other retired numbers for the home team. The diversity on Major League rosters and coaching staffs represents the best elements of Robinson's legacy. In his last public speech, Robinson noted that the Major Leagues had yet to embrace the practice of hiring African American coaches, field managers, or team executives. During the half century following his death, the Major Leagues made progress on all those areas. The roots of that progress extend back to April 15, 1947, and Ebbets Field in Brooklyn.

When Robinson took the field in his Dodgers jersey, he marked the passage of one era and the start of another that has continued into the early twenty-first century. Through fits and starts, Robinson brought diversity to the Major Leagues and left a legacy that no other ballplayer has matched.

Jack Roosevelt Robinson lived for less than fifty-four years, yet he stands as the most important and consequential African American athlete of the twentieth century. His success in reintegrating the Major Leagues mattered more than integration in other sports due to baseball's place as America's national pastime. Baseball held a special place in American society during Robinson's ten-season career, and his presence spoke to the changes that had happened and would happen to American society in the post–World War II era. Robinson also established a high standard for retired athletes by using his fame to press for civil rights and to engage in political advocacy. By his actions, Robinson demonstrated that athletes should look beyond the sports world and to consider ways they can best use their talents to advance causes that had little connections to their sports. Athlete, war veteran, civil rights activist, political advocate, husband, father—Robinson carried many different identities during his lifetime. His actions secured himself an elevated place in both baseball and American history, one that no other athlete can occupy. Robinson stands as the most important and consequential African American athlete of the twentieth century. His legacy extends well beyond the world of Major League Baseball. Robinson brought change to American society by bringing change to baseball. Near the end of this life, Robinson correctly noted that he "never had it made." Robinson, though, made it possible for countless others to play in the Major Leagues and to assert that they represented full citizens of the United States.

Timeline

1856
October 7: Moses Fleetwood Walker is born in Mount Pleasant, Ohio.

1858
March 16: John "Bud" Fowler is born in Fort Plain, New York.

1860
July 27: Weldy Wilberforce Walker is born in Steubenville, Ohio.

November 6: Abraham Lincoln of Illinois is elected the sixteenth president of the United States.

December 24: South Carolina passes its Ordinance of Secession and announces that it has seceded from the United States.

1861
February 4: The First Session of the Montgomery Convention commences; it lasts until March 16, 1861, and formally establishes the Confederate States of America.

March 4: Abraham Lincoln is inaugurated as the president of the United States.

April 12: Confederate forces fire upon Fort Sumter in South Carolina, thereby starting the United States' Civil War.

1865
March 4: Abraham Lincoln is inaugurated as the president of the United States for the second time.

April 9: Robert E. Lee surrenders his Confederate Army of Northern Virginia to the *Ulysees S. Grant* and the Army of the Potomac, thereby ending the Civil War.

April 15: Abraham Lincoln dies hours after being shot by John Wilkes Booth at Ford's Theater in Washington, D.C. Andrew Johnson becomes the seventeenth president of the United States.

December 6: The states ratify the Thirteenth Amendment, the amendment that abolishes slavery and all other forms of involuntary servitude.

1868
July 9: The states ratify the Fourteenth Amendment, the amendment that extended citizenship to all people born in the United States. Other provisions include punishments for states that refused to abide by the amendment.

1869
May 4: The Cincinnati Red Stockings make their official debut as the United States' first professional baseball team.

September 3: The Philadelphia Pythians play a game against the Olympics, an all-white baseball club based in Philadelphia. The contest marks the first time that an all-black club baseball team faces an all-white baseball team.

1870
February 3: The states ratify the Fifteenth Amendment, the amendment that prohibited states from using race as means to deny a citizen the ability to vote.

1876
February 2: The National League of Professional Baseball Clubs, the present-day National League, is founded in Manhattan.

1878
May: Bud Fowler becomes the first African American baseball player in an organized league when he joins a club that belongs to the International Association.

1881
December 20: Wesley Branch Rickey is born in Stockdale, Ohio.

1884
May 1: Moses Fleetwood Walker debuts with the Toledo Blue Stockings of the American Association, then one of baseball's major leagues. His brother Weldy joined him on the team; the 1884 season marks their own season in the major leagues.

1896
May 18: The Supreme Court issues is ruling in the case of *Plessy v. Ferguson*. The majority opinion asserts that racial segregation, as long as it followed the principle of separate but equal, did not violate African Americans' constitutional rights.

1901

January 28: The American League of Professional Baseball Clubs, the present-day American League, is founded in Milwaukee.

1909

February 12: The National Association for the Advancement of Colored People (NAACP) is founded in New York City.

1914

June 28: Archduke Franz Ferdinand and his wife are assassinated in Sarajevo. His assassination triggers a month-long stalemate between Austria-Hungary and Serbia.

July 28: Austria-Hungary declares war on Serbia, triggering the start of the Great War, also known as World War I.

1917

April 6: At Woodrow Wilson's urging, Congress formally declares war against Germany and enters World War I.

1918

November 11: An armistice officially ends World War I at 11:00 a.m.

1919

January 31: Jack Roosevelt Robinson is born in Cairo, Georgia.

June 28: The Treaty of Versailles' signing takes place; the treaty's provisions officially go into effect on January 10, 1920.

1922

July 19: Rachel Isum Robinson is born in Los Angeles, California.

1939

September 1: Nazi Germany invades Poland, triggering the start of World War II; the United Kingdom and France declare war on Germany on September 3.

September 29: The UCLA Bruins, with Jackie Robinson at running back, open their 1939 season with a victory over Texas Christian University.

1940

November 30: The UCLA Bruins' disappointing season ends with a loss to the crosstown rival USC Trojans. Jackie Robinson, again starred at running back, cements his place in UCLA history by making varsity in four sports. A few months earlier, Jackie Robinson had met Rachel Isum on UCLA's campus.

1941

December 7: Jackie Robinson is traveling on a boat from Hawaii to Pasadena when Japan bombs Pearl Harbor.

December 8: Congress declares war on Japan; the United States formally enters World War II.

1944

July 6: Jackie Robinson is taken into military custody after an altercation with a bus driver on an army bus. Robinson had entered the United States Army two years earlier and had been commissioned a Second Lieutenant in January 1943. He is acquitted in a court martial and is honorably discharged in November 1944.

1945

May 8: World War II officially ends in the European Theater of Operations. At the time, Jackie Robinson is in the midst of his one season with the Kansas City Monarchs.

September 2: Japan formally signs its surrender to the United States; World War II officially ends in the Pacific Theater of Operations.

October 23: Jackie Robinson officially signs his contract with the Brooklyn Dodgers' organization; he is assigned to the Montreal Royals, the top farm club in the Dodgers' Minor League system.

1946

February 10: Jackie Robinson and Rachel Isum Robinson are married.

April 18: Jackie Robinson debuts with the Montreal Royals. He becomes the first African American to play in the Minor League since the 1880s.

October 4: Jackie Robinson and the Montreal Royals win the Little World Series, the Minor League version of the World Series.

November 18: Jack Roosevelt Robinson Jr. is born in Los Angeles.

1947

April 15: Jackie Robinson becomes the first African American to play in the Major League since the Walker brothers in the 1884 season.

July 5: Larry Doby becomes the first African American to play in the American League when he makes his debut with the Cleveland Indians.

1949

July 18: Jackie Robinson delivers his prepared testimony to the House Un-American Activities Committee.

November 18: Jackie Robinson wins his first and only Most Valuable Player (MVP) award. He becomes the first African American to win the award.

1950

January 13: Sharon Robinson is born in New York City.

1952

May 14: David Robinson is born in New York City.

November 4: The Republican Party ticket of Dwight Eisenhower and Richard Nixon defeats the Democratic Party ticket of Adlai Stevenson and John Sparkman in the presidential election.

1954

May 17: The Supreme Court issues its unanimous ruling in the case of *Brown v. Board of Education*. The Court rules that racial segregation in public education is unconstitutional.

1955

October 4: Jackie Robinson and the Brooklyn Dodgers win their first, and only, World Series title.

December 5: Rosa Parks starts the Montgomery Bus Boycott by refusing to move to the back of a bus and facing arrest for her defiance.

1956

October 10: Jackie Robinson plays in his final Major League Baseball Game, a 9–0 loss to the New York Yankees in Game 7 of the World Series. In the same year, Robinson wins the NAACP's Spingarn Medal.

November 6: The Republican Party ticket of Dwight Eisenhower and Richard Nixon defeats the Democratic Party ticket of Adlai Stevenson and Estes Kefauver in the presidential election.

December 20: The Montgomery Bus Boycott ends with new rules in effect that eliminate racial segregation on the city's buses.

1957

September 4: The start of the school year sparks protests in Little Rock, Arkansas, over the integration of the city's Central High School. In that same year, Robinson starts to work for the Chock full o'Nuts company, joins the rank of the NAACP's leaders, and devotes more of his attention to civil rights.

1960

November 8: The Democratic Party ticket of John F. Kennedy and Lyndon B. Johnson defeats the Republican Party ticket of Richard Nixon and Henry Cabot Lodge Jr. in the Presidential Election.

1963

May 3: Bull Connor turns firehoses and attack guards on civil rights protesters in Birmingham, Alabama. His actions draw the ire of John F. Kennedy and compel him to support what will become the Civil Rights Act of 1964. In their home in Stamford, Connecticut, Robinson and Rachel raise money to help the protesters.

August 28: Dr. Martin Luther King Jr. delivers his "I Have a Dream" speech during the March on Washington. Robinson, Rachel, and their three children attend the March.

November 22: John F. Kennedy is assassinated in Dallas, Texas. Lyndon B. Johnson becomes the president of the United States.

1964

July 16: The Republican Party's national convention concludes with the nomination of Barry Goldwater for the upcoming presidential election. Goldwater's nomination effectively ends Robinson's hopes of supporting a Republican Party that fought for African American voters.

August 10: The U.S. Congress passes the Gulf of Tonkin Resolution, granting Lyndon B. Johnson power to expand America's involvement in the Vietnam War. In that same year, Jackie Robinson Jr. enters the United States Army.

1965

February 21: Malcolm X is assassinated in New York City.

1968

November 5: The Republican Party's ticket of Richard Nixon and Spiro Agnew defeats the Democratic Party's ticket of Hubert H. Humphrey and Edmund Muskie in the Presidential Election. Since their relationship had ended, Robinson took no pleasure in his former friend's victory.

1971

June 17: Jackie Robinson Jr. dies in a one-car accident at the age of twenty-four.

1972

October 18: Jackie Robinson makes his final public appearance when he attends Game 3 of the World Series featuring the Cincinnati Reds and the Oakland Athletics. He tosses the ceremonial first pitch and delivers a brief speech that challenged Major League officials to hire black coaches.

October 24: Jackie Robinson dies of a heart attack at his home in Stamford, Connecticut. He was fifty-three years old.

1997

April 15: On the fiftieth anniversary of Jackie Robinson's debut with the Brooklyn Dodgers, Commissioner Bud Selig announces that his number 42 is retired across all teams in Major League Baseball.

2004

April 15: Major League Baseball holds the first annual Jackie Robinson Day. Within a few years, on April 15 of each season, all players wear the number 42 in lieu of their actual jersey numbers.

PRIMARY DOCUMENTS

Jackie Robinson, Letter to President Dwight Eisenhower, May 13, 1958

During his retirement, Robinson moved away from the sports world and focused his energies on his twin goals of supporting his family and advancing civil rights for all African Americans. The violence surrounding the integration of Central High School in Little Rock, Arkansas, in 1957 attracted his attention as well as his anger. From his perspective, President Dwight Eisenhower took too long to act in support of the nine students who integrated the high school in the face of riots. Robinson also paid attention to a bill working its way through Congress, the bill that would become the Civil Rights Act of 1957. To Robinson, that bill fell far short of the promises and support that African American needed from the federal government in order to combat state and local authorities who opposed civil rights.

On May 13, 1958, Robinson expressed his disgust and disappointment with Eisenhower in a letter he sent directly to the White House on Chock full o'Nuts stationery. Robinson fired off the letter in response to a speech in which Eisenhower pleaded for patience from African Americans. Such a response galled Robinson who rightfully believed that African Americans had showed a tremendous amount of patience and who deserved more support from their president. Robinson wrote in a respectful manner, but his writing clearly reveals his anger and frustration with Eisenhower. At the end, he refers to the Constitution as a way of chiding Eisenhower and correctly noting that African Americans only wanted the rights promised to them in that important document.

My Dear Mr. President:

I was sitting in the audience at the Summit Meeting of Negro Leaders yesterday when you said we must have patience. On hearing you say this, I felt like standing up and saying, "Oh no! Not again."

I respectfully remind you sir, that we have been the most patient of all people. When you said we must have self-respect, I wondered how we could have self-respect and remain patient considering the treatment accorded us through the years.

17 million Negroes cannot do as you suggest and wait for the hearts of men to change. We want to enjoy now the rights that we feel we are entitled to as Americans. This we cannot do unless we pursue aggressively goals which all other Americans achieved over 150 years ago.

As the chief executive of our nation, I respectfully suggest that you unwittingly crush the spirit of freedom in Negroes by consistently urging forbearance and give hope to those pro-segregation leaders like Governor [Orval] Faubus who would take from us even those freedoms we now enjoy. Your own experience with Governor Faubus is proof enough that forbearance and not eventual integration is the goal the pro-segregation leaders seek.

In my view, an unequivocal statement backed up by action such as you demonstrated you could take last fall in dealing with Governor Faubus if it became necessary, would let it be known that America is determined to provide—in the near future—for Negroes—the freedoms we are entitled to under the constitution.

Respectfully yours,
Jackie Robinson

Source: White House Central Files Box 731; File: OF-142-A-3; Dwight D. Eisenhower Library; National Archives.

Jackie Robinson, Letter to President John F. Kennedy, February 9, 1961

In the 1960 presidential election, Jackie Robinson supported and campaigned for Richard Nixon. He did so because he regarded Nixon, the vice president under Dwight Eisenhower, as sincere and willing to use federal power to advance civil rights. Robinson did not trust John F. Kennedy or the Democratic Party because of the party's history of supporting segregation. Robinson even took a leave of absence from his job with the Chock full o'Nuts company in order to join Nixon's campaign. His efforts did not work; most African American voters supported Kennedy, the winner of the 1960 election.

Within one month of Kennedy's inauguration, Robinson wrote him a letter again using the Chock full o'Nuts stationery. The letter hints at an evolving relationship between Robinson and the president. Kennedy had made promises during the 1960 campaign and had used his influence to secure Dr. Martin Luther King Jr.'s freedom from a harsh jail sentence. Additionally, Kennedy had reached out directly to Robinson and had sought to reassure the former ballplayer about his own sincerity in regards to civil rights. Robinson refers to that note in his letter and uses it as a way to frame his own missive to the president. His letter to Kennedy shows his own sense of magnanimity and his willingness to give the new president a chance to prove himself. He briefly praises Kennedy for his actions thus far and asserts that those actions show promise for the rest of Kennedy's presidency. At the same time, Robinson pledges to remain vigilant and to use his voice when needed to nudge the president forward on civil rights.

My dear Mr. President:

I believe I now understand and appreciate better your role in the continuing struggle to fulfill the American promise of equal opportunity for all.

While I am very happy over your obviously fine start as our President, my concern over Civil Rights and my vigorous opposition to your election is one of sincerity. The direction you seem to be going indicates America is in for great leadership, and I will be most happy if my fears continue to be proven wrong. We are naturally keeping a wondering eye on what will happen, and while any opposition or criticism may not be the most popular thing when you are leading so well, you must know that as an individual I am interested because what you do or do not do in the next 4 years could have a serious effect upon my children's future.

In your letter to me of July 1, 1960, you indicated you would use the influence of the White House in cases where moral issues are involved. You have reiterated your stand, and we are very happy. Still, we are going to use whatever voice we have to awaken our people. With the new emerging African nations, Negro Americans must assert themselves more, not for what we can get as individuals, but for the good of the Negro masses.

I thank you for what you have done so far, but it is not how much has been done but how much more there is to do. I would like to be patient Mr. President, but patience has caused us years in our struggle for human dignity. I will continue to hope and pray for your aggressive leadership but will not refuse to criticise [sic] if the feeling persists that Civil Rights is not on the agenda for months to come.

May God give you strength and the energy to accomplish your most difficult task.

Respectfully Yours,
Jackie Robinson

Source: John Fitzgerald Kennedy Library, Harris L. Wofford Papers, File: Jackie Robinson, 7/28/61-9/5/61. National Archives.

Jackie Robinson, Letter to President Lyndon B. Johnson, April 18, 1967

On November 22, 1963, Lyndon Johnson became the president of the United States upon the assassination of John F. Kennedy. Johnson immediately stepped into the unfinished business that Kennedy had left behind. After supporting the Civil Rights Act of 1964, Johnson threw his weight behind a measure that became the Voting Rights Act of 1965. Johnson used the power of his office to advance civil rights, but he also sought to expand the United States' involvement in the Vietnam War. Two years after supporting the Voting Rights Act, Johnson came under fire from many for his expansion of the Vietnam War and witnessed the growth of a very vocal anti-war movement from young Americans.

In his letter to Johnson in April 1967, Robinson sought to secure the president's resolve to remain an advocate for civil rights. As he had with Kennedy, Robinson had initially distrusted Johnson to use the power of his office in support of civil rights legislation. Johnson's efforts had impressed Robinson, and that sentiment frames his letter to the president in April 1967. Robinson, however, feared that the growing militancy within the civil rights movement and the growing determination of the anti-war protesters would shift Johnson's focus away from civil rights. Additionally, Robinson feared that Dr. King's support for the anti-war effort would also sour Johnson on civil rights and lead him to crack down on all protesters.

Robinson pleading tone comes through in his letter to Johnson. He wrote the letter on stationery from New York governor's office because he worked for Nelson Rockefeller at the time of writing the letter. He copied both Rockefeller and Vice President Hubert Humphrey on the message, which shows his sense of urgency in wanting guarantees from the president.

Dear Mr. President:

First, Let me thank you for pursuing a course toward Civil Rights that no President in our history has pursued. I am confident your dedication will not only continue, but will be accelerated dependent on the needs of all Americans.

While I am certain your faith has been shaken by demonstrations against the Viet Nam war, I hope the actions of any one individual does not make you feel as Vice President Humphrey does, that Dr. King's stand will hurt the Civil Rights movement. It would not be fair to the thousands of our Negro fighting men who are giving their lives because they believe, in most instances, that our Viet Nam stand is just. There are hundreds of thousands of us at home who are not certain why we are in the war. We feel, however, that you and your staff know what is best and we are willing to support your efforts for a honorable solution to the war.

I do feel you must make it indefinitely clear, that regardless of who demonstrates, that your position will not change toward the rights of all people; that you will continue to press for justice for all Americans and that a strong stand now will have great effect upon young Negro Americans who could resort to violence unless they are reassured. Recent riots in Tennessee and Cleveland Ohio is warning enough. Your concern based on causes and not on whether it will hurt the Civil Rights effort, could have a wholesale effect on our youth.

I appreciate the difficult role any President has. I believe, also, yours is perhaps the most difficult any President has had. I hope God gives you the wisdom and strength to come through this crisis at home, and that an end to the war in Viet Nam is achieved very soon.

Again, Sir, let me thank you for your domestic stand on Civil Rights. We need an even firmer stand as the issues become more personal and the gap between black and white Americans get wider.

Source: Lyndon Baines Johnson Library, White House Central Files, Subject Files, File: EX-HU 2 2/4/67-5/31/67. National Archives.

Jackie Robinson, Letter to Roland L. Elliott, April 20, 1972

Richard Nixon finally won the presidency in November 1968, but he no longer embodied the type of politician Jackie Robinson hoped would lead the Republican Party. Even though Nixon had rebuffed an earlier meeting request, Robinson felt compelled to write letters to the Nixon administration. The letters came as Nixon prepped his run for a second term and as Robinson faced the end of his life. The letter that Robinson delivered on April 20, 1972, came in response to an earlier message he had sent to the Nixon administration. Tellingly, the letter did not go directly to the president. Robinson's letter went to Roland L. Elliott, a deputy special assistant to Nixon, someone who supervised the mail that the president received on a daily basis. The fact that the letter went to Elliott and not Nixon symbolized the breach between the once-close Robinson and Nixon and the outsider status that Robinson had near the end of his life. Robinson's dream of exerting political influence had long ended in failure, and the fact that he could not get an audience with the president cemented the demise of that dream.

Unlike his earlier letters, Robinson's letter appeared on the stationery for the Jackie Robinson Construction Corporation, a recently formed company that Robinson had created with the help of his friends and family. Since the start of his retirement, Robinson had dreamed of supporting his family financially and of helping them lead comfortable lifestyles. Robinson had succeeded in that dream, and the stationery he used for his April 1972 letter proved the success of that dream. Robinson would die about six months after he wrote the letter, and the corporation would continue to pay dividends for his family for many years after his death.

Dear Mr. Elliott:

Thanks for your letter of the 14th. I am sorry the President does not understand my concern. Black America, it seems, comes up short as Presidents study or give time to fashion standards that are designed to help all Americans when in reality it is a smoke screen.

Black America has asked so little, but if you can't see the anger that comes from rejection, you are treading a dangerous course. We older blacks, unfortunately, we willing to wait. Today's blacks are ready to explode! We had better take some definitive action or I am afraid the consequences could be nation shattering.

I hope you will listen to the cries of the black youth. We cannot afford traditional conflict.

Source: Nixon Presidential Materials, White House Central Files, National Archives.

Bibliography

WEBSITES

Baseball-Almanac.com
Baseball-Reference.com
Jackie Robinson, Civil Rights Advocate—National Archives
Jackie Robinson Foundation—jackierobinson.org
National Baseball Hall of Fame—baseballhall.org
Society of American Baseball Research—SABR.org

NEWSPAPERS

Baltimore Afro-American
Brooklyn Eagle
Chicago Defender
The Daily Worker
New York Amsterdam News
New York Post
New York Times
Philadelphia Bulletin
Philadelphia Daily News
Philadelphia Inquirer
Philadelphia Tribune
Pittsburgh Courier

ARTICLES

Alexander, Lisa Doris. "Effa Manley and the Politics of Passing." *Black Ball: A Journal of the Negro Leagues.* 1, no. 2 (Fall 2008): 83–94.

Alexander, Lisa Doris. "The Jackie Robinson Story vs. the Court-Martial of Jackie Robinson vs. 42." *Nine: A Journal of Baseball History & Culture*. 24, nos. 1 and 2 (Fall 2015–Spring, 2016): 89–102.

Alpert, Rebecca. "Jackie Robinson, Jewish Icon." *Shofar*. 26, no. 2 (Winter 2008): 42–58.

Branson, Douglas M. "The Integration of Baseball: Doby and Robinson." *Black Ball: A Journal of the Negro Leagues*. 9 (2017): 97–113.

Briley, Ron. "A Cold War State of Mind: Jackie Robinson and the Anticommunist Crusade." *Black Ball: A Journal of the Negro Leagues*. 8 (2015): 5–24.

Carroll, Brian. "A Crusading Journalist's Last Campaign: Wendell Smith and the Desegregation of Baseball's Spring Training." *Communication and Social Change*. 1 (2007): 38–54.

Carroll, Brian. "A Tribute to Wendell Smith." *Black Ball: A Journal of the Negro Leagues*. 2, no. 1 (Spring 2009): 4–11.

Carroll, Brian. "Rube Foster, C.I. Taylor, and the Great Newspaper War of 1915." *Black Ball: A Journal of the Negro Leagues*. 4, no. 2 (Fall 2011): 36–54.

DiFiore, Anthony. "Advancing African American Baseball: The Philadelphia Pythians andInterracial Competition in 1869." *Black Ball: A Journal of the Negro Leagues*. 1, no. 1 (Spring 2008): 14–28.

Dorinson, Joseph. "Paul Robeson and Jackie Robinson: Athletes and Activists at Armageddon." *Pennsylvania History: A Journal of Mid-Atlantic Studies*. 66, no. 1 (Winter 1999): 16–26.

Dorinson, Joseph. "Something to Cheer About: Paul Robeson, Monte Irvin, and Larry Doby." *Black Ball: A Journal of the Negro Leagues*. 6 (2013): 116–128.

Fetter, Henry. "The Party Line and the Color Line: The American Communist Party, the 'Daily Worker,' and Jackie Robinson." *Journal of Sport History*. 28, no. 3 (Fall 2001): 375–402.

Harnischfeger, Mark, and Mary E. Corey. "Cap, Jackie, and Ted: The Rise and Fall of Jim Crow Baseball." *OAH Magazine of History*. 24, no. 2 (April 2010): 31–36.

Henry, Patrick. "Jackie Robinson: An Athlete and American Par Excellence." *The Virginia Quarterly Review*. 73, no. 2 (Spring 1997): 189–203.

Kahn, Roger. "The Jackie Robinson I Remember." *The Journal of Blacks in Higher Education*. no. 14 (Winter 1996–1997): 88–93.

Kimball, Richard Ian. "Beyond the 'Great Experiment': Integrated Baseball Comes to Indianapolis." *Journal of Sport History*. 26, no. 1 (Spring 1999): 142–162.

Kreuz, Jim. "The Dodgers' First Choice Wasn't Jackie Robinson." *Black Ball: A Journal of the Negro Leagues*. 7 (2014): 114–126.

Lamb, Chris. "'I Never Want to Take Another Trip Like This One': Jackie Robinson's Journey to Integrate Baseball." *Journal of Sport History.* 24, no. 2 (Summer 1997): 177–191.

Lamb, Chris. "Did Branch Rickey Sign Jackie Robinson to Right a 40-Year Wrong?" *Black Ball: A Journal of the Negro Leagues.* 6 (2013): 5–18.

Lester, Larry. "Can You Read, Judge Landis?" *Black Ball: A Negro Leagues Journal.* 1, no. 2 (Fall 2008): 57–82.

Meriwether, James H. "'Worth a Lot of Negro Votes': Black Voters, Africa, and the 1960 Presidential Campaign." *Journal of American History.* 95, no. 3 (December 2008): 737–763.

Moore, Louis. "Doby Does It! Larry Doby, Race, and American Democracy in Post-World War II America." *Journal of Sport History.* 42, no. 3 (Fall 2015): 363–370.

Norwood, Stephen H., and Harold Brackman. "Going to Bat for Jackie Robinson: The Jewish Role in Breaking Baseball's Color Line." *Journal of Sport History.* 26, no. 1 (Spring 1999): 115–141.

Powell, Larry. "Jackie Robinson and Dixie Walker: Myths of the Southern Baseball Player." *Southern Cultures.* 8, no. 2 (Summer 2008): 56–71.

Simons, William. "Jackie Robinson and the American Mind: Journalistic Perceptions of the Reintegration of Baseball." *Journal of Sport History.* 12, no. 1 (Spring 1985): 39–64.

Smith, Ronald A. "The Paul Robeson—Jackie Robinson Saga and a Political Collusion." *Journal of Sport History.* 6, no. 2 (Summer 1979): 5–27.

Stout, Glenn. "Tryout and Fallout: Race, Jackie Robinson, and the Red Sox." *Massachusetts Historical Review.* 6 (2004): 11–37.

Vernon, John. "Beyond the Box Score: Jackie Robinson, Civil Rights Crusader." *Negro History Bulletin.* 28, nos. 3 and 4 (October–December 1995): 15–22.

Vernon, John. "A Citizen's View of Presidential Responsibility: Jackie Robinson and Dwight D. Eisenhower." *Negro History Bulletin.* 62, no. 4 (December 1999): 15–21.

Wiggins, David K. "Wendell Smith, *The Pittsburgh Courier*, and the Campaign to Include Blacks in Organized Baseball, 1933–1945." *Journal of Sport History.* 10, no. 2 (Summer 1983): 5–29.

BOOKS

Biddle, Daniel R., and Murray Dubin. *Tasting Freedom: Octavius Catto and the Battle for Equality in Civil War America.* Philadelphia: Temple University Press, 2010.

Breslin, Jimmy. *Branch Rickey: A Life.* New York: Penguin Books, 2012.

Browne, Paul. *The Coal Barons Played Cuban Giants: A History of Early Professional Baseball in Pennsylvania, 1886–1896.* Jefferson, NC: McFarland, 2013.

Brunson, James E., III. *Black Baseball 1858–1900: A Comprehensive Record of the Teams, Players, Managers, Owners, and Umpires.* Jefferson, NC: McFarland, 2019.

Corey, Mary E., and Mark Harnischfeger. *Before Jackie: The Negro Leagues, Civil Rights and the American Dream.* New York: Paramount Publishing, 2013.

Dickson, Paul. *Leo Durocher: Baseball's Prodigal Son.* New York: Bloomsbury, 2017.

Eig, Jonathan. *Opening Day: The Story of Jackie Robinson's First Season.* New York: Simon & Schuster, 2007.

Goldstein, Warren. *Playing for Keeps: A History of Early Baseball.* New York: Cornell University Press, 2014.

Heaphy, Leslie. *The Negro Leagues: 1869–1960.* Jefferson, NC: McFarland, 2003.

Henry, Ed. *42 Faith: The Rest of the Jackie Robinson Story.* Nashville: Thomas Nelson, 2017.

Hogan, Lawrence D. *The Forgotten History of African American Baseball.* Santa Barbara, CA: Praeger, 2014.

Hogan, Lawrence D., and Jules Tygiel. *Shades of Glory: The Negro Leagues and the Story of African-American Baseball.* Washington, D.C.: National Geographic, 2006.

Johnson, James W. *The Black Bruins: The Remarkable Lives of UCLA's Jackie Robinson, Woody Strode, Tom Bradley, Kenny Washington, and Ray Bartlett.* Lincoln: University of Nebraska Press, 2018.

Kahn, Roger. *The Boys of Summer.* New York: Harper & Row, 1972.

Kahn, Roger. *Rickey and Robinson: The True, Untold History of the Integration of Baseball.* New York: Potter, 2015.

Kashatus, William. *Jackie and Campy: The Untold Story of Their Rocky Relationship and the Breaking of Baseball's Color Line.* Lincoln: University of Nebraska Press, 2014.

Kirwin, Bill, ed. *Out of the Shadows: African American Baseball from the Cuban Giants to Jackie Robinson.* Lincoln: University of Nebraska Press, 2005.

Laing, Jeffery Michael. *Bud Fowler: Baseball's First Black Professional.* Jefferson, NC: McFarland, 2013.

Lamb, Chris. *Blackout: The Untold Story of Jackie Robinson's First Spring Training.* Lincoln: University of Nebraska Press, 2006.

Lamb, Chris. *The Conspiracy of Silence: Sportswriters and the Long Campaign to Desegregate Baseball.* Lincoln: University of Nebraska Press, 2012.

Lamb, Chris, and Michael G. Long. *Jackie Robinson: A Spiritual Biography: The Faith of a Boundary-Breaking Hero.* Louisville: John Knox Press, 2017.

Lanctot, Neil. *Fair Dealing and Clean Playing: The Hilldale Club and the Development of Black Professional Baseball, 1910–1932.* Jefferson, NC: McFarland, 1994.

Lanctot, Neil. *Negro League Baseball: The Rise and Ruin of a Black Institution.* Philadelphia: University of Pennsylvania Press, 2004.

Lanctot, Neil. *Campy: The Two Lives of Roy Campanella.* New York: Simon & Schuster, 2011.

Lester, Larry. *Rube Foster in His Time: On the Field and in the Papers with Black Baseball's Greatest Visionary.* Jefferson, NC: McFarland, 2012.

Martin, Brian. *Baseball's Creation Myth: Adam Ford, Abner Graves, and the Cooperstown Story.* Jefferson, NC: McFarland, 2013.

Marzano, Rudy. *The Brooklyn Dodgers of the 1940s.* Jefferson, NC: McFarland, 2005.

Marzano, Rudy. *The Last Year of the Brooklyn Dodgers: 1950–1957.* Jefferson, NC: McFarland, 2008.

McGregor, Robert Kuhn. *A Calculus of Color: The Integration of Baseball's American League.* Jefferson, NC: McFarland, 2015.

Moffi, Larry, and Jonathan Kronstadt. *Crossing the Line: Black Major Leaguers 1947–1959.* Lincoln: University of Nebraska Press, 2006.

Overmyer, James E. *Queen of the Negro Leagues: Effa Manley and the Newark Eagles.* New York: Rowan & Littlefield, 1993 and 2020.

Overmyer, James E. *Cum Posey of the Homestead Grays: A Biography of the Negro Leagues Owner and Hall of Famer.* Jefferson, NC: McFarland, 2020.

Peterson, Robert. *Only the Ball Was White.* New York: Oxford University Press, 1992.

Rampersand, Arnold. *Jackie Robinson: A Biography.* New York: Ballantine Books, 2011.

Ribowski, Mark. *A Complete History of the Negro Leagues, 1884 to 1955.* Secaucus, NJ: Citadel Press, 1995.

Riley, James A., ed. *Of Monarchs and Black Barons: Essays on Baseball's Negro Leagues.* Jefferson, NC: McFarland, 2012.

Robinson, Jackie, and Alfred Duckett. *I Never Had It Made.* New York: HarperCollins, 1972.

Robinson, Jackie, and Wendell Smith. *My Own Story.* New York: Greenberg Co., 1948.

Robinson, Rachel, and Lee Daniels. *Jackie Robinson: An Intimate Portrait.* New York: Harry N. Abrams, 1996.

Rogisin, Donn. *Invisible Men: Life in Baseball's Negro Leagues.* New York: Atheneum, 1983.

Ross, Charles K. *Outside the Lines: African Americans and the Integration of the National Football League.* New York: New York University Press, 1999.

Schutz, J. Christopher. *Jackie Robinson: An Integrated Life.* New York: Rowan & Littlefield, 2016.

Seymour, Harold, and Dorothy Seymour Mills. *Baseball: The Early Years.* New York: Oxford University Press, 1989.

Seymour, Harold, and Dorothy Seymour Mills. *Baseball: The Golden Age.* New York: Oxford University Press, 1989.

Seymour, Harold, and Dorothy Seymour Mills. *Baseball: The People's Game.* New York: Oxford University Press, 1991.

Silber, Irwin. *Press Box Red: The Story of Lester Rodney, the Communist Who Helped Break the Color Line in American Sports.* Philadelphia: Temple University Press, 2003.

Smith, Courtney Michelle. *Ed Bolden and Black Baseball in Philadelphia.* Jefferson, NC: McFarland, 2017.

Sokol, Jason. *All Eyes are Upon Us: Race and Politics from Boston to Brooklyn.* New York: Basic Books, 2014.

Threston, Christopher. *The Integration of Baseball in Philadelphia.* Jefferson, NC: McFarland, 2003.

Trembanis, Sarah L. *The Set-Up Men: Race, Culture, and Resistance in Black Baseball.* Jefferson, NC: McFarland, 2014.

Trotter, Joe William, Jr., and Eric Ledell Smith, eds. *African Americans in Pennsylvania: Shifting Historical Perspectives.* University Park: The Pennsylvania Historical and Museum Commission and Pennsylvania State University Press, 1997.

Tygiel, Jules. *Baseball's Great Experiment: Jackie Robinson and His Legacy.* New York: Oxford University Press, 1983.

Tygiel, Jules. *Past Time: Baseball as History.* New York: Oxford University Press, 2000.

Tygiel, Jules. *Extra Bases: Reflections on Jackie Robinson, Race, and Baseball History.* Lincoln: University of Nebraska Press, 2002.

Veeck, Bill, and Ed Linn. *Veeck as in Wreck: The Autobiography of Bill Veeck.* Chicago: University of Chicago Press, 1962.

Wiggins, David K., and Patrick B. Miller, eds. *Sport and the Color Line: Black Athletes and Race Relations in Twentieth-Century America.* New York: Routledge, 2004.

Young, William A. *J.L. Wilkinson and the Kansas City Monarchs: Trailblazers in Black Baseball.* Jefferson, NC: McFarland, 2017.

Zhang, David W. *Fleet Walker's Divided Heart: The Life of Baseball's First Major Leaguer.* Lincoln: University of Nebraska Press, 1998.

Index

About the Author

Courtney Michelle Smith is professor of history and political science and assistant dean of the core curriculum at Cabrini University in Radnor, Pennsylvania. Smith is a native and life-long resident of Delaware County, Pennsylvania, and is an avid fan of Philadelphia's four professional sports teams. She earned her bachelor's degree in history and in political science from Cabrini College. After leaving Cabrini, Smith earned her master's degree and doctorate in American history from Lehigh University in Bethlehem, Pennsylvania. Smith returned to Cabrini in August 2008 to pursue a full-time teaching career. Her research interests include sports history, Philadelphia history, Pennsylvania history, and American political history. She is the author of several articles and books and editor of Volume I of *American History through Its Greatest Speeches,* published by ABC-CLIO. Smith is grateful for the support she received while writing this book. She is also grateful for the love of baseball that came from her great-grandmother and grandmother, both of whom said the rosary for their Pirates during every game of the 1960 World Series.

CPSIA information can be obtained
at www.ICGtesting.com
Printed in the USA
LVHW081255270322
714516LV00003B/217